FROM ECONOMY TO SOCIETY? PERSPECTIVES ON TRANSNATIONAL RISK REGULATION

STUDIES IN LAW, POLITICS, AND SOCIETY

Series Editor: Austin Sarat

Recent Volumes:

Volumes 1–2:	Edited by Rita J. Simon
Volume 3:	Edited by Steven Spitzer
Volumes 4–9:	Edited by Steven Spitzer and Andrew S. Scull
Volumes 10–16:	Edited by Susan S. Sibey and Austin Sarat
Volumes 17–33:	Edited by Austin Sarat and Patricia Ewick
Volumes 34–61:	Edited by Austin Sarat
Volume 62:	Edited by Bettina Lange, Dania Thomas and Austin Sarat

STUDIES IN LAW, POLITICS, AND SOCIETY VOLUME 62

FROM ECONOMY TO SOCIETY? PERSPECTIVES ON TRANSNATIONAL RISK REGULATION

EDITED BY

BETTINA LANGE

Centre for Socio-Legal Studies, University of Oxford, Oxford, UK

DANIA THOMAS

Adam Smith Business School and School of Law, University of Glasgow, UK

AUSTIN SARAT

Department of Law, Jurisprudence & Social Thought and Political Science, Amherst College, Amherst, USA

Emerald

United Kingdom – North America – Japan
India – Malaysia – China

Emerald Group Publishing Limited
Howard House, Wagon Lane, Bingley BD16 1WA, UK

First edition 2013

British Library Cataloguing in Publication Data
A catalogue record for this book is available from the British Library

ISBN: 978-1-78190-738-2
ISSN: 1059-4337 (Series)

ISOQAR
REGISTERED
Certificate Number 1985
ISO 14001

ISOQAR certified Management System, awarded to Emerald for adherence to Environmental standard ISO 14001:2004.

INVESTOR IN PEOPLE

CONTENTS

PART II: APPLYING AND DEVELOPING POLANYIAN IDEAS

THEME 1: REGULATING THROUGH EMBEDDING SOVEREIGN DEBT DEFAULT

THEME 2: MORALIZING MARKETS THROUGH FAIR TRADE AND CORPORATE SOCIAL RESPONSIBILITY

THEME 3: EMBEDDING ECONOMIC ACTIVITY THROUGH EMOTIONS?

DISCUSSION PIECE

LIST OF CONTRIBUTORS

Mitchel Y. Abolafia	Rockefeller College of Public Affairs and Policy, University at Albany, Albany, NY, USA
Susan A. Bandes	DePaul University College of Law, Chicago, IL, USA
Sabine Frerichs	The Centre of Excellence (CoE) in Foundations of European Law and Polity, University of Helsinki, Finland
Mitu Gulati	Duke Law School, Durham, NC, USA
Anna Hutchens	The Regulatory Institutions Network, The Australian National University, Australia
Bettina Lange	Centre for Socio-Legal Studies, University of Oxford, Oxford, UK
John Paterson	Law School, University of Aberdeen, Aberdeen, UK
Petrina Schiavi	Regulatory Institutions Network, Australian National University, Australia
Dania Thomas	Adam Smith Business School and School of Law, University of Glasgow, UK
Aurora Voiculescu	School of Law, Advanced Legal Studies, University of Westminster, London, UK
W. Mark C. Weidemaier	School of Law, University of North Carolina, Chapel Hill, NC, USA

EDITORIAL BOARD

AFTER A ROMANTIC ASPIRATION TO SOCIETY: HARNESSING THE REGULATORY CAPACITY OF A SOCIAL SPHERE

Bettina Lange

ABSTRACT

This introduction unpacks the key question that informs the articles in this special issue. How does a social sphere inform regulation and, more specifically, how can the regulatory capacity of a social sphere be harnessed, as an alternative or significant complementary force to state regulation and reliance on the self-regulatory capacity of markets? This question is salient and topical also in light of the search for new regulatory strategies and perspectives in the aftermath of the 2007 financial and subsequent EU sovereign debt crises, which have led to a major realignment of economy and society in a number of countries.

This introduction argues that economic sociology is a crucial reference point for understanding more about the social practices that constitute business behavior. It enables to explore the scope and significance of often interlinked social and legal norms for regulating various transnational risks that economic activity can give rise to. The introduction

From Economy to Society? Perspectives on Transnational Risk Regulation
Studies in Law, Politics, and Society, Volume 62, 1–21

ISSN: 1059-4337/doi:10.1108/S1059-4337(2013)0000062001

therefore locates the quest for understanding more about the regulatory capacity of a social sphere in debates that draw on Karl Polanyi's analysis of the embedding, disembedding, and re-embedding of economic activity into social norms. The introduction highlights one of the key themes developed in this special issue, the idea of society within *economy which questions an assumed conceptual distinction between economy and society.*

This introduction concludes by specifying how the accounts of risk regulation developed in this special issue chart a path that is different from recent explorations of the role of a social sphere in regulation, which were conducted under the banner of "the sociological citizen," "regulatory sociability," and "collaborative governance."

Keywords: Economic sociology of law; transnational risk; financial crisis; social sphere; regulation; Karl Polanyi

CONTEMPORARY CRISES CALLING FOR NEW PERSPECTIVES ON TRANSNATIONAL RISK REGULATION

The current and still unfolding economic and political crises in the European Union (EU) and beyond raise the questions whether transnational regulation – in the public interest – of the risks posed by economic activity can be effective, and what role various types of social and legal norms play in this. The financial crisis of 2007 started with the sub-prime lending crisis in the United States, and has now been followed by a sovereign debt crisis in the EU. These economic crises are associated not just with a global economic downturn, but also with a crisis of political legitimacy for the state due to the highly contested nature of governments' responses to the financial crises, including the adoption of austerity budgets, for example, in the United Kingdom (Engelen et al., 2011, pp. 2, 11, 27, 30; Morgan, 2010). Financial losses arising from banks' private risk taking are being socialized, and partly paid for through deep cuts to welfare state provision, while banks' inefficient operation and financial gains seem to be beyond the scope of regulation. More fundamentally these crises call into question whether public regulators can steer and maintain economic activity through targeted policies in the interests of a population as a whole. More specifically, these economic and political crises highlight the limits of two key regulatory approaches: reliance on state regulation and self-regulatory markets, the latter having been a distinct feature of regulation in the run-up to the crises, especially of financial services regulation in the 1980s and 1990s in various EU Member States and the United States (Engelen et al., 2011, pp. 136–137). This special issue asks what role society can play in the regulation of transnational risks, as an alternative to or at least significant addition to reliance on state regulatory activity and the myth of the self-regulatory capacity of markets (Stiglitz, 2001, p. xiii). How can a social sphere contribute to the prevention and management of risks, often transnational in nature, posed by economic activity?

A renewed emphasis on the role of society has been a feature of some academic and public policy debates about regulation in the aftermath of the crises. Some of these debates mobilize a romantic aspiration to society, partly expressed, for instance, in new social movements such as "occupy the economy."

More specifically, this aspiration seeks to break with the old certainties of inegalitarian "neoliberal" governance (Saperstein, 2012; Wolff, 2012, pp. 63, 102; see also calls for a "social and solidarity economy" in the context of the "occupy" movement: http://vimeo.com/33187813). It responds to the threat of an increasing fragmentation of societies, as seen in the rise of political extremism, for example, in Greece, and increased economic migration in response to the recession (see, e.g., Hyslop, 2012). This romantic aspiration to society draws on utopian thinking and proposes collective responses to tackling the consequences of the economic and political crises in the name of "society" as an alternative to authoritarian state regulation or reliance on markets (Hann & Hart, 2011, p. 71). It also searches for new institutions of governance in the light of a crisis of confidence in traditional political institutions.

This aspiration to society echoes two key features of romanticism as an artistic movement. First, it invokes a consensus view of society which chimes with the emphasis of the artists of the early 19th century romantic period, such as the English poet Coleridge, on harmony, consensus, and the reconciliation of differences (Brown, 2001, p. 410; Knights, 2004, pp. 763, 765). Second, romanticism valued intuition as a guide to insight, and thus emphasized the responsiveness of thought to sentiments (Vaughan, 1978, p. 18). In the light of significant anger, despair, and tension between citizens affected by the economic crises, this is a relevant theme in current public policy debates. But what is the significance of this romantic aspiration to society for regulation researchers? Can it reinvigorate the regulatory imagination? Does it fundamentally question the technocratic, instrumental focus on sectional political interests and economic preferences of "stakeholders" in the analysis of regulatory strategies? What, if anything, can it contribute to debates about the regulatory capacity of a social sphere?

This special issue arises from a workshop that sought to critically explore a renewed interest in "big society"[1] solutions to regulatory crises, as a potential alternative to reliance on self-regulating markets and state regulation. The guest editors organized an international, interdisciplinary workshop in April 2010 at the Centre for Socio-Legal Studies, Oxford University. Forty-two risk regulation scholars from the United Kingdom, Germany, the Netherlands, France, Australia, and the United States, including lawyers, socio-legal researchers, political scientists, sociologists, and economists responded to our invitation.[2] This special issue draws together their key contributions. It explores whether and how the idea of harnessing the regulatory capacity of a social sphere provides a new analytical lens that can provide fresh insights into transnational risk regulation, and whether this idea helps to identify innovative approaches to regulating transnational risks.

HARNESSING THE REGULATORY CAPACITY OF A SOCIAL SPHERE

Harnessing the regulatory capacity of a social sphere involves to govern business through civil society, including economic actors themselves and lawyers, social norms, and institutional structures, such as nongovernmental organizations, as well as discourses arising from the normative political activism of citizens. We therefore define regulation from a socio-legal angle as involving various techniques of social and legal control deployed by civil society actors in order to prevent, minimize, or manage risks arising from economic activity. We use the term "social sphere" as a heuristic for citizens' imagined or real social bonds, mobilized in their interactions and informed by social norms. These social bonds stretch across different levels of governance, meshing together local, regional, national, and supranational public spheres (Habermas, 1996, p. 444). We distinguish a "social sphere" from the state and its regulatory institutions, such as public administration, and differentiate it from markets, one specific form of coordinating economic activity. But we also recognize links between a social sphere and specific state and economic institutions (see also Chng, 2012, p. 356). For instance, states and markets can also be institutional channels for the expression of social norms, though this is usually not perceived to be their primary or sole purpose. We understand a social sphere in reflexive terms, capable of regulating economic actors, but also regulating those who seek to harness its regulatory capacity. For instance, "fair trade" discourses can regulate the exchange of commodities, but also regulate the scope of citizens' consumptive behavior by constituting "the ethical, responsible, economic citizen." Drawing on Hood, Rothstein, and Baldwin (2001, p. 3) we define risk regulation through a social sphere as an activity which seeks to limit consequences labeled as "adverse" by specific regulatory regimes, with key elements of regulation having increasingly a transnational dimension. The objects of regulation, such as markets or social processes no longer operate merely within national spheres. Also the risks generated by economic activity travel beyond the boundaries of specific nation states, and finally regulating itself, that is, setting and enforcing standards, is increasingly a transnational activity. In developing the idea of harnessing the regulatory capacity of a social sphere, we start from a particular vantage point by drawing on economic sociology of law (Swedberg, 2003).

AN ECONOMIC SOCIOLOGY OF LAW TAKE ON THE REGULATION OF ECONOMIC ACTIVITY

We suggest that in order to gain new insights into transnational risk regulation we need empirical, sociologically informed accounts of business activity, different from those that neoclassical or even behavioral economics provide, though both these latter perspectives have been influential in regulation scholarship (Jolls, Sunstein, & Thaler, 2000; Ogus, 2006; Thaler & Sunstein, 2008). Neoclassical economics proceeds on the basis of abstract, "thin" assumptions about the utility maximizing and rational nature of individual economic agents. While behavioral economics recognizes a wider range of actually observed economic activity, it still works with key elements of the *homo oeconomicus* approach to economics, for instance, by rendering cognition central to economic action, thereby seeking to remedy what it perceives as heuristic shortcuts generated by the mobilization of emotions in economic reasoning (Bandes, 2013).

The articles in this special issue seek to develop a different perspective because their understanding of transnational risk regulation builds on sociological insights into actual business behavior. Hence, they provide a critical lens through which to view different concepts, such as market failure, competition, and economic self-interest that are more likely to be reified in risk regulation scholarship influenced by economic analysis (Driesen, 2012; Faure, Ogus, & Philipsen, 2009), and – somewhat puzzlingly – continue to be influential in current regulatory reform debates (Engelen et al., 2011, p. 159; Williams, 2013). In contrast to this, contributions to this special issue conceive of markets as institutions that are protected against "failure" through various social norms and political institutions (Abolafia, 2013). Competition is shown to be not a natural, neutral precondition for market-based economic exchange but revealed as a power relationship between market actors (Hutchens, 2013). Economic self-interest is understood to be a more complex social phenomenon than merely rational utility maximization. For Bandes (2013) it is also informed by emotional dynamics such as perceptions of self, relations to others, and appropriate risk taking.

In order to explore the regulatory capacity of a social sphere we draw on the classic and widely debated economic sociology text "The Great Transformation" by Karl Polanyi (2001 [1944]). For Polanyi regulation also occurs through the embedding of economic into social relationships. He suggests that we experience repeated cycles of embedding, dis-embedding, and re-embedding of economic in social relationships over the course of history. While in preindustrial societies economic relationships were embedded in social ones, the industrial revolution led to a disembedding of economic out of social relationships, also because markets which relied on the commodification of land, labor, and money, became central to the coordination of economic relationships. But through his historical analysis Polanyi seeks to show that this stage of disembedded economic relations does not last. It is followed by a "regulatory countermove" of society in which economic relationships are re-embedded again in social relationships, in order to reign in the socially destructive effects of the "myth" of self-regulatory markets (Stiglitz, 2001, p. xiii). The articles in this special issue explore the significance of these Polanyian ideas about the regulatory capacity of a social sphere in the context of contemporary risk[3] regulation regimes.

DEVELOPING POLANYIAN IDEAS ABOUT ECONOMY–SOCIETY INTERACTIONS

The articles explore whether and how embedding economic in social relationships can contribute to regulating contemporary transnational risks.

They thereby start from Polanyi's "embeddedness" metaphor. While some articles apply Polanyian ideas to regulatory activity, others also point toward new lines of inquiry and thereby transcend the original Polanyian framework. In particular some articles question under what conditions and in which fields of regulation it makes sense to think of economic and social relationships as distinct, a conceptual move that seems to be necessary before Polanyi's ideas about the disembedding and re-embedding of economic relationships can be applied. These articles question that we should start inquiry by assuming a distinction between a social and an economic sphere. Some articles also provide a reverse, though not entirely different take on Polanyi's idea of embedding economic into social relationships, by exploring how society works *within* economy.

More specifically three articles in Part I reflect critically on Polanyi's "embeddedness" metaphor also by comparing and contrasting Polanyi's ideas with both classical and contemporary social theorists, such as Weber, Marx, and Durkheim as well as Foucault, Bourdieu, and Luhmann (Frerichs, 2013; Lange, 2013; Paterson, 2013).

Frerichs' theoretical analysis reinterprets Polanyi's "embeddedness" metaphor. Frerichs suggests that embedding occurs not just on a behavioral, but also on a cognitive level. She shows that Polanyi focused on a behavioral dimension of embedding. He analyzed how economic relationships became actually embedded in social ones, for instance, through the redistribution of economic gains in medieval times between a town and its hinterland or through the exchange of economic goods in gift relationships. Frerichs, however, points to the importance also of cognitive resources in performing economic activity. She argues that the "market society," that is, a society in which economic exchange is mainly coordinated through markets, is "cognitively embedded" in neoclassical and neo-institutional economics, as specific professional practices. With reference to Bourdieu and Foucault she suggests that the market society is performed also by conceptual means, that is, by "symbolic violence," which takes effect "in the form of mental structures and categories of perception of thought" (Frerichs, 2013, referring to Bourdieu). Her introductory, contextualizing account thus also highlights the importance of a critical sociology of economic knowledges, which explain how different economic knowledge regimes underpin various types of organizing economic activity.

Lange further develops this theme of performativity with reference to an analysis of how "economy" and "society" are socially constructed. This provides a critical gloss on Polanyi's metaphor of "embedding" economy in society which seems to require some prior conceptual distinction between "economy" and "society." Lange illustrates close interconnections between a social and an economic sphere through an analysis of the EU regulatory regime for transgenic agricultural products. Attempts during administrative authorization processes to distinguish between "social" and "economic" advantages and risks of these products flounder, as various participants in this regulatory regime press for the recognition of "socioeconomic" impacts of transgenic agricultural products.

In contrast to this, Paterson's article suggests, also with reference to Luhmann, that Polanyi assumed a too close conceptual relationship between economy and society. Paterson contrasts Polanyi's "embeddedness" metaphor with the Luhmannian image of society and economy as separate autopoietic, self-referential spheres. Paterson identifies "finance" as a subsystem of the economy which resists "embedding" and thus external regulation, because it is cognitively open, but normatively closed to its societal environment. Hence, Paterson also suggests that some of Polanyi's ideas may have limited applicability in contemporary societies. In developed countries in the 21st century "the economy" is much more differentiated from "society" than in the industrialized countries of the 19th and 20th century, the latter being a key empirical reference for Polanyi in "The Great Transformation." Moreover, the system of finance can be further differentiated, as containing also the subfield of credit default swaps and bond contracts. The latter constitute a separate social subsystem of "finance," which is decoupled from the "real economy" in which actual goods and services are traded. But Paterson's argument also affirms some Polanyian ideas. In particular he extends Polanyi's notion of the "fictitious commodities," land, labor and nature which were created during the industrial revolution, to financial risk itself which is now being commodified through contemporary financial services.

The following six articles in Part II further develop the analytical lens of harnessing the regulatory capacity of a social sphere through engagement with the Polanyian idea that economic activity can be regulated by being embedded in social relationships (Voiculescu, 2013; Thomas, 2013; Gulati & Weidemaier, 2013; Hutchens, 2013; Bandes, 2013; Schiavi, 2013). On the basis of qualitative empirical data, academic literature and legal case-based analysis they locate "society" *within* "economy" by depicting social norms, interactions, and their institutional manifestations, as integral to economic activity. They thereby depart from a governmentality perspective that emphasizes "economy" in "society," that is, the intrusion of economic rationalities into social relationships in contemporary societies, for instance through "welfare to work" reforms of social security systems (Rose, 1996, p. 340). "Society" within "economy" seems to be a theme of wider significance, capturing also a shift in public sector reform. While under the banner of "new public management" in the 1980s and 1990s "economy," "efficiency," and "effectiveness" became key principles informing public service delivery, there is now a shift back to the consideration of "social" values in state economic activity. The Public Services (Social Value) Act 2012 in the United Kingdom requires English and Welsh public bodies to consider in their procurement decisions how the services and goods they obtain may improve "the economic, social and environmental well-being of the relevant area" (Sect. 1 (3) Public Services (Social Value) Act 2012).

By focusing on the regulatory capacity of a social sphere at the heart of economic activity we seek to avoid a reified, mythical conception of "society," which conceives of society as external to economic activity, and thus as a fundamental structural force that shapes economic activity "behind the back of economic actors" who primarily consider themselves as self-interested, rational utility maximizers. By locating "society" *within* economy we also seek to depart from a romantic aspiration to society which sees society as an essential counterforce to markets, and which has informed some reform debates in the wake of the contemporary economic and political crises and also features in some critiques of "neoliberalism" (Cruddas & Rutherford, 2010; Editorial, 2012; Gamble, 2001, pp. 70, 132–133; Tickell & Peck, 1995, p. 379; Williams, 2010, p. xii).

The first two articles in Part II of this special issue (Gulati & Weidemaier, 2013; Thomas, 2013) apply and develop Polanyian ideas about economy and society interactions in the context of sovereign debt markets, a type of market that now plays a much more significant role than in the early 1940s when Polanyi wrote "The Great Transformation" (Block, 2001, p. xviii). Weidemaier and Gulati develop the Polanyian idea of a market actor through their empirical analysis of elite law firms' rationalizations of anomalies in their drafting of sovereign bond contracts. Their analysis illustrates the "society within economy" theme in two ways. First, they reveal that the lawyers adopt a nonmarket narrative which suggests that they insert, for instance, unanimity requirements for dealing with creditor claims in bond contracts because they simply copy preexisting bond contracts. But Weidemaier and Gulati show that changes in bond contracts, such as the insertion of collective action clauses (CACs), reflect responsiveness to greater risks of default in sovereign bond markets. Hence, their analysis, which chimes with Hutchens' ideas, reveals that markets are not fixed institutional structures, but a set of social actor-mediated, dynamic strategies. Sovereign bond lawyers are in fact, even though they seek to deny this, powerful market actors. Second, CACs in bond contracts can help to coordinate creditor claims and ensure speedy debt workouts. A trustee, appointed through CACs, will owe duties to all of the bondholders as a group, rather than just to specific individual bondholders. Hence CACs keep the self-interested behavior of bondholders in check. Changes in bond drafting practices therefore reflect wider social norms about appropriate limits to the power of market actors which contribute to the regulation of sovereign debtor default, a further illustration of the society within economy theme.

Thomas presents a case-based analysis of sovereign debt litigation in relation to the Costa Rican and Argentinian debt crises in 1981 and 2001. She reveals the critical role of state intervention – through a debt restructuring policy – in giving effect to private law sanctions against defaulting debtors. Contrary to contemporary accounts that view private law as a necessary and sufficient check on sovereign debt markets, she argues that the effectiveness of private law remedies is both historically contingent and ideologically determined. Her analysis questions a classification of debates about sovereign debt regulation in noninterventionist, market led and interventionist, statutory law based responses. She proposes an alternative Polanyian reading of regulatory changes in sovereign debt markets, by highlighting that apparently self-regulating markets are sustained by political intervention. It remains to be seen whether future Eurozone debt workouts may be influenced by the faith of policy makers in the effectiveness of the private law, despite evidence to the contrary, in the absence of a Eurozone-wide debt restructuring policy.

Two further articles (Hutchens, 2013; Voiculescu, 2013) apply Polanyian ideas about society and economy interactions by discussing "fair trade" markets in food commodities, such as cocoa and coffee and "corporate social responsibility" more widely. Such "fair trade" markets appear at first glance to be less "disembedded" out of social relationships than sovereign bond markets. As the articles, however, show, harnessing the regulatory capacity of a social sphere by embedding economic into social relationships varies and needs to be analyzed with reference to the specific dynamics of particular markets at particular times. Contemporary financial markets can become re-embedded by being governed also by social norms, and some current fair trade markets can become dis-embedded through competitive pressures. But Hutchens' analysis of "fair trade" also shows that harnessing the regulatory capacity of a social sphere can entail the building of society. Higher pay for food stuffs producers in the developing world is used for infrastructure development, such as the building of schools and hospitals (Hutchens, 2009, pp. 139, 140, 2013, in this special issue).

Voiculescu applies Polanyian ideas by showing how his concepts of householding and reciprocity can further strengthen contemporary corporate social responsibility (CSR) discourse. She develops the notion of "gratuitous reciprocity" which involves unconditionality in the provision of economic activity. This form of economic activity, which is more akin to gift relationships, constitutes a departure from exchange-based forms of business. In the context of "gratuitous reciprocity" economic actors' commitment to "civil" values in economic life ensures that those values are pursued regardless of their cost. Two further articles (Bandes, 2013; Schiavi, 2013) develop a critique of Polanyian ideas by questioning clear-cut conceptual distinctions between a social and an economic sphere. Both of them highlight emotions as a shared feature of both an economic and a social sphere.

Emotions as a Shared Feature of Both an Economic and a Social Sphere

Bandes, Schiavi (and Hutchens and Lange) depict emotions as an important element of a social sphere because they are an integral aspect of social interactions and they are central to how social actors make sense of their worlds. But Bandes and Schiavi also depict emotions as a central aspect of economic activity (see also Perry-Kessaris, 2011, p. 404; Swedberg, 2003, p. 30). For instance, trust is indispensable for enabling economic exchange relationships, in particular when highly risky products are traded (Lange, 2013).

Bandes identifies a whole range of emotions including trust, fear, empathy, and disgust as shaping not just lay people's but also experts' reasoning about complex risks and appropriate regulatory responses. Hence Bandes questions Polanyi's argument that we witness over the course of history a cyclical, *automatic* dis- and re-embedding of economic out of and back into social relationships. Bandes' analysis suggests that there is nothing automatic about the re-embedding of economic into social relationships. Instead she argues that complex emotional dynamics mediate whether and when society's regulatory counter-movement springs into action and regulates risks. Emotions influence who is "within our circle of empathy and compassion," and thus what we consider as a fair distribution of risks, a point Bandes powerfully illustrates with reference to the 1995 Chicago Heat Wave and the 2005 Hurricane Katrina. Understanding emotional dynamics is thus important for understanding how regulation through "society" building within the "economy" occurs, a point further developed in Schiavi's analysis of the centrality of trust to facilitating and regulating mining operations.

Schiavi discusses trust-based strategies for regulating social and environmental risks in the Australian and US mining industry. She defines trust as the belief of a social actor that other social actors' behavior will not harm his or her interests. She argues that trust of various stakeholders, such as workers, regulators, and citizens living in the vicinity of mines, is central not just for mining corporations to build market share, but also to regulating mining. Mining corporations, for instance, seek to build reputations of trustworthiness with their stakeholders in order to lessen state regulatory interference, which, in turn, renders them susceptible to regulators' shaming strategies. But Schiavi also recognizes limits to trust-based regulatory strategies. She suggests that punitive state sanctions still matter, also in order to avoid that corporate actors abuse trust-based relationships with regulators and citizens. Schiavi thereby illustrates, like Hutchens, that emotions are crucial to the constitution and operation of both a social and economic sphere. Trust can promote both embedded and disembedded states of economic activity.

To summarize, the articles in this special issue provide a rich and nuanced analysis of harnessing the regulatory capacity of a social sphere to regulate transnational risks arising from economic activity. They highlight that the relevance of Polanyian ideas also varies with the particular cultural, market, and political contexts in which economic activity occurs. While the articles develop different facets of harnessing the regulatory capacity of a social sphere they also converge around common features. As Abolafia points out in his discussion appreciating the regulatory effects of a social sphere means to be aware of the importance of scripts that guide what constitutes appropriate behavior, for example, in a market. Market actors regulate themselves, for instance, by addressing in the context of each economic transaction how to balance opportunism with restraint, innovation with standard practice, as well as growth with stability. But this special issue also explores the limits of the regulatory capacity of a social sphere. Paterson draws attention to the resistance of financial markets to be regulated, and Schiavi points to the double-edged nature of enrolling a social sphere as regulatory actor. On the one hand, trust enables control of corporations for the purposes of wider social and environmental interests, while, on the other hand, it also facilitates maximization of shareholder returns, the pursuit of "accumulative norms" in Abolafia's terms. Similarly

Voiculescu points to the risk of CSR discourses becoming absorbed into a dominant, global neoliberal market paradigm.

While harnessing the regulatory capacity of a social sphere trains the spotlight on citizens' and economic actors' regulatory initiatives a number of articles in this special issue show that state law can frame such initiatives. For instance, Thomas argues that governments reassuring market actors that private law sanctions still play a role is an important aspect of contemporary regulation of sovereign debt markets. Also Abolafia emphasizes the importance of political institutions which help to enforce the resolutions that market actors find to their conflicts. Similarly Lange points to the continued significance of state law to harnessing the regulatory capacity of a social sphere. She suggests that legal regulation can be informed by both social norms that inform the operation of state law and social norms that inform business behavior. But what does harnessing the regulatory capacity of a social sphere – both as an analytical lens and as a regulatory strategy – contribute to contemporary regulation debates?

HARNESSING THE REGULATORY CAPACITY OF A SOCIAL SPHERE: A DISTINCT REGULATORY STRATEGY AND ANALYTICAL LENS?

We do not claim that exploring the regulatory capacity of a social sphere constitutes a new conceptual framework. But we argue that by reinterpreting Polanyi's social theory, in particular by questioning his "embeddedness" metaphor, also through exploring the idea of society *within* economy, we can develop a distinct analytical lens for understanding regulation, that can also frame empirical research. For instance, for the mining executives interviewed by Schiavi harnessing the regulatory capacity of a social sphere is a meaningful idea (see also Chng, 2012, p. 353). They themselves differentiate between mining regulation through state statutory provisions and the need to maintain "a social license" from the local communities in which they operate. Hence, we suggest that harnessing the regulatory capacity of a social sphere also captures a distinct regulatory strategy.

Exploring the regulatory capacity of a social sphere chimes with regulation scholarship that explores the role of civil society actors in regulation under various banners, such as co-regulation,[4] enforced self-regulation, smart regulation, meta-regulation, and regulatory mobilization (Braithwaite, 1982; Chng, 2012; Gunningham & Sinclair, 1998; Parker, 2002). More specifically, harnessing the regulatory capacity of a social sphere shares some features with, but is also distinct from three recent contributions to debates about the regulatory capacity of civil society actors in accounts of "regulatory sociability," "the sociological citizen," and "collaborative governance."

"Regulatory sociability" also builds on Polanyi's vision of markets being re-embedded in social relations (Findlay, 2012, p. 3). It shares with Polanyi a methodological approach that starts with "society" and is concerned about the fact that socially dislocated markets are failing society. This provides a counter-point to contemporary "better" regulation[5] and public choice perspectives (Farber & Frickey, 1991, p. 22) that focus on how the state may be failing markets, for instance, through excessive and bureaucratic "red tape" regulation, and the distortion of politicians' regulatory agendas by sectional economic interests.

Findlay's "regulatory sociability" perspective shares with the approach of harnessing the regulatory capacity of a social sphere an interest in enrolling citizens as a counterweight to bilateral, and often adversarial, relationships between regulators and regulated. Findlay (2013, p. 26) identifies as a drawback of such bilateral regulatory relationships the risk of regulators being captured by the interests of the regulated. He also considers bilateral regulation as resource intensive, requiring a developed public administration and regulatory expertise, that are not necessarily available in the global South. "Regulatory sociability" therefore seeks to devolve "regulatory power to a broader base of cooperative and mutualized stakeholder interests" (Findlay, 2012, p. 7). This development of "regulatory communities" may include "proxy advocates, technical experts, agency monitors, designated consumer representatives, and even ombudsmen" (Findlay, 2012, p. 10). Findlay also perceives a role for NGOs as private prosecutors, for instance, through class actions. This will be relevant in particular if there are strong legal provisions against anti-competitive behavior, if the state provides resources for NGOs to litigate and if the judiciary is not deferential toward economic interests. Moreover, "regulatory sociability" also seeks to understand markets in richer terms, that go beyond a neoclassical economic take, and takes into account their actual empirical operation. It suggests, for instance, that market failure is not an exception, but often endemic to the operation of markets (Findlay, 2012, p. 7). But "regulatory sociability" also differs from an exploration of the regulatory capacity of a social sphere. It pursues an explicit normative agenda, in particular a more equal distribution of wealth in a global context (Findlay, 2012, p. 3). It therefore advocates regulation that seeks simultaneously to reduce poverty and stabilize financial markets.

Silbey's (2011) less overtly normative "relational regulation"[6] approach explores how "sociological citizens" meet, in a pragmatic manner, occupational and professional obligations that help to accomplish organizational objectives, including those of regulatory agencies. Hence, Silbey is also interested in the regulatory force of social bonds. "Sociological citizens" are agents who use their own and sometimes their clients' dense professional networks in order to accomplish their professional work, not always in conformity with the formal rules of their workplace or even the commonly accepted moral standards of their profession (Silbey, 2011, p. 8).

Silbey's approach is concerned with the question how citizens in their professional roles handle norm conflicts, in particular how they seek to tackle gaps between regulatory standards and actual practices of the regulated. Related to this, but with a different emphasis, harnessing the regulatory capacity of a social sphere trains the lens on citizens' attempts to deconstruct such conflicts, through various strategies of building society *within* economy, and thereby transforming business activity by reducing its potential conflict with the "public interest," that is, "society's" regulatory standards. Moreover, Silbey's analysis of the everyday work of sociological citizens is located within the confines of formal organizations, for example, micro finance loan and prosecutors' offices, major industrial installations, Offices of Transport Security, as well as health and safety regulatory agencies. In contrast to this, exploring the regulatory capacity of a social sphere captures regulation beyond the limits of specific organizations, for instance through analysis of entire commodity chains (Hutchens, 2013) and within international markets, for example, in bond contract drafting services (Weidemaier & Gulati, 2013) or transgenic agricultural products (Lange, 2013). Finally, "relational regulation" is framed mainly through an interactional perspective, while harnessing the regulatory capacity of a social sphere also explores discourses and thus the constitution and limitation of agency by discursive means. Finally, an exploration of the regulatory capacity of a social sphere chimes with "collaborative governance" which explores the role of public–private partnerships in the delivery of public services.

Under the banner of "collaborative governance" government officials fulfill a public mandate through cooperation with private firms, groups, or individuals in order to create what is described in general terms as "public value" (Breyer, 2011, p. x; Donahue & Zeckhauser, 2011, p. 4). Similar to Polanyi's rejection of a class-based analysis, "collaborative governance" is rooted in a consensus approach, and therefore does not explore conflicts between different visions of "public value" held by different socioeconomic groups.

Collaborative governance shares with our interest in understanding the regulatory capacity of a social sphere an interest in mobilizing civil society actors in the accomplishment of public tasks. Donahue and Zeckhauser (2011, p. 36) point to the importance of mobilizing "the resourcefulness of citizens." They consider, for instance, individual citizens who adopt "healthy life styles" as an important third collaborator in the delivery of health care services. Donahue and Zeckhauser, however, focus mainly on the involvement of *organized* nonprofit and for profit private organizations in the delivery of public services, such as the development of the Chicago Millennium Park, the provision of emergency health care services, preschool education, and employee training, as well as the production of uranium fuel.

Like Silbey's "sociological citizen" perspective, "collaborative governance" values pragmatic approaches to regulation that build on lessons learnt from past mistakes (Donahue & Zeckhauser, 2011, p. 18). Moreover, like Silbey and Findlay, Donahue and Zeckhauser (2011, p. 281) foreground agency rather than social structures as key for explaining governance. In particular, they discuss "shared discretion" as a key feature of collaborative governance. This involves public and private actors determining jointly the specifics of the goal to be achieved and the means for realizing it (Donahue & Zeckhauser, 2011, p. 11). "Shared discretion" is located in the middle of a spectrum (Donahue & Zeckhauser, 2011, p. 16). "Contract" is located on one end of this spectrum. In contrast to "collaborative governance" it involves greater control by public bodies over private actors to whom the delivery of services is contracted out. It is also different from "charity," located on the other end of the spectrum, where private actors mainly exercise discretion in relation to the accomplishment of the public task. Donahue and Zeckhauser (2011, p. 286) advocate tight constraints on specific aspects of "shared discretion," such as preference and pay-off discretion, with preference discretion referring to the privileging of the agents' and thus private actors' tastes, preferences, and choices over those of public actors. In the case of "pay-off discretion" private benefits are realized to a greater extent than public ones (Donahue & Zeckhauser, 2011, pp. 25, 283).

This advocacy of tight constraints on private actors' discretionary powers illustrates that Donahue's and Zeckhauser's approach considers the state still as a key actor, since it sets limits to the exercise of discretion by private economic actors. This is different from the perspective of harnessing the regulatory capacity of a social sphere which perceives society as the key protagonist in interactions with economic actors. Moreover, "collaborative governance" does not seek to transcend the language of neoclassical economics in order to understand both public and private actors' behavior. It justifies the enrolment of the private sector in the delivery of public services on the grounds of "efficiency, including productive efficiency" and "effectiveness" as well as ownership of a greater range of "resources" (Breyer, 2011, p. xi; Donahue & Zeckhauser, 2011, pp. 38, 63).

CONCLUSION

This special issue starts to argue that harnessing the regulatory capacity of a social sphere is a distinct regulatory strategy and analytical lens which can help to develop new insights into transnational risk regulation. An inquiry into the regulatory capacity of a social sphere seeks to further develop Polanyi's macro-sociological idea of regulating by embedding economic in social relationships. But it also questions clear-cut distinctions between an economic and a social sphere by pointing to features shared by both social and economic action (see also Hann & Hart, 2011, p. 56). Moreover, an exploration of the regulatory capacity of a social sphere draws attention to "society" *within* "economy," for instance through society building elements of economic activity.

This points to a potentially more far-reaching vision for regulation of economic activity than Polanyi imagined. For him, society's regulatory counter-movement does no more than restore the strength of existing societies in the face of potentially destructive markets. More generally, harnessing the regulatory capacity of a social sphere seeks to develop academic literature at the intersection of a sociological take on economic activity and a sociological take on law. It seeks to contribute to developing debates that examine the legacy of Karl Polanyi, and economic sociology more widely, for regulation scholarship (Caparoso & Tarrow, 2009; Ebner & Beck, 2008; Hopkin & Blyth, 2011; Joerges, 2009; Joerges & Falke, 2011; Michael, 2008; Perry-Kessaris, Ashiagbor, & Kotiswaran, 2013; Tucker, 2010). It therefore aims to move debate about the regulation of transnational risks beyond a narrow, technocratic concern with "thin," instrumental, desocialized understandings of regulation that frame regulatory challenges mainly in terms of the need to focus on choosing the economically "optimal" or "efficient" regulatory strategies and models.

NOTES

1. In the United Kingdom this has taken on a particular, different meaning through the "big society" program of the current conservative–liberal coalition government that seeks to mobilize the third sector, such as charities and citizen volunteering, in order to provide public goods and services formally provided by the welfare state, also in order to promote social cohesion (see, e.g., the UK Prime Minister David Cameron's speech on the "big society," February 14, 2011, http://www.number10.gov.uk/news/pms-speech-on-big-society/; Lange, 2011).

2. We are grateful for financial support of the workshop through a UK Socio-Legal Studies annual seminar competition award.

3. Risk is defined as the probability of potentially not calculable adverse consequences materializing (Hood, Rothstein, & Baldwin, 2001, p. 3, fn. 1).

4. See, for example, the adoption of co-regulatory strategies which involve a degree of state oversight over economic actors' self-regulatory activities in the United Kingdom (http://www.bis.gov.uk/policies/bre/alternatives-to-regulation/co-regulation).

5. For instance, the UK government has set up a "Better Regulation Executive" which provides expert input into the development of regulatory policy and initiatives by developing alternatives to "command and control" state regulation, such as self- and co-regulation (http://www.bis.gov.uk/assets/biscore/better-regulation/docs/r/10-1155-reducing-regulation-made-simple.pdf; see also Weatherill, 2007).

6. Silbey defines "relational regulation" as a specific type of regulatory activity carried out by citizens, often in the context of their professional roles, in interaction with those subject to regulation. "Relational regulation" contributes to the achievement of regulatory objectives by pragmatically reducing gaps between regulatory standards and actual practices of the regulated. It chimes with Braithwaite's (2007) conception of responsive regulation that depicts a particular regulatory style of *state* regulators, which is responsive and relates to three key coping strategies ("feeling oppressed, thinking morally, and taking control") that make up motivational posturing adopted by regulatees.

ACKNOWLEDGMENT

I would like to thank Fiona Haines and Dania Thomas for comments on an earlier draft of this introduction.

REFERENCES

Abolafia, M. Y. (2013). Separate spheres? The cultural contradictions of markets. In B. Lange, D. Thomas, & A. Sarat (Eds.), *From economy to society? Perspectives on transnational risk regulation* (pp. 265–271). Bingley, UK: Emerald Group Publishing Limited.

Bandes, S. A. (2013). Emotions and risk regulation. In B. Lange, D. Thomas, & A. Sarat (Eds.), *From economy to society? Perspectives on transnational risk regulation* (pp. 219–237). Bingley, UK: Emerald Group Publishing Limited.
Block, F. (2001). Introduction. In K. Polanyi (Ed.), *The great transformation: The political and economic origins of our time* (pp. xviii–xxxviii). Boston, MA: Beacon Press.
Braithwaite, J. (1982). Enforced self-regulation: A new strategy for corporate crime control. *Michigan Law Review*, *80*(1), 1466–1507.
Braithwaite, V., Murphy, K., & Reinhart, M. (2007). Taxation threat, motivational postures, and responsive regulation. *Law and Policy*, *29*(1), 137–158.
Breyer, S. (2011). Foreword. In *Collaborative governance: Private roles for public goals in turbulent times* (pp. x–xiii). Princeton, NJ: Princeton University Press.
Brown, D. B. (2001). *Romanticism*. London: Phaidon Press. Reprint 2010.
Caparoso, C. J., & Tarrow, S. (2009). Polanyi in Brussels: Supranational institutions and the transnational embedding of markets. *International Organization*, *63*(4), 593–620.
Chng, N. R. (2012). Regulatory mobilization and service delivery at the edge of the regulatory state. *Regulation & Governance*, *6*, 344–361.
Cruddas, J., & Rutherford, J. (2010). The common table. In R. Williams & L. Elliott (Eds.), *Crisis and recovery: Ethics, economics and justice* (pp. 54–76). Basingstoke: Macmillan.
Donahue, J., & Zeckhauser, R. (2011). *Collaborative governance: Private roles for public goals in turbulent times*. Princeton, NJ: Princeton University Press.
Driesen, D. (2012). *The economic dynamics of law*. Cambridge: Cambridge University Press.
Ebner, A., & Beck, N. (2008). *The institutions of the market: Organizations, social systems, and governance*. Oxford: Oxford University Press.
Editorial. (2012). The economy: A calamitous strategy, with no end in sight. *Observer*, May 20. Retrieved from http://www.theguardian.com/commentisfree/2012/may/20/observer-editorial-governments-calamitous-economic-policy
Engelen, E., Ertürk, I., Froud, J., Sukhdev, J., Leaver, A., Moran, M., Nillson, A., & Williams, K. (2011). *After the great complacence: Financial crisis and the politics of reform* Oxford: Oxford University Press.
Farber, A., & Frickey, P. (1991). *Law and public choice: A critical introduction*. Chicago, IL: University of Chicago Press.
Faure, M., Ogus, A., & Philipsen, N. (2009). Curbing consumer financial losses: The economics of regulatory enforcement. *Law and Policy*, *31*(2), 161–191.
Findlay, M. (2012). Fictional commodities in asset bubbles – Was Polanyi right all along? Legal Studies Research Paper No. 12/09, Sydney Law School, February. Retrieved from http://ssrn.com/abstract=2001730
Findlay, M. (2013). Corporate sociability: Analyzing motivations for collaborative regulation. *Administration and Society*, 1–32, on-line pre-publication. Retrieved from http://aas.sagepub.com/content/early/2012/08/09/0095399712454115.abstract
Frerichs, S. (2013). Polanyi in an hourglass: The two lives of a sociological classic. In B. Lange, D. Thomas, & A. Sarat (Eds.), *From economy to society? Perspectives on transnational risk regulation* (pp. 25–47). Bingley, UK: Emerald Group Publishing Limited.
Gamble, A. (2001). Neo-liberalism. *Capital and Class*, *25*, 127–134.
Gulati, M., & Weidemeier, M. (2013). How markets work: The lawyer's version. In B. Lange, D. Thomas, & A. Sarat (Eds.), *From economy to society? Perspectives on transnational risk regulation* (pp. 107–133). Bingley, UK: Emerald Group Publishing Limited.
Gunningham, N., & Sinclair, D. (1998). *Smart regulation: Designing environmental policy*, Oxford: Clarendon Press.

Habermas, J. (1996). *Between facts and norms* (William Rehg, Trans.). Cambridge: Polity Press.

Hann, C., & Hart, K. (2011). *Economic anthropology: History, ethnography, critique*. Cambridge: Polity Press.

Hood, C., Rothstein, H., & Baldwin, R. (2001). Oxford: Oxford University Press.

Hopkin, J., & Blyth, M. (2011). What can Okun teach Polanyi? Efficiency, regulation and equality in the OECD. *Review of International Political Economy*, *69*, 1–33.

Hutchens, A. (2009). *Changing big business: The globalisation of the fair trade movement*. Cheltenham: Edward Elgar.

Hutchens, A. (2013). Defiance in the social sphere: The complexity of risk regulation in the case of fair trade. In B. Lange, D. Thomas, & A. Sarat (Eds.), *From economy to society? Perspectives on transnational risk regulation* (pp. 163–187). Bingley, UK: Emerald Group Publishing Limited.

Hyslop, L. (2012). Emigration from Ireland soars. *The Telegraph*. Retrieved from http://www.telegraph.co.uk/expat/expatnews/9584756/Emigration-from-Ireland-soars.html

Joerges, C. (2009). Ch. 21: Sound science in the European and global market: Karl Polanyi in Geneva. In M. Everson & E. Vos (Eds.), *Uncertain risks regulated* (pp. 415–426). London: Routledge.

Joerges, C., & Falke, J. (2011). *Karl Polanyi, globalisation and the potential of law in transnational markets*. Oxford: Hart Publishing.

Jolls, C., Sunstein, C. R., & Thaler, R. H. (2000). A behavioural approach to law and economics. In C. Sunstein (Ed.), *Behavioural law and economics* (pp. 13–59). Cambridge: Cambridge University Press.

Knights, B. (2004). From the idea of the clerisy: Samuel Taylor Coleridge. In N. Halmi, P. Magnuson, & R. Modiano (Eds.), *Coleridge's poetry and prose* (pp. 755–767).

Lange, B. (2011). Socializing economic relationships: A critique of business regulation: Introduction. *Northern Ireland Legal Quarterly*, *62*(4), 393–339.

Lange, B. (2013). After a romantic aspiration to society: Harnessing the regulatory capacity of a social sphere. In B. Lange, D. Thomas, & A. Sarat (Eds.), *From economy to society? Perspectives on transnational risk regulation* (pp. 1–21). Bingley, UK: Emerald Group Publishing Limited.

Michael, F. (2008). Law as the interplay of ideas, institutions, and interests: Using Polanyi (and Foucault) to ask TWAIL questions. *International Community Law Review*, *10*, 455–465.

Morgan, G. (2010). Legitimacy in financial markets: Credit default swaps in the current crisis. *Socio-Economic Review*, *8*, 17–45.

Ogus, A. (2006). *Costs and cautionary tales: Economic insights for the law*. Oxford: Hart Publishing.

Parker, C. (2002). *The open corporation: Effective self-regulation and democracy*. New York, NY: Cambridge University Press.

Paterson, J. (2013). A systems theory perspective on Polanyi's great tranasformation: The case of financial derivative contracts. In B. Lange, D. Thomas, & A. Sarat (Eds.), *From economy to society? Perspectives on transnational risk regulation* (pp. 49–71). Bingley, UK: Emerald Group Publishing Limited.

Perry-Kessaris, A. (2011). Reading the story of law and embeddedness through a community lens: A Polanyi-meets-Cotterrell economic sociology of law? *Northern Ireland Legal Quarterly*, *62*(3), 401–413.

Perry-Kessaris, A., Ashiagbor, D., & Kotiswaran, P. (2013). *Towards an economic sociology of law*. London: Wiley-Blackwell.
Polanyi, K. (2001 [1944]). *The great transformation: The political and economic origins of our time*. Boston, MA: Beacon Press.
Rose, N. (1996). The death of the social? Re-figuring the territory of government. *Economy and Society*, *25*(3), 327–356.
Saperstein, Z. (2012). *Occupy movement: Origins and future*. Amazon Self-Publication.
Schiavi, P. (2013). Trust and regulation: Insights from the mining industry. In B. Lange, D. Thomas, & A. Sarat (Eds.), *From economy to society? Perspectives on transnational risk regulation* (pp. 239–261). Bingley, UK: Emerald Group Publishing Limited.
Silbey, S. (2011). The sociological citizen: Pragmatic and relational regulation in law and organization. *Regulation and Governance*, *5*, 1–13.
Stiglitz, J. (2001). Foreword. In K. Polanyi (Ed.), *The great transformation: The political and economic origins of our time* (pp. vii–xvii). Boston, MA: Beacon Press.
Swedberg, R. (2003). The case for an economic sociology of law. *Theory and Society*, *32*(1), 1–37.
Thaler, R. H., & Sunstein, C. (2008). *Nudge: Improving decisions about health, wealth and happiness*. New Haven, CT: Yale University Press.
Thomas, D. (2013). Sovereign debt restructuring in the Eurozone: A Polanyian reading of private law enforcement. In B. Lange, D. Thomas, & A. Sarat (Eds.), *From economy to society? Perspectives on transnational risk regulation* (pp. 135–159). Bingley, UK: Emerald Group Publishing Limited.
Tickell, A., & Peck, J. (1995). Social regulation after Fordism: Regulation theory, neo-liberalism and the global-local nexus. *Economy and Society*, *24*(3), 357–386.
Tucker, E. (2010). Renorming labour law: Can we escape labour law's recurring regulatory dilemmas? *Industrial Law Journal*, *39*(2), 99–138.
Vaughan, W. (1978). *Romanticism and art*. London: Thames and Hudson Ltd.
Voiculescu, A. (2013). "Etiquette and magic": Between embedding and embedded corporate social responsibility. In B. Lange, D. Thomas, & A. Sarat (Eds.), *From economy to society? Perspectives on transnational risk regulation* (pp. 189–216). Bingley, UK: Emerald Group Publishing Limited.
Weatherill, S. (Ed.). (2007). *Better regulation*. Oxford: Hart Publishing.
Williams, R. (2010). Foreword. In R. Williams & L. Elliott (Eds.), *Crisis and recovery: Ethics, economics and justice* (pp. x–xiii). Basingstoke: Palgrave Macmillan.
Williams, T. (2013). Continuity not rupture: The persistence of neoliberalism in the internationalisation of consumer finance regulation. In T. Wilson (Ed.), *International responses to the credit crisis: Credit and over-indebtedness*. Farnham: Ashgate.
Wolff, R. (2012). *Occupy the economy: Challenging capitalism, Richard Wolff in conversation with David Barsamian*. San Francisco, CA: Open Media Series, City Light Books.

PART I
THEORETICAL ENGAGEMENT WITH POLANYI: CONTEXT AND CRITIQUE

POLANYI IN AN HOURGLASS: THE TWO LIVES OF A SOCIOLOGICAL CLASSIC

Sabine Frerichs

ABSTRACT

This article aims to show that studies of transnational risk regulation can benefit from Polanyian and neo-Polanyian research agendas in the field of law, economy, and society. Risk regulation would then be understood as a corrective force within the market society. Drawing on the relevant literature in the field, Karl Polanyi's work is contextualized both in the past ("scholarship before and beside Polanyi") and in the present ("scholarship after and beyond Polanyi"). The review considers developments within sociology, its neighboring disciplines economics and jurisprudence, and the interdisciplinary research fields of "economy and society," "law and society," and "law and economy." The article demonstrates that Polanyi is a "late classic" who shares the holistic orientation of classical historical scholarship. At the same time, it is argued that his "early revival" is due to the topicality of his criticism of the market society, and its inherent risks, in an era of neoliberalism and globalization. By going back and forth in time, the article situates Polanyi in a line of holistically minded scholarship that combines insights of general,

From Economy to Society? Perspectives on Transnational Risk Regulation
Studies in Law, Politics, and Society, Volume 62, 25–47

ISSN: 1059-4337/doi:10.1108/S1059-4337(2013)0000062002

economic, and legal sociology in what can be called the "economic sociology of law." This is "old" and "new," at the same time.

Keywords: Karl Polanyi; market society; classical sociology; contemporary sociology; economic sociology of law; general review

INTRODUCTION: WHY POLANYI?

Why engaging with Polanyi in a special issue on transnational risk regulation? Karl Polanyi (1886–1964), an economic historian and sociologist, can be understood as a theorist of risk regulation avant la lettre. In fact, his famous study "The Great Transformation" (1957 [1944]) is about nothing less than how a policy of unrestricted economic liberalism puts society, as a whole, at risk, that is, how it destroys its very foundations. More specifically, it is about how this "systemic risk" is produced, or instituted, by the so-called "fictitious commodities" of land, labor, and money (*ibid.*, Ch. 6). In a "market society," all of these are subject to the price mechanism and, hence, follow the logic of demand and supply. Sure enough, the creation of the "self-regulating market" – which was, first of all, a chimera of economic thinking – requires legal regulation (of subjects, objects, and means of exchange) as much as legal *de*regulation (in order to unleash the price mechanism). What results are unprecedented risks for the "substance" of economic life (Polanyi, 2001 [1957]), that is, for its natural substrate, which is turned into "land," for its social content, which is turned into "labor," and for capitalist production itself, which is subjected to "money capital." The volatility of the "factor markets" for land, labor, and money affects the stability and viability of market society itself.

In Polanyi's terms, risk regulation thus amounts to the "self-protection of society" against the destructive forces of the "self-regulating market" (1957 [1944], part II.2). While sweeping agendas of legal and economic deregulation have, in the first place, created these risks, substantive policies of environmental regulation, social regulation, and financial regulation act as counter-forces to the commodification of economic life. What is new today, compared to Polanyi's time, is the degree of economic integration and interdependence in the "globalized" market society. The free movement of goods and services, of capital and – less so – persons across national and regional borders ranks high on the (neo-) liberal agenda, and the resulting risks and remaining regulatory options have, more than ever, to be conceived from a transnational (or global) point of view. In this regard, it is worth mentioning that, other than the work of many of his contemporaries, Polanyi's account is not biased by "methodological nationalism." Instead, he started from the international political economy, that is, the larger institutional and ideological context, in which nation states and national economies themselves are "embedded" (*ibid.*, part I). Under conditions of Europeanization and globalization, this "holistic" point of view is gaining ever more importance (Frerichs, 2012a). For all these reasons, Polanyi's work deserves a fresh look.

SETTING THE FRAMEWORK

When Karl Polanyi completed, in a rush, "The Great Transformation" (1957 [1944]), he had much bigger worries than matching the works of the sociological classics. Published at the height of the Second World War, the book aims at explanations for the civilizational breakdown that people were witnessing and experiencing at that time, and at critical lessons for the future. One may think that Polanyi's in-depth study of "nineteenth century civilization" and its ultimate "collapse" bears little relevance to readers in the twenty-first century who are preoccupied with the problems of the present. However, his story of the "rise and fall of market economy," which originally ends with the Second World War, has found its continuation in the "rise and fall of the *social* market economy," as Wolfgang Streeck (2009) shows for postwar Germany. Whereas Polanyi's focus was on the social transformations which were once brought about by modern capitalism, Streeck's emphasis is on the more recent reformation of capitalism in post-welfarist societies. In both cases, the key observation is the loss of protective social institutions in the relentless play of the market forces. This is but one example of how Polanyi's historical analysis, and diagnosis of his time (*Zeitdiagnose*), also informs present scholarship about still ongoing developments. In fact, it seems that in times of increasing global interdependencies and recurrent crises, scholars across the social sciences seek, once again, inspiration from Polanyi's work and, notably, his concept of "social embeddedness" (see, e.g., Ashiagbor, Kotiswaran, & Perry-Kessaris, 2013; Beckert, 2007; Gemici, 2008; Joerges & Falke, 2011; Krippner & Alvarez, 2007; Krippner et al., 2004; Rizza, 2006).

It is in the definition of a "true classic" – be it in the realm of fiction (Sainte-Beuve, 2001 [1850]) or academia – that he or she engages not only his or her contemporaries but also speaks to the present. Against this background, one can identify two different ways to approach the work of a classic (Fine & Kleinman, 1986): One may either study the original concerns of the author, and of his or her time, or one may address present concerns through the eyes of the classic, by reframing the questions and refining the methodology of the original. Both roads have been taken in recent scholarship on Karl Polanyi, a renowned classic, first and foremost, in the field of economic sociology. In her review of "neo-Polanyian" scholarship, Sally Randles (2003) can thus distinguish between "Polanyi-*given*" and "Polanyi-*inspired*" research designs (p. 409; original emphasis). The first category encompasses scholars who either content themselves with a close reading of Polanyi's work or "contextualize" it within the "author's life and times," thus furthering "a broader understanding of Polanyi's concerns and normative position" (*ibid.*). In contrast, scholars in the second group take Polanyi's writings only as a starting point to develop their own views of contemporary society, which is increasingly perceived in terms of a globalized market society. According to Randles, "[t]hey are inspired by the view that Polanyian insights, worked out over a period of some 30 years of the 20th century, appear to provide such a high degree of relevance and application to problems facing the world today" (*ibid.*, p. 410).

In the following, I want to explore the two lives that Polanyi developed as a sociological classic, one in the past and one in the present. More precisely, I will "contextualize" his work both within his own time and within the present time. Like in an hourglass which runs both ways (and can thus, figuratively, "reverse" time), Polanyi's work will, hence, be approached from two different ends: from his classical mentors and from his contemporary audience. In doing so, I want to highlight what Polanyi learnt, or inherited, from the sociological classics, and what his current "revival" also imports into the present debate. At the same time, certain ideas of our time can also be read into Polanyi's writings, thus reinterpreting them from within. By locating Polanyi's work in the middle of a timeline which encompasses both scholarship "before and beside Polanyi" and scholarship "after and beyond Polanyi," I want to demonstrate continuities as well as discontinuities in the field of law, economy, and society. With his "holistic-historical" approach, Polanyi was still rooted in the legacy of the "founding fathers" of sociology – namely, Karl Marx, Emile Durkheim, and Max Weber – who were often advancing general sociology, legal sociology, and economic sociology at the same time. Moreover, they were also prolific in some of the neighboring disciplines (such as history, philosophy, economics, and jurisprudence). Compared to contemporary sociology, classical sociology was thus both more integrated across its different subfields and less insulated from the other social-scientific disciplines. As I will argue below, a Polanyian framework can, therefore, best be identified with some form of substantive and methodological "holism."

CONTEXTUALIZING POLANYI'S WORK IN THE PAST

The first step in my argumentation is to contextualize Polanyi's work in the past. For the purposes of this article, I will equate "the past" with "scholarship before and besides Polanyi," and "the present" with "scholarship after and beyond Polanyi." In the same vein, Polanyi's work can be taken as a reference point in order to distinguish between "classic" and "contemporary" scholarship. If we concentrate on Polanyi's most famous work, "The Great Transformation" (1957 [1944]), this separating line actually coincides with the Second World War. This is, of course, no mere "coincidence" but has deeper historical reasons. As Polanyi's own life and work demonstrates, the academic careers and research interests of many promising scholars were seriously affected by the dramatic events and developments that triggered – or were triggered by – the two world wars. The distinction between pre- and postwar scholarship is thus, by no means, arbitrary. In distinguishing, in the following, between scholarship "before" and "beside" Polanyi, I want to point to two different currents, or "generations," of sociological thinking, including its equivalents in socio-legal and socioeconomic thinking. These will be referred to as "historical-holistic" perspectives on the one hand, and "institutional-realist" perspectives on the other. Third, I will relate Polanyi's work to these two classic strands of thought and, thereby, account for his position as a sociological classic with regard to the context of his lifetime.

Scholarship Before Polanyi

The generation, or rather "era," of sociologically minded scholarship that preceded Polanyi's work, and which he could still draw upon, can best be characterized as "historicism." Historicism is here understood in the wider (and non-pejorative) sense of historical scholarship which puts social phenomena into a historical, and often comparative, perspective (Frerichs, 2011b, pp. 204–236, 2012b, pp. 18–36). It is characteristic of the nineteenth century and namely encompasses historical jurisprudence, historical economics, and historical sociology. The historical paradigm thus united scholarship across different social-scientific disciplines. More precisely, it apparently "spilled over" from jurisprudence, where it was developed first, to economics, and from economics to sociology. This spill-over effect can be illustrated both in terms of the leading persons and the guiding principles of historical scholarship. As to the persons, the ideas of Friedrich Carl von Savigny (1779–1861), the founder of the German historical school of jurisprudence, inspired not only English and American schools of historical jurisprudence, but also scholarship in the (emerging) disciplines of economics and sociology. For example, Wilhelm Roscher (1817–1894), a leader of the German historical school of economics, drew explicitly on its jurisprudential forerunner, while Emile Durkheim (1858–1917), one of the main representatives of classical historical sociology, made ample reference to historical economics. As to the principles, we can point to the "spirit of the people" which von Savigny found to be reflected in legal customs that emerged organically, without a need for codification. The same "collective spirit" seems at work in the minds of historical economists and sociologists when they study the moral foundations of the (national) economy and the (national) community, respectively.

The "holistic" orientation of historical scholarship consists in a certain predilection for collective entities, and perhaps, first and foremost, for national collectives. Law, economy, and society were thus preferably studied in a national frame of reference, including the (national) legal culture in jurisprudence, the (national) political economy in economics, and the (national) solidarity community in sociology. There are several technical terms which describe this analytical preference, such as "methodological collectivism" for an emphasis on collective rather than individual entities, "methodological nationalism" for an emphasis on national rather than global entities, and "methodological holism" for a more general emphasis on the "whole" rather than its "parts." I will here opt for the latter, most encompassing term since it captures best what I consider paradigmatic about historical scholarship. This term can then be respecified in several dimensions, including the relation between individual and collective entities, and the relation between national and global entities. Interestingly, historical scholarship seems more "holistic" in the former dimension than in the latter: It is collectivist but not globalist. However, there is yet another dimension which we can add to this methodological grid. In this third dimension, holism extends to the moral qualities that many historical scholars consider to be inherent to their subject matter, and also pertinent to their own scientific engagement. In other words, historical scholarship is often explicitly value-related, and inasmuch it derives these values from the material studied, it can be said to follow some sort of moral substantivism.

Scholarship "before" Polanyi thus forms part of an era in which sociology – and social science, more generally – was ultimately conceived as a moral science. For Durkheim (1887), sociology contributes a "positive science of morality" which aims at the moral cohesion of a given society. In the introductory lesson to his new "course of social science" (Durkheim, 1888) – the first of its kind in France – he declares: "[T]he collective spirit has weakened in our country. Each of us is so exorbitantly concerned with himself that he does not perceive the boundaries that constrain him everywhere" (*ibid.*, p. 24; my translation). Accordingly, the new sociological discipline was envisioned to "restore the consciousness of [society's] organic unity" (*ibid.*, my translation). "It will teach the individual what the society is, how he is complemented by it, and how little is due to his own forces. It will make clear that he is not an empire among other empires, but the organ of an organism" (*ibid.*; my translation). Regarding the moral ambitions underlying much of classic historical sociology, Durkheim's work is, perhaps, most explicit. But we can find similar features also in the works of other sociological classics, such as Karl Marx (1818–1883), at the one end, and Max Weber (1864–1920), at the other.

Marx's theory of social change entails a vision of human progress in technological as well as in moral respects. In capitalist times, the collective spirit, which includes a "natural" sense of right and wrong, seems, however, corrupted (Marx, 1842). It is the "economic structure of society" which determines not only the "legal and political superstructure" but also the related "forms of social consciousness" (Marx, 1859). The "alienations" brought about by the capitalist economy and its political ally, the bourgeois state, were meant to be overcome in a socialist, and later communist, society. Weber, in turn, combines a macro-sociological approach, which relies on the historical development and comparison of collective entities as a whole, with a micro-sociological approach, which starts from the "meaning" that individuals attach to their (inter-) action. Both aspects, historicity and meaning, form part of what Weber considers the moral underpinning of social science, namely its orientation toward the "cultural significance" of the phenomena studied. Accordingly, the "objectivity" of social-scientific, namely empirical, knowledge is qualified by its relation to "evaluative ideas" which render the reality "meaningful" to us (Weber, 2004 [1904], pp. 377, 382).

All in all, historical scholarship was thus holistic, first of all, in *social* terms. Its basic entities were collectives rather than individuals, or individuals in their social context. Hence, the frame of reference of historical scholarship was macro- rather than micro-sociological. As importantly, it was holistic in *historical* terms. It aimed for an understanding of modern society – or, more precisely, of the modern Western civilization – from a historical point of view. Its all-encompassing orientation in time was complemented by its intended completeness on a *spatial* scale, even though the comparison of different cultures, or nations, was still predominant. Today, notions of world history and world society imply, in contrast, a genuinely global perspective. Furthermore, society was not only studied from the observable and measurable outside but also from the evaluative inside, that is, its inherent values. Historical scholars were thus not only interested in the causes and effects but also in the cultural meaning of social developments, and in the *moral* lessons to be drawn. Finally, the social-scientific field was still integrated in a way that scholars could relatively easily move from one (emerging) discipline to the other – such as Weber, whose academic career led from law to economics and from economics to sociology (Swedberg, 2006, p. 74). It was thus a certain holism also in *substantial* terms which allowed the historical paradigm to flourish across the social sciences, or, vice versa, substantial comprehensiveness was itself furthered by the holistic perspective of historical scholarship.

Scholarship Beside Polanyi

While the nineteenth century was mainly characterized by historical-holistic scholarship, the field of law, economy, and society already looked much different in the early twentieth century, when Karl Polanyi started his academic career. A historical contextualization of his work therefore also has to take account of the developments that took place at, or around, the turn of the twentieth century, here including the decades leading to the two world wars. In this period, some important shifts took place which mark, at the same time, the beginning of a "positivist" era of (social) science that left moral questions largely aside, or rather, moved them outside the sphere of scientific enquiry (Frerichs, 2012b, pp. 36–55). Since the label "positivism" is often used in a negative sense – notably, to criticize others and not to identify oneself – some qualifications seem in place.

"Logical positivism" denotes a specific school of thought – the so-called Vienna Circle – which formed in the 1920s and set out to rid science of all metaphysical speculations. Due to its "empiricist criterion of meaning and a broadly logicist conception of mathematics" it is also referred to as "logical empiricism" (Uebel, 2011). Accordingly, truth is a matter of logical forms and measurable facts, and not of morality. Against this ideational background, positivism has, more generally, come to stand for a strong emphasis on empirical facts, while abstracting as much as possible from underlying value-relations. Such a positivist/empiricist orientation eventually seems to prevail in the disciplines of economics and sociology by the middle of the twentieth century. However, also the dominant school of thought within jurisprudence is, at that time, known as "legal positivism." In this case, though, the term positivism does not refer to the empirical study of law, or legal behavior, which is the subject of "legal realism," but to the study of law as something that has been "posited" by courts or legislators (Green, 2009). It is, thus, the legal text – and not the social context or moral subtext – that legal positivists start from. What the different "positivisms" in economics, sociology, and jurisprudence do have in common is, however, a clear abdication of moral judgments as far as the empirical analysis of social facts or the textual analysis of legal norms is concerned.

The stage for these positivist developments was, at least in the German-speaking countries, set by the so-called "battles of methods" (*Methodenstreits*) which economists and (prospective) sociologists fought out in the late nineteenth century (first battle of methods) and in the early twentieth century (second battle of methods, also called *Werturteilsstreit*, i.e., battle of value judgements). The same term is also used in jurisprudence, albeit only when legal positivism came itself under attack in the 1920s. What is important here is that, at least in economics and sociology, the methodological debates largely consisted of a fierce criticism (and a passionate defence) of historical scholarship, which was attacked both for its analytical deficiencies and its moral ambitions. One of the main goals of the positivist camp, which subscribed to the postulate of "freedom from value judgements" (*Wertfreiheitspostulat*), was to draw a clear line between social science, properly speaking, and social policy. These debates affected not only the methodological outlook of law, economics, and sociology as independent disciplines but also the relationship between them, notably in the fields of "economy and society," "law and society," and "law and economy" (Frerichs, 2009, pp. 20–22). Against these odds, I want to emphasize two developments which can be understood as a continuation of holistically minded scholarship "between the disciplines." The first concerns "old" institutional economics, the second "old" legal realism. Both strands of thought are, first and foremost, connected with U.S. American scholarship in the first half of the twentieth century.

The continuity between the historical school of economics and "old" institutional economics can be demonstrated as follows. Writing in 1890, the English economist Alfred Marshall (1920 [1890]) praises the achievements of the German historical school of economics, which actually spans over three academic generations (from Wilhelm Roscher via Gustav Schmoller to Max Weber). He explicitly acknowledges its historical-comparative orientation and its link with legal history. "[German historical economists] have taken the lead in the 'comparative' study of economic, as well as of general history. They have brought side by side the social and industrial phenomena of different countries and of different ages; have so arranged them that they throw light upon and interpret one another, and have studied them all in connection with the suggestive history of jurisprudence" (1920 [1890], Appendix B, § 8). A few lines later Marshall claims that historical economics has thus enlightened "the history of economic *habits* and *institutions*" and "the *evolution* of man's moral and social life" (*ibid.*; emphasis added). A very similar research agenda, using quite similar terms, was also developed on the other side of the Atlantic, notably in the realm of "old" institutional economics. As Geoffrey Hodgson (1998) summarizes, the main focus of this school of economic thought, which emerged from "the evolutionary controversies of the 1890s and early 1900s" (*ibid.*, p. 190), was on "institutions, habits, rules, and their evolution" (*ibid.*, p. 168). After the First World War, it was even considered "dominant in economics departments in American universities" (*ibid.*, p. 166). Main representatives of this "old" institutionalism were Thorstein Veblen (1857–1929), who is known best for his concept of "conspicuous consumption," and John Rogers Commons (1862–1945), who published, among others, a book entitled "The Legal Foundations of Capitalism" (Commons, 1924) – and thus links, once again, economic and legal scholarship.

The continuity between the historical school of jurisprudence and "old" legal realism is, despite all differences, based on similar notions of the spirit of the people (von Savigny) and the spirit of the time (Pound). The American counterpart of German historical jurisprudence is connected with the name of James Coolidge Carter (1837–1905) and, actually, "became the dominant school of legal theory in the United States in the late nineteenth and into the first decades of the twentieth century, both among legal scholars and in the courts" (Berman 2005, p. 16). However, soon after the turn of the century, a strong "cross-disciplinary" competitor emerged in the form of sociological jurisprudence, which is the "oldest" form of American legal realism. This initial movement is mainly connected with the name of Roscoe Pound (1870–1964), who coined the famous distinction between "law in books" and "law in action" (1910). Pound criticized Carter's approach, and historical jurisprudence, more generally, as being preoccupied with the past and its expression in customary law (legal rules as social habits), thereby neglecting the present and its (possible) expression in statutory law (Grossman, 2009). In other words, he promotes a more progressive, or proactive, view of law (as shaping social habits): "Let us not be afraid of legislation, and let us welcome new principles, introduced by legislation, which express the spirit of the time" (Pound, 1910). While law is thus explicitly considered as political instrument – and less in its organic or systemic nature – the idea of a moral consciousness is still there. In fact, lawyers are encouraged "to induce a consciousness of the role of ideal pictures of the social and legal order both in decision and in declaring the law" (Pound, 1923, p. 958). Foreshadowing the opening-up of legal realism toward law and economics, Oliver Wendell Holmes (1841–1935) already claimed at the turn of the twentieth century that "the man of the future is the man of statistics and the master of economics" (Holmes, 1897, p. 469).

Polanyi as "Old School"

As an interim conclusion, I will provide some evidence for the fact that Karl Polanyi was, in many ways, one of the old school – without identifying him with any of the historical-holistic or institutional-realist schools of thought in particular. Polanyi was an original thinker but also a child of his time and, notably, an heir to the holistic currents of scholarship, which marked the nineteenth century. At the same time, he was, apparently, not much affected yet by the methodological debates that took place at the turn of the twentieth century, and the upcoming analytical and empirical "positivism" (and disciplinary purism). In order to substantiate this argument, I will make use of the methodological grid elaborated above, that is, the five (ideal-typical) dimensions of "methodological holism," and illustrate them with regard to Polanyi's work. Not surprisingly, his overall approach is best expressed in the "embeddedness" paradigm, which has actually come to be equated with his work, but which has also been reinterpreted in less holistic terms, namely in "new" economic sociology. In "The Great Transformation," the embeddedness term is rarely used as such but it does play a prominent role in the depiction of the market society: "Instead of economy being embedded in social relations, social relations are embedded in the economic system" (Polanyi, 1957 [1944], p. 57). More generally, the idea of embeddedness can be understood as the essence of Polanyi's holistic way of thinking. With his "substantivist" emphasis on the institutions that shape the economy, Polanyi shares, at the same time, in the legacy of "old" institutionalism (2001 [1957]).

Polanyi's notion of embeddedness starts from the macro-social level, namely from the "interior relationship of the economic and the social" (Krippner & Alvarez, 2007, p. 233). According to this view, economy and society – or, with a different accent, the economy and the state – are mutually constitutive and not separate spheres per se. An example of this holistic argument is Polanyi's characterization of the self-regulating market: "A self-regulating market demands nothing less than the *institutional separation of society* into an economic and political sphere. Such a dichotomy is, in effect, merely the restatement, from the point of view of *society as a whole*, of the existence of a self-regulating market" (1957 [1944], p. 71; emphasis added). Polanyi's reasoning is, at the same time, holistic also in historical terms when he continues: "Neither under tribal, nor feudal, nor mercantile conditions was there, as we have shown, a separate economic system in society. Nineteenth century society, in which economic activity was isolated and imputed to a distinctive economic motive, was, indeed, a singular departure" (*ibid.*). Moreover, according to Polanyi, the economic theory underlying the attempt "to establish a self-regulating economic system on the motive of individual gain" gives only a "distorted view of life and society" (*ibid.*, p. 269). In order to complement and correct this approach, a substantive – or interdisciplinary – holism seems necessary, which reunites economic theory with economic history and economic sociology. Referring to the "testimony of modern research in various fields of social science such as social anthropology, primitive economics, the history of early civilization, and general economic history," Polanyi thus concludes that "there is hardly an anthropological or sociological assumption – whether explicit or implicit – contained in the philosophy of economic liberalism that has not been refuted" (*ibid.*).

Substantively, Polanyi distinguishes between four "institutional patterns and principles of behavior [which] are mutually adjusted" (*ibid.*, p. 43). Accordingly, in nonmarket societies, institutional patterns of symmetry, centricity, and/or autarchy, which are themselves based on behavioral principles of reciprocity, redistribution, and/or householding, were still prevailing. In contrast, the dominant mode of organization, and related behavior, in the modern market society is "[b]arter, truck, and exchange" (*ibid.*, p. 56). A similar argument is behind Polanyi's criticism of the "commodification" of man and nature, namely in the form of land and labor, which are then only seen in their exchange value and no longer in their intrinsic properties. To complete this account, we also have to consider the spatial and the moral dimension of Polanyi's methodological holism. As to the spatial scope of his work, Polanyi's analysis goes, from the outset, beyond national economies and polities and suggests a global frame of reference. This becomes already clear at the beginning of his book when he postulates that "[n]ineteenth century civilization rested on four institutions," "two of [which] were national, two international" (*ibid.*, p. 3). Even more compelling is, however, the argument that the market society which rests on these institutions is ultimately a global one. In this respect, Polanyi speaks of "[t]he global sweep of economic liberalism," since "[n]othing less than a self-regulating market on a world scale could ensure the functioning of this stupendous mechanism" (*ibid.*, p. 138). Since a fully fledged market society is, at least in the long run, doomed to failure in Polanyi's account, he sides with the social counter-movements that represent, for him, the "self-protection of society" (*ibid.*, part II.2) against the "satanic mill" of the market (*ibid.*, part II.1). His vision of a "liberal socialism" is itself rooted in the embeddedness paradigm and completes Polanyi's holistic approach (Frerichs, 2011a, p. 73). Like the historical sociologists, economists, and even jurists that Polanyi drew inspiration from, he thus studied the history, or genesis, of the modern market society, last but not least, in moral terms (Frerichs, 2011b, pp. 230–232; Gemici, 2008, pp. 20, 23).

CONTEXTUALIZING POLANYI'S WORK IN THE PRESENT

After establishing Polanyi's rank as a sociological classic, and a late representative of classical methodological holism, the second step in my argumentation is to contextualize his work in the present, that is, with regard to contemporary scholarship. Contemporary scholarship in the field of law, economy, and society includes research within and, more importantly perhaps, at the margins of the respective academic disciplines, namely economics, sociology, and jurisprudence. Furthermore, it includes interdisciplinary research in the fields of "economy and society," which is broader than economic sociology alone, "law and society," which is broader than legal sociology alone, and "law and economy," which goes beyond the economic subdiscipline of law and economics. In the following, I will, however, only summarize some of the developments which seem relevant for the present revival and reappraisal of Polanyi's work. I will first give a brief account of the developments in, and the present state of, social (or sociological) theory "after Polanyi," then recapitulate what happened, at the same time, in the three interdisciplinary research fields mentioned above and, finally, draw conclusions for what scholarship "beyond Polanyi" would – or should – look like.

Scholarship After Polanyi

In the previous section, the core of classical sociology was represented by Karl Marx, Emile Durkheim, and Max Weber, who were themselves related to a much broader stream of historical-holistic scholarship. The question is thus which contemporary social thinkers could be considered equivalent to the classical sociological canon, both in terms of their "comprehensiveness" and their actual prominence. With regard to the interrelations of law, economy, and society one may come to think of the following four theorists: Niklas Luhmann and Jürgen Habermas (who are both combining legal and social theory), on the one hand, and Pierre Bourdieu and Michel Foucault (who focus on the interplay of politics and economics), on the other. As the first overarching postwar theorist, one may also add Talcott Parsons. All of these thinkers draw on macro-sociological categories (from fields and systems to power and culture) and bear, albeit in different ways, on economic as well as legal sociology. Otherwise, the selection remains, of course, somewhat subjective (Frerichs, 2011b, pp. 236–275). Because of their conflict-theoretical underpinnings (which remind of Polanyi's account of movements and counter-movements), the works of Bourdieu and Foucault will only be discussed in the next section. The present section will, instead, also include an update of the developments in the interdisciplinary research fields between law, sociology, and economics (Frerichs, 2012b, pp. 36–55).

Talcott Parsons (1902–1979) is the closest contemporary of Polanyi, in that he was born and died only some 15 years later. But while Polanyi still shares his historical-holistic outlook and moral ambitions with the sociological classics, Parsons is already more of a thinker of the positivist age even though he was, strictly speaking, no positivist himself. He thus took value orientations seriously, which often evade an empiricist account. However, he is a representative of twentieth-century thinking notably in his respect for, and fortification of, disciplinary boundaries. He namely furthered the division of labor between (neoclassical) economic theory, on the one hand, and (institutional) economic sociology, on the other – thereby ruling out "old" institutional economics. Somewhat ironically, the subdiscipline of economic sociology did not really take off until its "renewal" in the 1980s, thus leaving neoclassical economics largely uncontested (Velthuis, 1999). As to the relationship between sociology and jurisprudence, Parsons (1977) aimed to revive the tradition of the sociological classics in studying and theorizing about the law. However, he did not seriously engage with legal discourse (Cotterrell, 2005, p. 70), and his rather abstract interest in the field, did not reverse the divergent pathways of positivist legal theory and empirical legal sociology.

Niklas Luhmann (1927–1998) and Jürgen Habermas (born 1929) follow in the footsteps of Talcott Parsons in developing rather comprehensive theories about the functioning of modern society in terms of different, highly specialized function systems. However, both have become antagonists in the ways their respective "systems theories" developed, notably with regard to the role of "morality." In Parsons' theory, value orientations were still represented in the cultural system, the function of which is "latent pattern maintenance" and which is considered to "interpenetrate" with all other function systems, such as the economic system, the political system, and the system of the "societal community," that is, civil society. His starting point was, thus, a moral consensus that granted the stability, or equilibrium, of society as a whole and was, more or less, taken as given. This changes in Luhmann's as well as in Habermas' approach. Whereas the former "de-constructs" any notion of a moral consensus and refuses to side with any moral project, the latter "reconstructs" moral consensus as the result of an "enlightened" rational discourse, which he also strives for as a scholar. Luhmann's reservations are reflected, on a theoretical plane, in what can be depicted as an a-moral side-by-side of different function systems, whereas Habermas' engagement is expressed in a call to reconnect economic and administrative function systems to the legitimating spheres of the (rationalized) "lifeworld."

In a way, social theory, as discussed in this article, was never really positivist in its essence. Rather, it always aimed for an understanding of modern society as a whole, which can hardly be translated into piecemeal empiricist research designs. This is somewhat different in the more empirically and practically oriented research fields around the law, which notably emerged from (American) legal realism, the origins of which we illustrated above with Roscoe Pound's sociological jurisprudence. However, whereas Pound's early legal realism still bore traces of the holistic methodology of historical scholarship, including its moral undertones, the more mature legal realism is also, more decisively, characterized by an at least "*temporary* divorce of Is and Ought for purposes of study." Karl Llewellyn (1893–1962), one of the main representatives of this movement, specifies this as follows: "[V]alue judgments must always be appealed to in order to set objectives for inquiry, yet during the inquiry itself into what Is, the observation, the description, and the establishment of relations between the things described are to remain *as largely as possible* uncontaminated by the desires of the observer or by what he wishes might be or thinks ought (ethically) to be" (Llewellyn, 1931, pp. 1236–1237; original emphasis). He thus replicates the postulate of "freedom from value judgements" and, thereby, subscribes to the more "positivist" state of the art of his time.

Both the "law and society" movement and the "law and economics" movement, which formed, in the middle of the twentieth century – and which followed, otherwise, very different ambitions – are rooted in this positivist – or legal realist – tradition. In a way, the interdisciplinary endeavor of law, economy, and society was thus split into two different movements, one of which "borrows concepts and methods from economics proper" and also "inherits the controversies to which they are subject in the mother discipline" (Mackaay, 2000, p. 66), whereas in the other, "sociology has played a leadership role" (Hagan, 1988, p. 648), even though other disciplines, such as anthropology, history, or political science, were involved as well (Galanter & Edwards 1997, p. 379). Nowadays, there is even talk of a "new" legal realism which is advertised, once more, for its empirical (and non-axiomatic) qualities. Among its many "varieties" are notably listed "behaviorists," "contextualist," and "institutionalists" (Nourse & Shaffer, 2009). At the same time, an "empirical legal studies" movement has formed in the last decade, and there is, obviously, also a more general attempt to strengthen the capacities of "empirical legal research" (Cane & Kritzer, 2010, p. 1).

However, a shared interest in empirical research does not yet imply a substantive reintegration of research on law, economy, and society. Ambitions that point into this direction have lately been discussed both by law and society scholars, who aim for a reconstruction, or reintegration, of law and economics (Edelman, 2004; Edelman & Stryker, 2005), and by economic sociologists, who have "rediscovered" the law – and its relevance for the economy – not least, in the works of the sociological classics (Ashiagbor et al., 2013; Swedberg, 2003, 2006). Such efforts to advance an "economic sociology of law" can systematically be linked with a critical reappraisal of the work of Karl Polanyi, who was, admittedly, more of an economic sociologist than of a legal sociologist (Frerichs, 2009, 2011a, 2012c). Until recently, the mainstream of scholarship in the field of "economy and society" was, however, less holistically minded than required for such an undertaking. In fact, the leading ventures in this field, such as "new" economic sociology and "new" institutional economics, were, by and large, characterized by approaches that focus on the micro- and meso-levels of social reality, that is, on how social institutions come into being and how they affect individual action, rather than on the macro- and meta-levels of complex institutional regimes and their underlying rationalities, which were still in the focus of "old" economic sociology and "old" institutional economics. More comprehensive approaches could only be found in the field of (comparative) political economy, which is, from the outset, interested in the interplay of politics and economics, or of state and markets.

Scholarship Beyond Polanyi

At the beginning, we distinguished, with Sally Randles, between Polanyi-given and Polanyi-inspired research agendas in contemporary scholarship (2003, p. 409). In the group of "inspired" neo-Polanyians, Randles identified two subgroups which either work with a more empirical focus or with a more theoretical focus. While the former update, so to speak, the material basis on which Polanyi's considerations and conclusions rest, the latter upgrade the conceptual framework itself. In their review of the divergent "intellectual projects" of "old" and "new" economic sociology, Greta Krippner and Anthony Alvarez (2007) also consider a couple of scholars "Polanyians" who have not explicitly made reference to his work but otherwise share its general outlook, such as Neil Fligstein, whose work "substantively shares with Polanyi a broad interest in the role of law, politics, and the state in organizing market economies and methodologically engages in a critique of the analytically autonomous economy" (*ibid.*, p. 221, note 1). In this final section, I will even go one step further and only include one explicitly Polanyi-inspired scholar, namely Wolfgang Streeck, but also two less explicitly (or even non-) inspired ones who, nevertheless, take us "beyond" Polanyi's original work, namely Pierre Bourdieu and Michel Foucault.

Wolfgang Streeck represents a current of "neo-Polanyian" scholarship which does not arise from "new" but from "old" economic sociology. On a similar rank, in the German context, is Christoph Deutschmann (both were born 1946). Both scholars deal, in their latest works, with the inherent dynamic of modern capitalism, a phenomenon which, arguably, cannot be studied without a minimum of methodological holism (Deutschmann, 2009; Streeck, 2009). As already mentioned in the introduction, Streecks "Reforming Capitalism" can be read as a continuation of Polanyi's "The Great Transformation" with regard to the "rise and fall of the *social* market economy," namely in the political economy of postwar Germany (Frerichs, 2010, p. 829). Accordingly, it is the "slowly grinding force" of capitalism itself, which also undermines the German model (Streeck, 2009, p. 146). In the present context, I want to relate this argument to the distinction between "old" and "new" economic sociology, and "old" and "new" institutionalism, respectively. Streeck speaks, in this respect, of "Durkheimian" as opposed to "Williamsonian" institutions and, thereby, confronts the institutional perspective of an "old" European sociologist with that of a "new" US American economist. The latter, Oliver Williamson (born 1932), is considered the founder of new institutional economics, for which he was awarded the Nobel Memorial Prize in Economic Sciences in the year 2009.

In Streeck's argumentation, Durkheim's name stands for (noncontractual) institutions that impose social obligations "from above" whereas Williamson's name is equated with (privately contracted) institutions that result from individual choices "from below." Whereas the former form part of the public order, or authoritative forms of organization, the latter belong to systems of private ordering that facilitate voluntary coordination. Streeck argues, in a nutshell, that the capitalist dynamic always tends to undermine "obligational" institutions and replace them with "voluntaristic" ones (*ibid.*, pp. 154–155). However, "*Polanyian institutions* that are market-breaking rather than market-making probably need to be Durkheimian in character: public rather than private, obligatory rather than expedient, and political instead of economic" (*ibid.*, p. 252; original emphasis). While Streeck's emphasis is on how institutions work in the real world and not in the mind of scholars, his analysis also illustrates the shift from "old" to "new" institutionalism in *conceiving* of institutional embeddedness. We could thus rephrase Polanyi's above dictum about the market society in the following way: "Instead of economy being embedded in social (i.e., Durkheimian) institutions, society is embedded in economic (i.e., Williamsonian) institutions." In cognitive terms, new institutional economics (and, to a certain extent, also new economic sociology) is thus concomitant with the market society, or the "reformation" of capitalism, itself.

The "cognitive embeddedness" of the market society in neoclassical and neo-institutional economics can further be elucidated with the help of scholarship that emphasizes the link between power and knowledge and addresses, at the same time, the relationship between politics and economics, or the economic and the social, more generally (Frerichs, 2011a, pp. 69–71, 2011b, pp. 262–275). This is where Bourdieu's and Foucault's respective works come in. Pierre Bourdieu (1930–2002) does not confine himself to a sociological analysis of the economy but has, instead, developed what he calls an "economics" of social practices. His starting point is "the immersion of economy in the social dimension" which makes it worthwhile to study "the economy of the conditions of production and reproduction of the agents and institutions of economic, cultural and social production and reproduction" (Bourdieu, 2005, p. 13). While Bourdieu uses the term "economy" here in a much wider sense and for other fields than the economy proper, it also helps to clarify how other social practices, such as political or legal practices, are related to distinctly economic practices. This is demonstrated in his writings on the law and the state, and the "*nomos*," that is, the "cognitive and evaluative structures" they impose (Bourdieu, 1994, p. 13; original emphasis; cf. Bourdieu, 1987, p. 837, note 55). In this sense, the market society – or the capitalist political economy – is implemented, last but not least, by, conceptual means, that is, by "symbolic violence," which takes effect "in the form of mental structures and categories of perception and thought" (*ibid.*, pp. 3–4).

This interpretation is supported by the account that Michel Foucault (1926–1984) gives of the genesis of the modern "governmental" state which is, first and foremost, characterized by its incorporation, or embodiment, of economic rationalities. The "new economy of power relations," which Foucault (1982, p. 779) investigates in a figurative sense, can thus also be understood literally. His history of the state is based on "men's actual practice," that is, on "what they do and how they think" (Foucalt, 2009, p. 358). And these ideas and practices are shaped, last but not least, by political economy, both as a sphere of reality and as economic discipline, which made its way into politics. Accordingly, good government has to obey the laws of the market, and, hence, accept the "truth" postulated by modern economists, notably (neo-) liberal ones. Ultimately, even the (statutory) law would then speak the language of the market; jurisdiction would become "veridiction." Both scholars, Bourdieu and Foucault, thus reach out for the "whole" of law, economy, and society, in all its cognitive and normative complexity. In principle, their methodologies are socially and substantially, spatially and historically as encompassing – or holistic – as

Polanyi's. Only their moral claims could be considered more cautious, self-reflected, and self-restrained, due to the "disenchantment" (*Entzauberung*) of social science (Weber, 1946 [1922]) as well as its "constructivist," or cognitive, turn (Frerichs, 2012b, pp. 55–74).

CONCLUSION: SOCIETY AT RISK

Polanyi is a "late" classic with an "early" revival. He is a "classic" in his comprehensive interest in the institutional foundations of the modern market society. And his early "revival" can be attributed to the fact that the problems he wrote about never really disappeared but have only been put on hold for a while. This is, at least, suggested by Wolfgang Streeck's (2009) account of the "reformation" of capitalism in Germany's *social* market economy – which remained, after all, a *market* economy. Similarly, Sally Randles (2003) observes that "neo-Polanyian research agendas" are often preoccupied with the new challenges the national welfare states of the postwar era are facing in an increasingly globalized market economy. The main concern would, hence, be "to uncover the implications for world political-economy of the *crisis* of the Keynesian Welfare State, interpreted as the result of a contagion of world forces and events" (*ibid.*, p. 416; original emphasis). The challenge neo-Polanyian scholars are confronted with today is, thus, the return of economic liberalism. While Polanyi studied the detrimental effects of "classical liberalism," the "embedded liberalism" of the postwar decades apparently kept these risks in check. However, with the turn to "neoliberalism" in a framework of "Europeanization" and "globalization," national prerogatives in financial regulation, social regulation, and also environmental regulation are again on trial. In Polanyi's terms, the new wave of deregulation and "commodification" brings new hazards to society, or the substance of economic life. Society is once more at risk.

REFERENCES

Ashiagbor, D., Kotiswaran, P. & Perry-Kessaris, A. (Eds.) (2013). Special issue: Towards an economic sociology of law. *Journal of Law and Society, 40*(1), 1–171.

Beckert, J. (2007). *The great transformation of embeddedness: Karl Polanyi and the new economic sociology*. MPIfG Discussion Paper No. 07/1. Retrieved from http://www.mpifg.de/pu/mpifg_dp/dp07-1.pdf

Berman, H. J. (2005). The historical foundations of law. *Emory Law Journal, 54* (Special Edition), 13–24.

Bourdieu, P. (1987). The force of law: Toward a sociology of the juridical field. *Hastings Law Journal, 38*, 805–853.

Bourdieu, P. (1994). Rethinking the state: Genesis and structure of the bureaucratic field. *Sociological Theory, 12*(1), 1–18.

Bourdieu, P. (2005). *The social structures of the economy*. Cambridge: Polity Press.

Cane, P., & Kritzer, H. M. (2010). Introduction. In P. Cane & H. M. Kritzer (Eds.), *The Oxford handbook of empirical legal research* (pp. 1–7). Oxford: Oxford University Press.

Commons, J. R. (1924). *Legal foundations of capitalism*. New York, NY: Macmillan.

Cotterrell, R. (2005). *Law's community: Legal theory in sociological perspective*. Oxford: Clarendon Press.

Deutschmann, C. (2009). *Soziologie kapitalistischer Dynamik*. MPIfG Working Paper No. 09/5. Retrieved from http://www.mpifg.de/pu/workpap/wp09-5.pdf

Durkheim, E. (1887). *La science positive de la morale en Allemagne*. Retrieved from http://classiques.uqac.ca/classiques/Durkheim_emile/textes_1/textes_1_12/sc_pos_morale_allemagne.pdf

Durkheim, E. (1888). *Cours de science sociale: Leçon d'ouverture*. Retrieved from http://classiques.uqac.ca/classiques/Durkheim_emile/sc_soc_et_action/texte_1_01/cours_sc_sociales.rtf

Edelman, L. B. (2004). Rivers of law and contested terrain: A law and society approach to economic rationality. *Law and Society Review, 38*(2), 181–197.

Edelman, L. B., & Stryker, R. (2005). A sociological approach to law and the economy. In N. J. Smelser & R. Swedberg (Eds.), *The handbook of economic sociology* (pp. 527–551). Princeton, NJ: Princeton University Press.

Fine, G. A., & Kleinman, S. (1986). Interpreting the sociological classics: Can there be a 'true' meaning of Mead? *Symbolic Interaction, 9*(1), 129–146.

Foucault, M. (1982). The subject and power. *Critical Inquiry, 8*(4), 777–795.

Foucault, M. (2009). *Security, territory, population: Lectures at the Collège de France 1977–1978* (M. Sennelart, Ed., G. Burchell, Trans.). Basingstoke: Palgrave Macmillan (Picador).

Frerichs, S. (2009). The legal constitution of market society: Probing the economic sociology of law. *Economic Sociology – The European Electronic Newsletter, 10*(3), 20–25.

Frerichs, S. (2010). Review of Wolfgang Streeck: Re-forming capitalism: Institutional change in the German political economy. *Management International Review, 50*(6), 827–832.

Frerichs, S. (2011a). Re-embedding neo-liberal constitutionalism: A Polanyian case for the economic sociology of law. In C. Joerges & J. Falke (Eds.), *Karl Polanyi, globalisation and the potential of law in transnational markets*. Oxford: Hart Publishing.

Frerichs, S. (2011b). What sociological backing for the conflicts-law approach? A gallery of candidates. In C. Joerges & T. Ralli (Eds.), *After globalization – New patterns of conflict and their sociological and legal re-constructions* (pp. 199–278). Oslo: ARENA. RECON Report No. 15.

Frerichs, S. (2012a). Law, economy and society in the global age: A study guide. In A. Perry-Kessaris (Ed.), *Socio-legal approaches to international economic law: Text, context, subtext* (pp. 36–49). Abingdon, UK: Routledge.

Frerichs, S. (2012b). *Studying law, economy, and society: A short history of socio-legal thinking*. Helsinki Legal Studies Research Paper No. 19. Retrieved from http://papers.ssrn.com/sol3/papers.cfm?abstract_id=2022891

Frerichs, S. (2012c). The law of the market society: A Polanyian account of its conflicts and dynamics. In H.-W. Micklitz & Y. Svetiev (Eds.), *A self-sufficient European private law: A viable concept?* (pp. 45–66). EUI Working Paper LAW 2012/31. Retrieved from http://cadmus.eui.eu/handle/1814/24534

Galanter, M., & Edwards, M. A. (1997). Introduction: The path of the law ands. *Wisconsin Law Review*, *72*(3), 375–387.

Gemici, K. (2008). Karl Polanyi and the antinomies of embeddedness. *Socio-Economic Review*, *6*(1), 5–34.

Green, L. (2009). Legal positivism. In E. N. Zalta (Ed.), *The Stanford encyclopedia of philosophy* (Fall 2009 Edition). Retrieved from http://plato.stanford.edu/archives/fall2009/entries/legal-positivism/

Grossman, L. A. (2009). *'From Savigny through Sir Henry Maine': Roscoe Pound's flawed portrait of James Coolidge Carter's historical jurisprudence*. American University, WCL Research Paper No. 2009-21. Retrieved from http://ssrn.com/abstract=1407623

Hagan, J. (1988). Review: The law and society movement comes of age. *Contemporary Sociology*, *17*(5), 648–650.

Hodgson, G. M. (1998). The approach of institutional economics. *Journal of Economic Literature*, *36*(1), 166–192.

Holmes, O. W. (1897). The path of the law. In: *Harvard Law Review*, *10*(8), 457–478.

Joerges, C. & Falke, J. (Eds.) (2011). *Karl Polanyi, globalisation and the potential of law in transnational markets*. Oxford: Hart Publishing.

Krippner, G. R., & Alvarez, A. S. (2007). Embeddedness and the intellectual projects of economic sociology. *Annual Review of Sociology*, *33*, 219–240.

Krippner, G., Granovetter, M., Block, F., Biggart, N., Beamish, T., Hsing, Y., … O'Riain, S. (2004). Polanyi symposium: A conversation on embeddedness. *Socio-Economic Review*, *2*(1), 109–135.

Llewellyn, K. (1931). Some realism about realism: Responding to Dean Pound. *Harvard Law Review*, *44*(8), 1222–1264.

Mackaay, E. (2000). History of law and economics. In B. Bouckaert & G. De Geest (Eds.), *Encyclopedia of law and economics, Vol. 1. The history and methodology of law and economics* (pp. 65–117). Cheltenham: Edward Elgar.

Marshall, A. (1920 [1890]). *Principles of economics*. London: Macmillan. (Appendix B: The growth of economic science). Retrieved from http://www.econlib.org/library/Marshall/marP57.html

Marx, K. (1842). Debates on the law on thefts of wood. *Rheinische Zeitung, Supplement*. Retrieved from http://www.marxists.org/archive/marx/works/1842/10/25.htm

Marx, K. (1859). *A contribution to the critique of political economy*. (Preface). Retrieved from http://www.marxists.org/archive/marx/works/1859/critique-pol-economy/preface.htm

Nourse, V., & Shaffer, G. (2009). Varieties of new legal realism: Can a new world order prompt a new legal theory? *Cornell Law Review*, *95*(1), 61–137.

Parsons, T. (1977). Law as an intellectual stepchild. *Sociological Inquiry*, *47*(3–4), 11–58.

Polanyi, K. (1957 [1944]). *The great transformation: The political and economic origins of our time*. Boston, MA: Beacon Press.

Polanyi, K. (2001 [1957]). The sociology of economic life. In M. Granovetter & R. Swedberg (Eds.), *The economy as instituted process* (2nd ed., pp. 31–50). Boulder, CO: Westview Press.

Pound, R. (1910). Law in books and law in action. *American Law Review*, *44*(1), 12–36.

Pound, R. (1923). The theory of judicial decision, Part III. *Harvard Law Review*, *36*(8), 940–959.

Randles, S. (2003). Issues for a neo-Polanyian research agenda in economic sociology. *International Review of Sociology*, *13*(2), 409–434.

Rizza, R. (2006). The relationship between economics and sociology: The contribution of economic sociology, setting out from the problem of embeddedness. *International Review of Sociology*, *16*(1), 31–48.

Sainte-Beuve, C. A. (2001 [1850]). What is a classic? In C. W. Eliot (Ed.), *Harvard classics, 1909–14, Literary and philosophical essays: French, German and Italian* (*Vol. 32*), New York, NY: P.F. Collier & Son. Retrieved from http://www.bartleby.com/32/202.html

Streeck, W. (2009). *Re-forming capitalism: Institutional change in the German political economy*. Oxford: Oxford University Press.

Swedberg, R. (2003). The case for an economic sociology of law. *Theory and Society*, *32*(1), 1–37.

Swedberg, R. (2006). Max Weber's contribution to the economic sociology of law. *Annual Review of Law and Social Science*, *2*, 61–81.

Uebel, T. (2011). Vienna circle. In E. N. Zalta (Ed.), *The Stanford encyclopedia of philosophy* (summer ed.). Retrieved from http://plato.stanford.edu/archives/sum2011/entries/vienna-circle/

Velthuis, O. (1999). The changing relationship between economic sociology and institutional economics: From Talcott Parsons to Mark Granovetter. *American Journal of Economics and Sociology*, *58*(4), 629–649.

Weber, M. (1946 [1922]). Science as a vocation. In H. H. Gerth & C. W. Mills (Eds.), *From Max Weber: Essays in sociology* (pp. 129–156). New York, NY: Oxford University Press.

Weber, M. (2004 [1904]). The 'objectivity' of knowledge in social science and social policy. In S. Whimster (Ed.), *Essential Weber: A reader*. London: Routledge.

A SYSTEMS THEORY PERSPECTIVE ON POLANYI'S *GREAT TRANSFORMATION*: THE CASE OF FINANCIAL DERIVATIVE CONTRACTS

John Paterson

ABSTRACT

Whereas much of the renewed interest in Polanyi's Great Transformation *speculates that the rebalancing of economy and society he foresaw might now be emerging in the context of the financial crisis, the systems theory perspective adopted in this article concludes that there are good reasons to believe that such a shift may be no closer. From an examination of credit default swaps and corporate bonds, the article suggests that finance may best be understood as an internally differentiated subsystem of the economy and thus perhaps peculiarly proof against efforts to exert control over it. Concluding that Polanyi's analysis lacks the conceptual tools to cope with contemporary conditions when compared to systems theory, the article nevertheless suggests that his approach may usefully*

From Economy to Society? Perspectives on Transnational Risk Regulation
Studies in Law, Politics, and Society, Volume 62, 49–71

ISSN: 1059-4337/doi:10.1108/S1059-4337(2013)0000062003

be extended by adding a fourth fictitious commodity – risk – to the familiar trio of land, labor, and money.

Keywords: Polanyi; systems theory; economy; society; markets; contracts

INTRODUCTION

The possibility of a fundamental rebalancing between economy and society in the aftermath of the financial crisis of 2008 is a very seductive idea – perhaps more so because it has been replaced by a new variant, the sovereign debt crisis. That there could – perhaps even that there must – be a shift in power away from markets and in favor of other less economically driven social institutions will appeal to many as only right and fitting. This situation accounts for the renewed interest in recent years in the work of Karl Polanyi and in particular in his 1944 work *The Great Transformation* (2001). The proposition in essence is that even if Polanyi was wrong about such a rebalancing in the aftermath of the Second World War, there may well be features of the financial crisis that indicate that the time is now ripe for the reestablishment of society as preeminent in relation to markets, thus reversing the previous position.

As seductive as this notion undoubtedly is, there is surely plenty of evidence to suggest that it may once again prove to be a false dawn. Financial markets may well have collapsed spectacularly and once mighty financial institutions may well have failed or been saved from that fate only by unprecedented bailouts, but as the months go by there is little sense of any seismic shift in the balance of power. Thus, policy makers and regulators around the world talk tough but then hold back from any intervention that might scare the markets and lead to capital flight. Similarly, the treatment of heavily indebted countries in the Eurozone is driven as much by considerations of what will be acceptable to the markets as it is by concern with what voters in more stable Member States will think.

If there is any notion that Polanyi's time has come, therefore, it may well be once again premature. The tenacity of markets and their ability, in Polanyi's terms, to prevail as against society is accordingly in need of explanation. At first sight it is by no means obvious that such an explanation will emerge from investigations in the realm of legal theory. The starting point for this article is, however, specifically *systems theory*. While this shares with Polanyi a functionalist perspective (and could in fact be regarded as of less utility given the degree of abstraction evident in some of its variants) there is a growing awareness of both its potential as a critical tool (Philippopoulos-Mihalopoulos, 2009) and even as possessing normative potential (Paterson, 2006, pp. 13–35). More immediately, the choice of systems theory is driven by the observation that this is an approach that, on the basis of its particular understanding of functional differentiation, conceptually is not surprised by the resistance of the economy to outside intervention (for other systems theory perspectives on the financial crisis, see Kjaer, Teubner, & Febbrajo, 2011). More specifically, the approach adopted by the article is motivated by the observation that the financial instruments at the heart of the crisis are *contracts*. The article considers what a systems theory analysis of such contracts reveals about the nature of the crisis and draws conclusions for the prospects of a Polanyian transformation.

The article begins by reviewing briefly Polanyi's analysis and considering its relevance to the financial crisis. Noting the apparent resistance of markets to any rebalancing efforts in their relations with other social institutions, the article then introduces systems theory and its potential utility in analyzing the contractual instruments at the heart of the crisis. The next following section introduces derivative financial instruments before the article moves on to demonstrate what systems theory can add to the understanding of such contracts. Concluding that the findings of the analysis can best be understood on the basis that the financial system has evolved into an internally differentiated subsystem of the economy, the argument then moves on to consider what the implications are for the prospects of the sort of *Great Transformation* predicted by Polanyi. Observing that these are not positive, the article concludes by suggesting what may be needed to be added to Polanyi's analysis in order to account for this situation – specifically, the addition of a fourth fictitious commodity (risk) to the familiar trio of land, labor, and money.

POLANYI'S *GREAT TRANSFORMATION* AND THE FINANCIAL CRISIS

The great transformation that Polanyi is principally concerned with in his 1944 work is the shift from a position where the market is something peripheral to social relations to one where it is central. He is thus concerned to provide an explanation of the emergence of 19th-century civilization and especially the European liberal state. By the time Polanyi was writing in 1944, he was also concerned, of course, with a second great transformation, namely the rise of fascism, which he perceived to be both a system that came close to a dominance of markets as well as the final playing out of the inevitable failure of the dominance of markets over society. While Polanyi sees the emergence of 19th-century civilization in Europe as the product of a complex array of factors, it is noteworthy that he sees the development of the complex machines of the Industrial Revolution as playing a key role. The fact that these machines require significant capital means that investments will not be made unless the wherewithal to render their functioning profitable is available (Polanyi, 2001, pp. 42ff). As a consequence, everything required for their profitable operation becomes a factor of production – including labor. This is what Polanyi refers to as the emergence of the fictitious commodities of land, labor, and money – which come to be traded notwithstanding that they do not fit the usual category of things that have been produced with a view to trade. With both humankind and nature now commoditized, there is nothing in principle to stop these being driven to destruction in the relentless drive to feed the demands of industrial processes. Faced with this unattractive truth, Polanyi is convinced that society will always eventually resist, will always in the end fight back against the insidious march of the market in order to avoid such destructive effects (Polanyi, 2001, pp. pp. 71ff).

To put this in other words, while for Polanyi markets in preindustrial societies had always been adjuncts to those societies (with economic relations being characterized in the main by reciprocity, redistribution, and householding) (Polanyi, 2001, pp. 51–57), in the context of industrialization, the relationship is reversed and society becomes an adjunct to the market (p. 60). But while the market thus seeks to disembed itself from society, this is never actually achieved. The market always relies to some extent on society. Nevertheless, in the process of assuming a central role, the market has destructive effects on the fictitious commodities that it creates. In such circumstances, society will take steps to protect itself and to see the market re-embedded in society (pp. 3, 42).

From the perspective of the lawyer, of course, what is particularly interesting in Polanyi's analysis is that, in the course of this first great transformation in the context of the emergence of the liberal state, social relations are transformed into contractual relations (Polanyi, 2001, p. 266). It is the case, therefore, in Polanyi's view, that contract (and by extension law) itself plays a role in the disembedding of the market from society and, more disturbingly, in the destructive effects of the commoditization of the labor and land (pp. 141ff).

Before that question can be examined further, however, it is necessary to consider in greater detail why there is a resurgence of interest in Polanyi's work. In 1944, Polanyi was convinced that the end of the 100 years' peace and the fact of the second 30 years' war marked the final catastrophe for markets. The 100 years' peace from the end of the Napoleonic Wars to the opening of the First World War had been a remarkable achievement, but it had been bought at a terrible price as markets essentially dominated everything else in the context of the European liberal state. The failure of society in some jurisdictions to achieve an appropriate rebalancing in the aftermath of the failure of markets left the way open for fascism in Polanyi's view – something he regarded as the second great transformation – but the defeat of fascism left the way open for the reemergence of society with markets as their adjunct and thus for a third great transformation (Block, 2001, p. xxviii).

The following years, however, turned out quite differently. There are certainly examples that could be read as society pushing back against the market or occupying ground that the market has been unable or unwilling to occupy. In this regard, the postwar expansion of the welfare state, as well as developments in the provision of free health care and education might have seemed to be a vindication of Polanyi's analysis (for the United Kingdom, see Lowe, 2005, more generally Ruggie, 1982). Similarly, the progressive expansion of regulatory law in the same period could be read as a significant effort to ensure that markets served desirable social functions (e.g., competition law) or to correct or compensate for market failures (e.g., environmental and occupational safety regulation) (for a discussion, Parker & Braithwaite, 2003). Notwithstanding these apparently positive signs, however, the period from the 1980s onwards must surely raise doubts that any societal push back against markets (if such it was) has been successful. Reaganomics, Thatcherism, the characterization of the welfare state as something pernicious and the reification (if not indeed the deification) of the market argue strongly that such rebalancing as there might have been up to that point was at best incomplete and at worst wholly illusory (Evans, 2004; Rousseas, 1982). Social relations became more dominated by contract than ever before, while regulation was explicitly not about taming the market or compensating for its failures but rather about facilitating its operation (see the contributions in Campbell & Vincent-Jones, 1996; and in Deakin & Michie, 1997). Beyond the domestic realm, the globalization of markets could be read as a turbo-charged version of the 19th-century international trade that Polanyi had documented with such mixed feelings and once again contract was at the core with international trade law seeking to ensure that barriers to the freedom to contract were removed (Love & Lattimore, 2009). Add to all of this the exponential expansion of the financial markets on the back of explicit policies of deregulation or of regulatory restraint and it is easy to make the argument that by the first decade of the 21st-century society, far from having pushed back against the market, had become more of an adjunct to the market than ever before and had even appeared complicit in its inexorable rise to domination (see the contributions in McCrudden, 1999).

There is, however, another interpretation, not least one that could yet vindicate Polanyi. What the previous potted history of the last 60 years has conveniently ignored is the fact of the financial crisis. Might it not therefore be suggested that the trajectory of the society–market relationship over that period was indeed to the advantage of society during the first three decades or so, followed by a shift in favor of markets thereafter, but that with the recent unprecedented travails in the realm of finance the point has finally been reached when the inescapably destructive effects of markets have at last been revealed and thus only now has the time of Polanyi's hoped for great transformation arrived? In other words, is there something about the crisis that would promote at last a truly transformative rebalancing between society and market? Or are Polanyians to be disappointed once again?

A SYSTEMS THEORY PERSPECTIVE ON FINANCIAL INSTRUMENTS

In order to attempt an answer to these questions this article looks at matters from a different perspective. Insofar as markets in the postwar era, far from going into reverse or becoming society's servants, actually appeared to tighten their grip on society, it does not seem unreasonable to choose a perspective which predicts precisely that dynamic. Systems theory, which paints a picture of functionally differentiated society, is by no means taken by surprise by the ability of the economy once differentiated to continue and deepen that differentiation rather than going through periods of advance and retreat (Luhmann, 1995). This section of the article, therefore, takes seriously some of Polanyi's key observations, but then suggests that his account makes better sense when his discussion of society and economy is given a specifically systems character. The observation of Polanyi, which is the starting point for the argument, is that *social* relations become *contractual* relations in the context of a situation where society has become an adjunct to markets. The question then is: what emerges when contractual relations are considered from a systems' perspective? Given that the immediate interest is the financial crisis, the focus of attention will be on one of the financially engineered contracts that have been most deeply implicated in that event, and which, at the time of writing in late 2011, are reappearing as a potentially significant factor in the sovereign debt crisis – the credit default swap (CDS). This may seem like an inordinate jump from the macro to the micro level, but it is worth remembering that Polanyi himself extrapolated from the minute observation of micro-relations in preindustrial societies to develop his ideas of reciprocity, redistribution, and householding (Polanyi, 2001). Furthermore, although looking at individual contractual arrangements is indeed to descend to the micro-level, these arrangements in aggregate constitute some of the most all-pervasive and influential forces in the world today (see Strange's prescient account, 1997). While only one derivative instrument (and its real economy counterpart) is examined here given the constraints of space, it is suggested that the conclusions drawn for finance and the economy may be generalized. The methodology developed here could equally be utilized to investigate other derivative instruments.

Despite the undoubted complexity of derivative financial instruments, the basic ideas behind them are relatively simple. They are instruments whose value depends upon underlying "more elementary" transactions, whether commodity trades or loans (see Kolb, 1996, p. viii; see also McDonald, 2009, p. 2). They exist as a means of hedging risk as well as generating profit. In order to understand specifically what a CDS is, the following example can be considered. A company Y needs to raise capital to develop a new product and therefore issues a corporate bond. Pension fund X buys the bond as part of its diversified portfolio of investments, attracted by the promise of the coupon payments and by the fact that the yield on the bond is high compared to less risky government bonds.[1] X is now a creditor of Y and while anticipating the financial benefits of the transaction is also aware of the risk that the company will default on the coupon payments. X accordingly needs to hedge that credit risk and does so by buying a credit default swap from investment bank Z. This involves pension fund X making periodic premium payments to investment bank Z, in return for which Z promises to pay X in the event that company Y defaults on coupon payments. In essence, then, the CDS is nothing more than a sort of insurance policy and the simplicity of its relationship with a corporate bond is illustrated in Fig. 1.

On the face of it, this appears to be a well-adjusted hedging arrangement that amply meets the needs of the three parties involved: the need for capital on the part of company Y; the need for a return on investment on the part of the pension fund X and of the investment bank Z; and finally the need to hedge credit risk on the part of the pension fund X. Nevertheless, simple arrangements such as these proved to be a significant factor in the 2008 financial crisis. The fact that credit default swaps proved so popular meant that by the end of 2007 the market had a gross nominal value of $60 trillion. This extraordinary figure is apt to mislead, however, as clearly it is the net value of outstanding positions that will ultimately matter. But even that latter figure, standing at just under $4 trillion at the end of 2007 (Turner, 2009, para. 2.5(iii)), is equivalent to more than a quarter of the GDP of the United States in the same year, which stood at $14 trillion (OECD, 2011). The global market in CDSs is, therefore, enormous and the dire consequences of a market failure can be more readily understood. But how could such an extraordinary market have emerged in a way that was largely invisible not only to the general public but also in many cases to policy makers and regulators as well? It is important first of all to understand that the market for CDSs – and indeed other derivative financial instruments – exists primarily because there is a need to hedge risk. Financial engineering is in essence the process of producing instruments that respond to the precise risk profile of the customer, whether they are concerned with the possibility of adverse movements in commodity prices, currency values or interest rates, or the possibility that a counterparty will default. The recognition of this phenomenon is perhaps an early indication

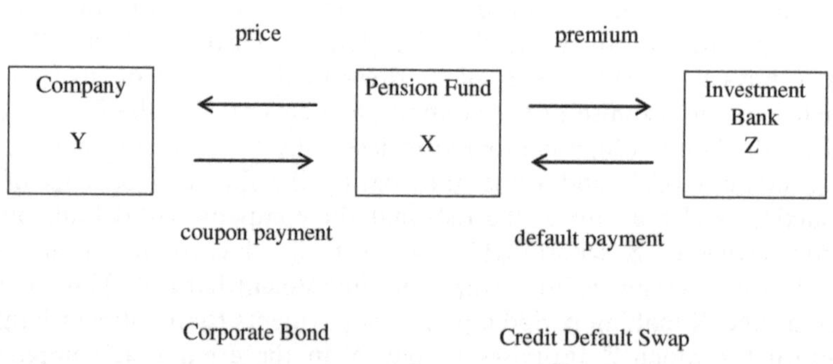

Fig. 1. The Relationship of a Credit Default Swap to a Corporate Bond.

that something new has emerged since Polanyi was writing in 1944 which may fundamentally alter the force of his analysis.

A first suggestion as to the nature of this new phenomenon may be gleaned from the way in which the relationship between derivative instruments (such as CDSs) and underlying transactions is frequently described. As was mentioned above, the derivative financial instrument is a contract which depends for its value upon an underlying "more elementary" commodity or loan transaction (see Kolb, 1996, p. viii; see also McDonald, 2009, p. 2), and such underlying transactions are often said to belong to the "real economy," whereas the derivative financial instrument is often referred to as a product of "financial markets."[2] It is possible that such terms are sometimes used relatively loosely, but in the context of discussion of the financial crisis, it is not unusual to come across the claim that finance has actually become "decoupled" from the real economy (this suggestion was, indeed, already current before the crisis, see Menkhoff & Tolksdorf, 2001). From a Polanyian perspective, might it even be ventured that finance has been *disembedded* from the real economy?

A systems theory perspective can assist in making sense of this situation. To begin with, it is important to recognize that although the corporate bond and the credit default swap are closely related – and indeed the latter depends upon the former for its existence – they nevertheless represent two distinct contracts: one between Y and X (the bond-issuing company and the bond-buying pension fund) and one between Z and X (the CDS-selling investment bank and the CDS-buying pension fund). No contractual relationship exists between Y (the company) and Z (the investment bank). Whereas the usual assumption is that a contract represents a unity, a concretization of the agreement reached between the parties, systems theory draws attention to the extent to which a contract is actually characterized by fragmentation (Luhmann, 2004; Teubner, 2000; Teubner, 2007). It does this by shifting the focus away from the instrument itself, and toward its multiple existences within a variety of social subsystems where it is involved in a variety of transformations. Notwithstanding this emphasis on fragmentation and the multiple existences of a contract in, say, the subsystems of law, economy, and science, the instrument is also understood within systems theory as an example of *structural coupling*, that is, as a means by which the "twofold membership of events" in different systems can occur (Luhmann, 1987, p. 342; Teubner, 2007, p. 54). To be clear, structural coupling does not imply that the autopoiesis of the subsystems involved can be overcome: there is still no transfer of information between subsystems in the way assumed by linear–causal models (Paterson & Teubner, 1998,

p. 457). It remains the case that the contract is internally constructed by each of the subsystems in play in a given situation (Luhmann, 1995, p. 41). What the contract adds is the requirement for the subsystems involved to conduct their self-transformations simultaneously, if only momentarily (Teubner, 2007, pp. 52 and 58). If this perspective is adopted, then, it is possible to represent the corporate bond contract from the example described above in Fig. 2.

What this diagram reveals is that the subsystems in play in the example are the economy (E), law (L), and science (S). (In this last regard, of course, any of the other productive[3] subsystems could equally be involved, e.g., medicine.) The fact that the contract (c) is present – and therefore a means by which structural coupling is achieved – is signified by a broken line. Importantly, however, the contract also appears as a construct of each of the involved subsystems (c^E), (c^L), and (c^S). The diagram shows the subsystems as they coevolve through one simultaneous transformation along the temporal dimension. As regards the question of how the corporate bond is constructed by each of the subsystems through that simultaneous transformation, the following answers may be given. As regards the subsystem of science, the corporate bond is a means of raising capital to develop the new product. For the economy, the corporate bond is a means of continuing productive activity to generate future payments. And for law, the corporate

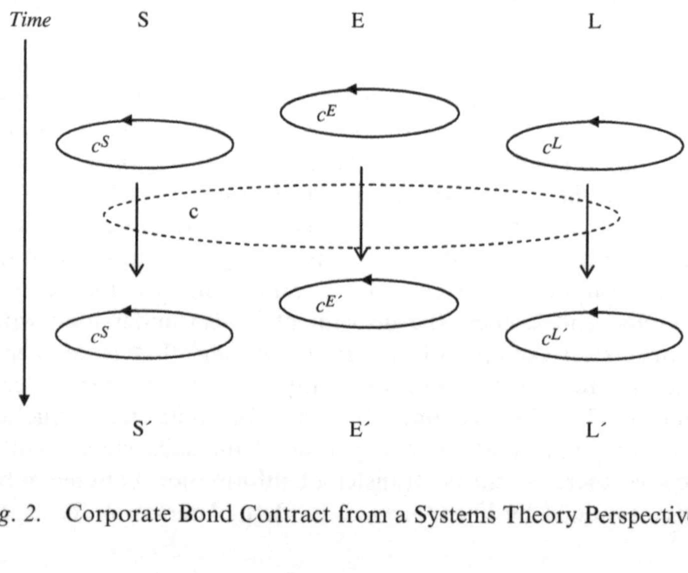

Fig. 2. Corporate Bond Contract from a Systems Theory Perspective.

bond is a means of stabilizing normative expectations within the context of the specific activity covered by the agreement.

The fact that systems theory allows the generation of these multiple and obviously different constructions of the same contract clearly raises the possibility that a more sophisticated analysis of the corporate bond might be achieved, but it is not immediately clear what it might reveal that is of interest in the context of the questions raised by the renewed interest in Polanyi's analysis of the relationship between society and markets. It is suggested, however, that the insight emerges only when this systems perspective on a corporate bond contract is compared with that on a credit default swap contract. Modeling the CDS in the same way, we obtain the diagram given in Fig. 3.

From the discussion above, it is clear that the most interesting information to emerge from this systems analysis is the differential constructions of the contract by the different subsystems in play. So how is the CDS constructed through one simultaneous transformation along the temporal dimension? As regards, the economy, it appears that the CDS is both a means of reducing credit risk by guaranteeing payment in the event of default by the bond issuer and a means of continuing productive activity to generate future payments. For law, the CDS is a means of stabilizing normative expectations within the context of the specific activity covered by the agreement.

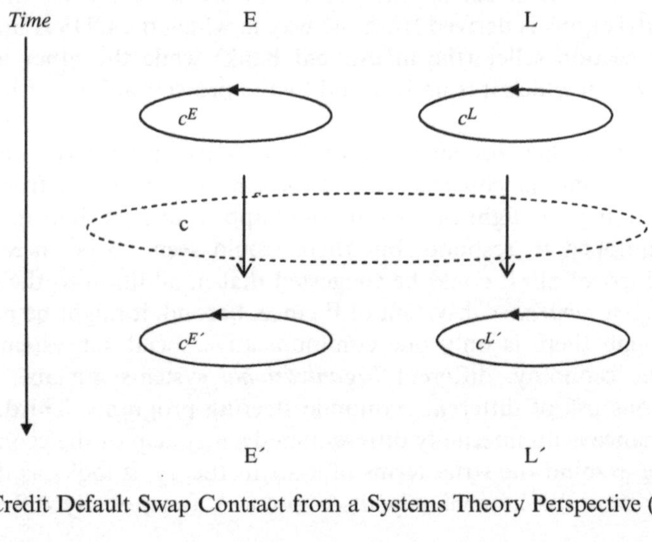

Fig. 3. Credit Default Swap Contract from a Systems Theory Perspective (version 1).

There are, therefore, obviously two important differences between the two contracts, as well as one important similarity. To deal with the similarity first, the legal construction of the CDS contract is exactly the same as for the corporate bond. Moving on to the differences, the first is that there is no productive subsystem (science in the present example) in play in the case of the CDS, while the second is that there are no less than two separate economic constructions of that contract: one that is the same as for the corporate bond and another that is totally different. To take these observations further, it is first of all clear that law is essentially indifferent to the content of contracts. For law, the contract is no more than a means of stabilizing the normative expectations of the parties, but the precise activity in which they are engaged (loan, sale, hire, insurance, etc.) is unimportant unless it breaches contract law to produce a void or voidable agreement.[4] Second, it is possible to point to a difference in systems terms between a contract from the "more elementary" world of the real economy and one from the more rarefied atmosphere of financial markets: it would appear that in the latter case no productive subsystem is in play. It is true that the CDS only exists because there is an underlying corporate bond, but the derivative contract does not itself include any such transaction. It may thus be suggested that a derivative financial instrument is defined in systems theory terms by the fact that it does not engage a productive subsystem. Third, and most importantly, it is necessary to explain why (and, indeed, how it is possible that) there are two quite different economic constructions of the contract in the case of the CDS. It is clear that one of these constructions is derived from the way in which the CDS is understood by the protection seller (the investment bank) while the other is derived from the way in which it is understood by the protection buyer (the pension fund).

The question then becomes one of how to account for the presence of two distinct economic constructions of the same contract. Far from systems theory shedding any light on this, it could appear at first sight to be singularly ill-equipped to respond, but there would seem to be three possible answers. First of all, it could be suggested that in addition to the economy there is also a *separate* subsystem of finance. Second, it might be postulated that although there is only one communicative social subsystem in play, namely the economy, different *organizational* systems are able to make simultaneous use of different economic steering programs. Third, it could be that finance is an internally differentiated subsystem of the economy.

Bearing in mind the strict terms of systems theory, it looks as if the first possibility must be immediately discounted. A functionally differentiated social subsystem is identified by its binary code: payment/nonpayment in the case of the economy. If the code used in the construction of the "real" economic contract (the corporate bond) and that used in the construction of the financial market contract (the CDS) are compared, it is clear that they are the same in each case. Accordingly, insofar as only one code is employed, only one subsystem can be in play. The second possibility, on the other hand, can at least be accommodated by the theory. Luhmann observes in this regard that while a subsystem's binary code is invariable, it is nevertheless possible for more than one difference-minimizing steering programme to be deployed (Luhmann, 1997). Accepting that second possibility, however, does not rule out the third – and might indeed even depend upon it. But what would it mean to say that finance is an internally differentiated subsystem of the economy? Luhmann provides an insightful and very suggestive account of the concept as follows: "[i]nternal differentiation connects onto the boundaries of the already-differentiated system and treats the bounded domain as a special environment in which further systems can be formed." This basic fact produces a number of important consequences. First of all, insofar as the internal environment of the "already-differentiated system" represents a reduction of the external complexity, this represents a valuable resource which any emergent process of internal differentiation can take advantage of. As Luhmann expresses it, "certain capacities for regulation" are accordingly presupposed which provide a platform for "[n]ew, more improbable system formation." Furthermore, insofar as further internal system formation is improbable, it can only survive to the extent that it "can mobilize processes of deviation-amplification (positive feedback) to [its] own advantage and keep [itself] from being leveled out again." Lastly, Luhmann makes the point that far from internal differentiation compromising or weakening the surrounding system, the fact that the process depends upon the system's boundary actually serves to strengthen that boundary (Luhmann, 1995, pp. 189–190).

It is necessary then to consider the application of these ideas to the question in hand: the possibility that finance could be an internally differentiated subsystem of the economy. First of all, it can be observed that it is the case that the economic social subsystem has indeed achieved a quite remarkable reduction of complexity on the basis of its binary code of payment/nonpayment.[5] As such, any further process of internal system formation starts with the advantage of that greatly simplified account of the environment on which to operate. Second, it is certainly possible to characterize the emergence of an internally differentiated subsystem of finance as improbable: recall the extent to which the gross (and even net) value of derivative contracts can grow to quite astonishing levels on the back of real economic contracts of comparatively little value.[6] Third, notwithstanding the improbability of its existence and continued operation when viewed in these terms, it is possible to see how finance has been able to sustain itself and prevent its dissolution by successfully mobilizing positive feedback to its own advantage. It does this by simultaneously offering benefits in terms both of the amplification of payments and of the reduction of risk. In other words, finance offers opportunities that are attractive from whichever angle they are viewed making it difficult to argue against irrespective of any difficulties that may arise.[7] Finally, the fact that finance depends for its existence upon the system boundary established by the economy means that that boundary is itself reinforced. The extent to which the years since Polanyi wrote *The Great Transformation* have been characterized by the progressive commoditization of practically every other aspect of every other system, communicative or living, offers compelling evidence of the success of finance in strengthening the boundary between the economy and its environment.[8] Accepting the possibility that finance is indeed an internally differentiated subsystem of the economy allows a more accurate diagram of the CDS contract from a systems perspective to be drawn, which is given in Fig. 4.

The CDS as a pure financial contract has a constructed existence both within the internally differentiated financial subsystem (F) and within that

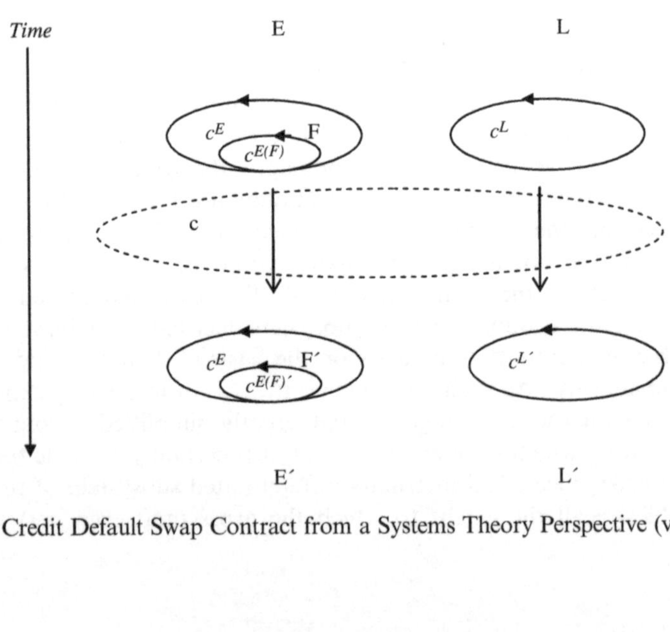

Fig. 4. Credit Default Swap Contract from a Systems Theory Perspective (version 2).

part of the economy that constitutes the bounded environment of finance (E). It is the fact that the CDS has this dual economic existence that allows it to be used simultaneously for two separate economic difference-minimizing steering programmes, one directed at payment amplification, the other at risk reduction. The improbability of this double existence confirms the success that finance has achieved in establishing and maintaining its self-reproduction as an internally differentiated subsystem of the economy. Nor is that success difficult to understand when one considers the irresistibility of a subsystem which can simultaneously amplify payments (even exponentially) and enhance the management of risk (even to a point where the claim is made that the risk has effectively been removed).

Bearing this systems theory perspective on the relationship between financial markets and the "real economy" in mind, does it add anything to the popular notion of a "decoupling" of the former from the latter? It seems clear that a quite different relationship emerges and that the notion of "decoupling" would have to be reconsidered. Insofar as the self-reproduction of the financial subsystem is dependent on the self-reproduction of the economy, the relationship between them is very close from the outset and remains so however intense the internal differentiation becomes. And yet it is the case that the financial subsystem is able to produce its own internal constructions of contracts that must be quite distinct from those of the subsystem of the economy beyond the internal boundary of finance. Insofar as that is so, then it may be said that what can appear to be a "decoupling" of the two is actually – almost paradoxically – a matter of *differential internal constructions of reality on the basis of the same binary code.*[9]

THE IMPLICATIONS OF THE SYSTEMS PERSPECTIVE FOR POLANYI'S ANALYSIS

Given the present concern with the relevance of the insights of systems theory for the consideration of Polanyi's analysis, what does this mean in terms of his discussion of *embeddedness*? Recall that his view was that although liberal economics promoted the disembedding of markets from society, moves in this direction were doomed to failure because of the inevitable destructive effects they threatened and because of the inevitable reaction on the part of society to protect itself (and nature) that these threats provoked. In other words, try as it might, the economy could never succeed in disembedding itself from society. Is there a sense, however, in which the systems reading of the relationship between economy and finance developed above suggests that, even as the economy remains embedded (however tenuously) in society, *finance* has been able to disembed itself while using *economy* as its cover? In other words, has the disembedding that Polanyi always suggested could not happen actually happened?

This might provide a neat and eye-catching conclusion to this article, but it would surely be incorrect. For a start, it is necessary to be accurate in reporting Polanyi's ideas on embedding and disembedding – ideas which have given rise to a degree of confusion and controversy (see Block, 2001, p. xxiii). On the very first page of *The Great Transformation*, he writes: "[o]ur thesis is that the idea of a self-adjusting market implied a stark utopia. Such an institution could not exist for any length of time without annihilating the human and natural substance of society" (Polanyi, 2001, p. 3). In other words, if finance has indeed succeeded in disembedding itself from society, then this is not a situation that will subsist for long once any destructive effects have become apparent. Given the scale of the problems witnessed over the past few years, the expectation would accordingly be that society will have taken steps to protect itself against these destructive effects and will be in the process of achieving a rebalancing. Well, governments have been nothing if not active in responding to the financial crisis. One may cite a whole range of policies and interventions from quantitative easing, through bank bailouts and guarantees to outright nationalizations of financial institutions, not to mention a comprehensive new regulatory architecture (for an indication of the complex responses at the EU level, see Snowdon & Lovegrove, 2011).

Can these developments accordingly be characterized as something that systems theory might not have expected – namely a *de*differentiation – but nevertheless something which is absolutely in tune with Polanyi's ideas about the self-preserving instincts of society when confronted with economic disembedding? The answer is, unfortunately, not clear, but it may be that the question itself offers guidance on the possible directions in which answers may be sought. For a start, is it clear that the state actions taken in response to the financial crisis are most appropriately characterized as societal reactions to the potentially destructive effects of economic disembedding? It is surely just as plausible to paint them as efforts by society to *restore* the markets. Again, this need not necessarily trouble the Polanyian perspective inasmuch as this was never antimarket, but rather only concerned that markets should serve society and not the other way round.

Insofar as these efforts accordingly are directed at curbing future excesses on the part of financial markets, then it is possible to be relatively sanguine. And after all, the political rhetoric does seem to be focused on the need to restore markets with a view to ensuring the necessary growth in the real economy to provide the wherewithal to meet ongoing societal needs. But is it not the case that that very statement sets alarm bells ringing? Is this simply to do no more than to set up the next fall? Are the determinedly centrist politicians who dominate most liberal democracies these days really all Keynesians or Polanyians in the aftermath of the crisis? Or are they actually all simultaneously – and paradoxically – Hayekians as well? Or, as the weeks and months go by, does the Hayekian imperative come to dominate the Keynsian or Polanyian?

Having said, therefore, that the answer is not clear, the systems theory predilections of the present author nevertheless lead him to fear the worst. But this is not simply unfounded fatalism or even pessimism. Rather it is based on the analysis of financial contracts outlined above. The demand for financial contracts, for derivative instruments, stems from the need on the part of a whole range of actors engaged in transactions in the real economy involving commodities and loans to hedge the risks associated with trading in an increasingly complex environment. Insofar as there is a demand for these risk management tools there will be suppliers competing to meet it. And as soon as these suppliers provide risk management tools, they in turn must look for ways to manage the risk that they themselves have taken on. And so it goes on. Each level of complexity in turn generates greater complexity which in turn creates a demand for yet more complex risk management instruments. Policymakers and regulators may bemoan the exponential growth in the financial markets and worry over the spiraling disconnection from the underlying transactions in the real economy (see, e.g., Haldane, Brennan, & Madouros, 2010), but these are clearly futile worries when one understands the dynamics of the internally differentiated financial subsystem – the upward spiral of complexity is inevitable and inexorable.

How can this be explained in Polanyian terms? One proposal would be to suggest that while Polanyi spoke in terms of there being three fictitious commodities (land, labor, and money) it is now necessary to speak in terms of there being a fourth, namely risk (this is a proposal also made by Guyer, 2009). It is interesting to note that while Polanyi in *The Great Transformation* does mention the idea of insurance at various points this is almost uniformly in terms of social insurance. In other words, for him, the risks that confront the individual are most appropriately dealt with in the context of social relations. And yet as soon as economic means of dealing with risk arise, these are the very innovations which permit, for example, long-distance trade and thus the eventual emergence of the sorts of markets that so trouble Polanyi. Risk beyond that which can be mitigated in the context of social relations has been present for a long time.[10] It was surely present when *The Great Transformation* was written, but it could perhaps at that time be subsumed within the fictitious commodity of money. Since that time, however, it has assumed extraordinary importance, leading to the sort of developments discussed in this article. It could be proposed that it is the absence of the discussion of risk in these terms which prevents Polanyi's analysis from providing adequate conceptual tools to deal with the emerging highly sophisticated relationship between finance and economy. Notwithstanding that possibility, might it nevertheless be suggested that the rise in the importance of this fourth fictitious commodity is implicated in a further great transformation, one that is characterized by the internal differentiation (or disembedding) of finance? The demonstration of that possibility is beyond the scope of this article, but one might already point to some of the components: thus, in addition to the idea of risk as the fourth fictitious commodity, might it be suggested that the rise of computers (and especially the exponential growth in computing power and the emergence of instantaneous global connections) has played a significant role? In the same way that the emergence of complex machines requiring significant investment set in train the commoditization of humankind and nature during the 19th century, is it not the case that the emergence of computers and their impact on trading (and indeed calculation) set in train the commoditization of risk that is such a feature of contemporary conditions?

CONCLUSIONS

What is the direction of travel from here? Is this dynamic of the internal differentiation of finance one that is reversible? Policymakers and regulators are now busy coming up with plans to clip the wings of financial markets and prevent a recurrence of the crisis (in the United States, see Department of the Treasury, 2009; in the United Kingdom, see Turner, 2009), but does the experience of the period following the publication of *The Great Transformation* indicate that another 60 years from now a future Polanyi (or Luhmann) will be sitting amidst the ruins (a situation, after all, that was only narrowly avoided this time) or charting the latest unexpected development of the market dynamic, exploiting the commoditization of something whose "value" even now has not been noticed? As regards regulatory responses, what amounts to an intriguing experiment is already underway. While there have already been moves to take CDS transactions away from the unregulated over-the-counter market and on to regulated exchanges,[11] regulators are facing the difficulty that a significant proportion of these contracts are not standardized – precisely because they are engineered to respond to specific risk profiles – and are thus not amenable to exchange transactions (the regulatory challenges revealed by this sort of analysis are considered further in Paterson, 2013). Tensions are emerging between those states who are making the case for stronger regulation and those who are at least perceived to see the tightening of US and EU regulation of financial derivative contracts as an opportunity to attract business.[12] If society really is now keen to take steps to protect itself from the worst excesses of destructive markets, it is certainly not going to find markets simply sitting waiting to be disciplined. Systems theorists would not be sanguine about the prospects of success. Would Polanyians in the light of the experience of the last 60 years really be any more positive?

At the conclusion of this article, in view of the themes of the conference at which the initial version was presented, it is also appropriate to reflect critically on the socio-legal methods that have informed the development of the argument. If one were to look for a common criterion to apply to the two distinctive sets of analytical tools that have been deployed above, one might well consider the degree of inherent optimism or pessimism that each possesses. These are, after all, times of great uncertainty, and individuals and corporations are continually asked about their own attitudes to the future in the aftermath of the crisis (e.g., in the context of a range of confidence indices) or bombarded by the media with data on the attitudes of others (with, of course, the possibility of feedback, self-fulfilling prophecies and the like). It is surely not unreasonable then to ask whether analytical tools applied to the crisis possess inherent biases one way or the other. Adopting this rather loose and unscientific criterion, it will come as no surprise to readers familiar with the socio-legal and related literatures that Polanyi is regarded as essentially optimistic while systems theory is regarded as essentially pessimistic. And yet what the foregoing analysis reveals is that each of these approaches is considerably more sophisticated and capable of much more nuanced findings than these popular perceptions routinely allow. In each case, there is an effort to identify and understand deep currents within social phenomena. In each case, these efforts are of particular relevance in the context of the events of recent years on financial markets and their effects on the broader society. Precisely what is to be made of these efforts, however, appears to differ in each case. In the case of Polanyi, there appears to be a sense in which the identification of the deep currents is in large part about predicting the next significant shift, but less about providing indications of how that might be achieved – albeit that one may infer that the very identification and prediction might have been intended to encourage a particular direction of travel. In the case of systems theory, on the other hand, it depends which particular strand one chooses to follow. If one follows Luhmann, then it would appear as if one may admire the sophistication of the analysis but then have to accept that the very autopoetic closure that allows the theory's nuanced and genuinely new insights also precludes any opportunity to intervene so as to make things better. If one follows Teubner, on the other hand, then one may feel less constrained about considering possible interventions while remaining modest about the possibility of success. Neither approach, therefore, whether Polanyi's or systems theory, is rushing to offer policy or regulatory solutions. That should not be read negatively, however. In the context of considerable uncertainty, a sense of the deep currents in the relationship between economy and society has considerable value in and of itself. And while the suggestion here is that Polanyi's analysis lacks the conceptual tools to cope with the developments that have been at the heart of the financial crisis, this is not to suggest that systems theory must have the final word. While the argument here has been that systems theory does offer a richer picture of the precise relationship between finance and economy, it should also be read as indicating one of the ways in which Polanyi's undoubtedly suggestive analysis could be taken forward in the context of the addition of a fourth fictitious commodity (risk). After all, if there is a lesson from the financial crisis that must be drawn, then it is surely that there is the greatest need to be concerned when the conviction is strongest that one has the right answer.

NOTES

1. This is not, of course, to suggest that all government bonds are less risky. One thinks in particular of Greece and certain other members of the Eurozone. It is worth noting that the CDS is a feature also of the sovereign debt crisis, although at the time of writing (October 2011) the jury is still out on whether the voluntary fifty per cent "haircut" for private holders of Greek bonds will constitute a default event and trigger CDSs.

2. See, for example, the definition of the "real economy" provided by the Financial Times (2011): "The part of the economy that is concerned with actually producing goods and services, as opposed to the part of the economy that is concerned with buying and selling on the financial markets."

3. "Productive" is used here in the sense of a subsystem which in the context of a contract engages in "a productive act that, in accordance with the intrinsic logic of the relevant social context (e.g., technology, medicine, media, science, art, and other social areas where goods and services are produced), changes the productive situation" (Teubner, 2007, p. 52).

4. While it is true that law can distinguish between different types of contract and can provide different regulatory frameworks for them, it remains the case from a systems theory perspective that the contract is concerned with stabilizing normative expectations.

5. This complexity reduction is so complete that economists are warned to beware of assuming that economic models bear any relation to reality when it comes to making policy recommendations (see Lawson, 1997).

6. Recall in this regard the scale of the CDS market reported at note 19 above and associated text. To be clear, the suggested improbability is not that a larger internally differentiated subsystem could not be physically accommodated within the subsystem of the economy (as communicative systems, such spatial constraints do not apply) but rather that so much that is intangible depends for its ultimate value on so little that is tangible.

7. For a measure of the extent to which the belief grew that structured credit effectively reduced risk while simultaneously creating value, see Turner (2009, pp. 13–14).

8. Among examples of the inventiveness of finance in seeking new ways to create value, life settlement-backed securities or "death bonds" must rank particularly highly. For details, see Stone and Zissu (2006). For an accessible overview, see Goldstein (2007). I am grateful to Katayoun Baghai for drawing my attention to this example.

9. It could be objected that this picture of the relative positions of finance and economy from a systems theory perspective implies also a rupture of the link between the risk of default on the corporate bond and the premium charged in the context of the CDS, but, of course, this is precisely what the CDS has done. While it can be bought as a hedging instrument by the purchaser of a corporate bond, its very existence depends upon a liquid market and therefore on the presence of speculators. Thus, the vast majority of CDSs are held by parties with no "insurable interest," as it were – that is, parties who do not hold the corresponding corporate bond.

10. One could think here of the risks involved in industrialization, international trade, and speculation, in short, the phenomena that are the key focus of Polanyi's account of the 19th century. More recently, one could think in terms of the risks associated with the continued development of these phenomena during the 20th century and thus of the shift identified by Beck from *industrial* society to *risk* society. See Beck (n.d., p. 12).

11. For example, see in relation to the US Title VII of the Dodd-Frank Act (The Wall Street Transparency and Accountability Act 2010).

12. See the remarks by the US Treasury Secretary to the International Monetary Conference, Atlanta, Georgia, June 6, 2011. Available online at http://www.treasury.gov/press-center/press-releases/Pages/tg1202.aspx. See also the response from the outgoing Chief Executive of the Hong Kong Securities and Futures Commission, 9 June 2011, reported online at http://www.risk.net/asia-risk/news/2077744/outgoing-sfc-chief-slams-geithner-regulatory-arbitrage-comments. (Both accessed 9 June 2011.)

REFERENCES

Beck, U. (n.d.). *Risk society*. London: Sage.

Block, F. (2001). Introduction. In K. Polanyi (Ed.), *Great transformation*. Polany (2001).

Campbell, D., & Vincent-Jones, P. (Eds.). (1996). *Contract and organisation: Socio-legal initiatives*. Aldershot: Dartmouth.

Deakin, S., & Michie, J. (Eds.). (1997). *Contracts, co-operation and competition: Studies in economics, management and law*. Oxford: Oxford University Press.

Department of the Treasury. (2009). *Financial regulatory reform – A new foundation: Rebuilding financial supervision and regulation*. Washington, DC: Department of the Treasury.

Evans, E. J. (2004). *Thatcher and thatcherism*. London: Routledge.

Financial Times. (2011). Retrieved from http://lexicon.ft.com. Accessed on June 9, 2011.

Goldstein, M. (2007). Profiting from mortality. *Business Week* (cover story), July 30, 2007.

Guyer, J. I. (2009). Composites, fictions and risk: Toward an ethnography of price. In C. Hann & K. Hart (Eds.), *Market and society: The great transformation today* (pp. 203–220). Cambridge, MA: Cambridge University Press.

Haldane, A., Brennan, S., & Madouros, V. (2010). What is the contribution of the financial sector: Miracle or mirage? In A. Turner, A. Haldane, P. Woolley, S. Wadhwani, C. Goodhart, A. Smithers, A. Large, J. Kay, M. Wolf, P. Boone, S. Johnson & R. Layard (Eds.), *The future of finance: The LSE report* (pp. 87–120). London: London School of Economics.

Kjaer, P. F., Teubner, G., & Febbrajo, A. (Eds.). (2011). *The financial crisis in constitutional perspective: The dark side of functional differentiation*. Oxford: Hart.

Kolb, R. W. (1996). *Financial derivatives* (2nd ed.), Cambridge, MA: Blackwell Business.

Lawson, T. (1997). *Economics and reality*. London: Routledge.

Love, P., & Lattimore, P. (2009). *International trade: Free, fair and open?* Paris: OECD.

Lowe, R. (2005). *The welfare state in britain since 1945*. Basingstoke: Palgrave Macmillan.

Luhmann, N. (1987). Closure and openness: On reality in the world of law. In G. Teubner (Ed.), *Autopoietic law: A new approach to law and society* (p. 335–348). Berlin: de Gruyter.

Luhmann, N. (1995). *Social systems*. Stanford, CA: Stanford University Press.

Luhmann, N. (1997). Limits of steering. *Theory, Culture and Society*, *14*(1), 41–57.

Luhmann, N. (2004). *Law as a social system*. Oxford: Oxford University Press.

McCrudden, C. (Ed.). (1999). *Regulation and deregulation: Policy and practice in the utilities and financial services industries*. Oxford: Clarendon Press.

McDonald, R. L. (2009). *Fundamentals of derivatives markets*. Boston, MA: Pearson.

Menkhoff, L., & Tolksdorf, N. (2001). *Financial market drift: Decoupling of the financial sector from the real economy?* Berlin: Springer-Verlag.

OECD statistics. (2011). Retrieved from http://stats.oecd.org/Index.aspx. Accessed on June 9, 2011.

Parker, C., & Braithwaite, J. (2003). Regulation. In P. Cane & M. Tushnet (Eds.), *The Oxford handbook of legal studies*. Oxford: Oxford University Press.

Paterson, J. (2006). Reflecting on reflexive law. In M. King & C. Thornhill (Eds.), *Luhmann on politics and law: Critical appraisals and applications*. Oxford: Hart.

Paterson, J. (2011). Financial instruments, functional differentiation and regulatory challenges. In A. Febbrajo & G. Harste (Eds.), *Law and intersystemic communication: Understanding structural couplings*. Aldershot: Ashgate.

Paterson, J., & Teubner, G. (1998). Changing maps: Empirical legal autopoiesis. *Social and Legal Studies*, *4*, 451–486.

Philippopoulos-Mihalopoulos, A. (2009). *Niklas luhmann: Law, justice, society*. London: Routledge.

Polanyi, K. (2001 [1944]). *The great transformation: The political & economic origins of our time*. Boston, MA: Beacon Press.

Rousseas, S. (1982). *The political economy of reaganomics*. Armonk, NY: ME Sharpe.

Ruggie, J. G. (1982). International regimes, transactions, and change: Embedded liberalism in the postwar economic order. *International Organisations*, *36*(2), 379–415.

Snowdon, P., & Lovegrove, S. (2011). The new European supervisory structure. *Compliance Officer Bulletin*, *83*, 1–39.

Stone, C. A., & Zissu, A. (2006). Securitization of senior life settlements: Managing extension risk. *The Journal of Derivatives*, *13*(3), 66–72.

Strange, S. (1997). *Casino capitalism*. Manchester: Manchester University Press.

Teubner, G. (2000). Contracting worlds: The many autonomies of private law. *Social and Legal Studies*, *9*, 399–417.

Teubner, G. (2007). In the blind spot: The hybridization of contracting. *Theoretical Inquiries in Law*, *8*(1), 51–71.

Turner, L. (2009). *A regulatory response to the global banking crisis*. London: Financial Services Authority.

FROM POLANYI TO DISCOURSE THEORY

Bettina Lange

ABSTRACT

This article starts from the assumption that economic sociology, including Karl Polanyi's work, can contribute fresh perspectives to regulation debates because it opens up new understandings of the nature of economic activity, a key target of legal regulation. In particular this article examines Polanyi's idea that society drives regulation. For Polanyi the "regulatory counter-movement" is society's response to the disembedding – in particular through the proliferation of markets – of economic out of social relationships. Section One of the article identifies three key challenges that arise from this Polanyian take on regulation for contemporary regulation researchers. First, Polanyi focuses on social norms restraining business behavior, but neglects social norms embedded in law as also shaping regulation. Second, he seems to imply a clear-cut conceptual distinction between "economy" and "society." Third, his analysis sidelines the role of interest politics in the development of regulation.

Addressing the first of these three key challenges, Section Two of this article therefore argues that a Polanyian vision of "socialized" legal regulation should build on contemporary accounts of responsive law and regulation, which focus attention on social norms informing legal regulation.

From Economy to Society? Perspectives on Transnational Risk Regulation
Studies in Law, Politics, and Society, Volume 62, 73–101

ISSN: 1059-4337/doi:10.1108/S1059-4337(2013)0000062004

Section Three of this article tackles the second key challenge raised by Polanyi's work for contemporary regulation researchers, that is, how to transcend a modernist perspective of "economy" and "society" as clearly demarcated, distinct fields of social action. It argues that discourse theory is an important alternative theoretical resource. Drawing on Laclau and Mouffe, the article suggests that understanding "economy" and "society" as performed by open and relationally constructed discourses helps to capture interconnections between "economy" and "society" that become particularly visible when we analyze how specific regulatory regimes work at a medium- and small-scale level. These points are further brought to life in Section Four through a discussion of the European Union (EU) regulatory regime for trade in risky, transgenic agricultural products, and in particular the current reform debates about the consideration of the "socioeconomic impacts" of such products.

Keywords: Transgenic agricultural products; responsive regulation; discourse theory; European Union regulation; socio-economic impacts

POLANYI'S MACRO-SOCIOLOGICAL AND HISTORICAL PERSPECTIVE: REGULATION AS THE OUTCOME OF CHANGING ECONOMY–SOCIETY RELATIONSHIPS

Polanyi's regulation concept is wide. It encompasses, first, the regulatory force of social norms, and second, distinct political, economic and legal strategies, and institutions for regulating economic activity, such as trade unions, central banking, and monetary policy, as well as state-enforced competition law (Polanyi, 2001, pp. 138, 214). For Polanyi, regulatory institutions come into being at a time in history when economic activity becomes increasingly coordinated through markets. In fact regulation is part of a "double-movement" (Dale, 2012, p. 7). On the one hand, it enables the development of a distinct economic sphere and markets in particular, for instance by guaranteeing private property rights, while, on the other hand, it reins in the worst social side-effects of markets (Dale, 2010a, p. 61). Regulation thus both enables and restrains economic activity.

Polanyi (1944, 2001) develops his ideas about economy–society interactions through a wide-sweep, macro-sociological, and historical analysis of some preindustrial societies, such as Dahomey (Bognár, 1990, p. 15) and the industrializing countries of Western Europe, in particular England, as well as the United States. He shows that the market society and its key elements, such as economic rationality, the pursuit of individual material gain, and markets as the dominant form for coordinating economic exchange, are not universal and natural, but historically exceptional and predicated upon specific cultural conditions, such as the rise of industrial entrepreneurialism (Hann & Hart, 2011, p. 57; Salsano, 1990, p. 143; Somers, 1990, p. 153; Waller & Jennings, 1991, p. 489).

Polanyi suggests that during the first phase of preindustrial, precapitalist societies, economic activity was still embedded in social relationships, even though markets may have been more prevalent in such societies than acknowledged by Polanyi (Hann & Hart, 2011, p. 71). According to Polanyi, distinct regulatory institutions play only a minor role in preindustrial and precapitalist societies (Dale, 2011, p. 319; Salsano, 1990, p. 141). Regulation is not imposed externally on citizens, but reflects commonly accepted norms of self-governance of a community:

> Custom and law, magic and religion cooperated in inducing the individual to comply with rules of behaviour which eventually, ensured his functioning in the economic system. (Polanyi, 2001, p. 57).

For instance, before the rise of the market society, wages for laborers were regulated according to the custom and rule of the guild and the town (Polanyi, 2001, p. 73). During the second, mercantilist phase, lasting from the 16th until the late 18th century, more economic activity in Europe became coordinated through markets. Now the liberal state started to organize trade on the scale of the national territory, also by dismantling traditional forms of regulation which had restricted trade to the town, its surrounding countryside, and specific trade routes between a few municipalities, such as the Hanse along the Baltic sea coast (Polanyi, 2001, p. 68). Regulation began to promote markets, not just for internal unification, but also to support external war efforts (Polanyi, 2001, p. 70; Somers, 1990, p. 155). New tasks were opening up for regulation, such as preventing the rise of national monopolies (Polanyi, 2001, p. 69). But during mercantilism, state legal regulation ensured that economic activity was in tune with the wider social purposes of the political community (Polanyi, 2001, pp. 58, 73). For instance, the principle of self-sufficiency continued to be applied to national economic activity, as well as the household economy (Polanyi, 2001, p. 71).

During the third phase, starting in the late 18th century in Britain, regulation became central to the establishment of a "market society." This radically altered relations between "economy" and "society," also because labor, land, and money were now commodified (Dale, 2010a, p. 51).[1] The market society is characterized by a *belief* in the self-regulatory capacity of markets, though regulation is central to its functioning. Regulation ensures that prices are the main organizing principle of markets and that incomes are achieved only through market transactions (Polanyi, 2001, p. 72). Moreover, regulation now expands by transcending national boundaries. Tariffs, for instance, control trade between England and its colonies. Polanyi's historical take on the role of regulation of economic activity poses, however, a number of challenges for contemporary regulation researchers.

THREE KEY CHALLENGES FOR CONTEMPORARY REGULATION RESEARCHERS

How to Avoid Essentializing "Economy" and "Society"?

This historical, social–theoretical Polanyian take on the development of regulation poses three key challenges for contemporary regulation researchers. First, it seems to imply a clear conceptual distinction between "economy" and "society" which leaves no room for a potential blurring of boundaries between these spheres during the actual operation of specific regulatory regimes. In particular, Polanyi's "embeddedness" metaphor – which is central to his thinking about regulation – seems to rely on a clear distinction between "economy" and "society," though it is not entirely clear from *The Great Transformation* (2001, pp. 178, 209) how the idea of embedding economic in social relationships should be interpreted. Polanyi's claim that the economy is *always* embedded in social relationships seems to detract from a clear conceptual distinction between "economy" and "society" (Dale, 2010b, p. 382). This lack of clarity has also been attributed to the fact that Polanyi fused various, sometimes opposing intellectual traditions when writing *The Great Transformation* (Dale, 2010b, p. 370).

So how can we start to make sense of Polanyi's idea of embedding economic in social relationships? It implies that "the economic system is, in effect, a mere function of social organization" (Polanyi, 2001, p. 52). It also involves the subordination of economic activity to value systems, such as politics and religion (Block, 2001, p. xxiv). Economic activity is understood to be motivated by social gains, such as status, expressed through rank, influence, respect, responsibility, and security (Polanyi, 2001, p. 160). Satisfaction of material needs may be a visible token of the pursuit of these social gains, but is not, according to Polanyi and in contrast to some

Marxist perceptions, the driver of change in society (Polanyi-Levitt, 1990, p. 115). Polanyi therefore seeks to mark out "social" motivations for economic activity that are distinct from the play of economic interests themselves, but he does not address whether such "social" motivations are defined by powerful economic interests. Hence, Polanyi's analysis rests on a conceptual distinction, though not necessarily empirical difference, between a "social" and an "economic" sphere. Only if we think of economic action as distinct from social action does the idea of embedding economic in social relationships make sense. Moreover, even when Polanyi analyzed how economic relationships become embedded in social ones, the analysis was geared toward understanding the economy as a distinct, stable field:

> The study of how economies are instituted should start, according to Polanyi, from how the economy acquires **unity and stability**, i.e., how the interdependence and recurrence of **its** parts come to be secured. (emphasis added, Jessop, 2002, p. 194).

Moreover, Polanyi does differentiate clearly between an economic and a social sphere in his analysis of "disembedded" economic activity in 19th-century Britain (Polanyi, 2001, pp. 101–103; Waller & Jennings, 1991, p. 491). At that time, the state was no longer a key economic actor, but enforced merely the rules of the market (Dale, 2010a, p. 50). Hence, the economy was governed by laws of its own because it had been taken out of "a social whole" (Dale, 2010a, p. 192). The claim that a distinct economic sphere developed in 19th-century Britain is further buttressed by the mirror-claim that also a separate sphere of "society" emerged during the second half of the 19th century (Polanyi, 2001, p. 157). Not just the economy but also society now works according to its own laws, geared to the progress of the community as a whole, as an entity distinct from the state and the market. Moreover, society's rules are now seen to act upon the character of citizens who become part of a "social whole," with society setting limits to human progress, a perspective different from Malthus and Ricardo who perceived the laws of the market as key determinants of human progress. Given this clear distinction between "economy" and "society," Polanyi's work has therefore been criticized for reifying economic life, in comparison to Marx who analyzed the specific *social* relations between those who sell and buy, and thus explored the nature of private property and control enabled by it (Dale, 2012, pp. 9, 21; Dale, 2010a, p. 198; Polanyi-Levitt, 1990, p. 118). Another line of critique argues that Polanyi failed to see that during the rise of the market society social linkages did not disappear, but that simply old social bonds were replaced with new ones. Polanyi's claim that social bonds are less central to economic activity during the rise of the market society than during mercantilism may be founded on a mistaken perception of how people actually lived their lives. Strong links between economic activity, reproductive family lives, and political intervention were also important during the rise of the market society (Waller & Jennings, 1991, pp. 492–493). For some economic sociologists, the key issue therefore is whether economic activity is governed by individualist or collectivist values, with neither of these value orientations being specific to "economy" or "society." From this perspective the regulatory counter-movement is not necessarily a move to embed markets into the values of society, with these values being understood in collectivist terms. Instead it can reinforce individualistic values, manifested in regulatory objectives, such as "equality, fairness, and opportunity," that underpin, also according to Adam Smith, the operation of markets (Waller & Jennings, 1991, p. 495). In Section Three below I suggest that contemporary discourse theories are an important theoretical resource for moving further away from essentialized and clearly demarcated conceptions of economy and society. Before developing this discussion, it is, however, necessary to outline two more challenges that Polanyi's work poses for contemporary regulation researchers.

Acknowledging the Regulatory Force of Social Norms that Inform State Legal Systems

A second key challenge that Polanyi's work poses for contemporary regulation researchers is that he did not explore the implications of his assumption of the "primacy of society" for state *legal* regulation of economic activity. If social relationships already regulate how economic activity is conducted, what are the consequences of this for the form and content of state legal regulation? Moreover, Polanyi's "primacy of society" idea requires to also examine the social norms that underpin the operation of state legal regulation, such as the social norms that shape how regulatory agencies work (Hawkins, 1984, 2003; Reichman, 1998). In *The Great Transformation* (1944, 2001) Polanyi explores how entire markets are governed by social norms. Section Two below suggests that this macro-sociological take needs to be complemented by contemporary accounts of responsive law and regulation which explore at a medium and micro-sociological level how social norms govern the behavior of individual business actors, sectors of industry, and most importantly regulation itself, including state legal regulation.

I therefore argue that combining Polanyi's economic sociology with a sociology of law enables to develop a conception of "socialized" legal regulation. Socialized legal regulation explores how legal regulation opens up to social norms that inform the operation of law, as well as social norms that inform business behavior. It therefore retains a distinct conception of legal regulation, separate from the regulatory force of social norms. In Section Two below I address how the responsive regulation literature points toward a way of doing this.[2] But before that, a third challenge for contemporary regulation researchers arising from Polanyi's work should be briefly mentioned here.

Injecting Interest Politics Into Explanations of the Rise of Regulation

Polanyi's analysis sidelines the specific and small-scale political forces that contribute to the development of regulation. He projects a general regulatory tendency into society and portrays the regulatory counter-movement as a nearly automatic response to the disembedding of economic out of social relationships during the rise of the market society (Dale, 2012, p. 10; Polanyi, 2001, p. 156; Rotstein, 1990, p. 100; Waller & Jennings, 1991, p. 493):

> The legislative spearhead of the countermovement against a self-regulating market as it developed in the half century following 1860 turned out to be **spontaneous, undirected by opinion, and actuated by a purely pragmatic spirit**. (emphasis added, Polanyi, 2001, p. 147)

This perspective flows also from Polanyi's methodological assumption of the "primacy of society" which was a reaction to the "naturalism" of classical economists, such as Ricardo and Malthus, who focused on population growth and the availability of natural resources as key structural forces shaping human development (Polanyi, 2001, pp. 131). Polanyi's insistence on the "reality of society" (Somers, 1990, p. 153) turns "society" into a transhistorical, unified explanatory category that sidelines the fragmentation of societies into interest groups and thus interest politics as drivers of regulation (see e.g., Haines, 2011). For Polanyi "social interests," not class can explain regulation (Hann & Hart, 2011, p. 71; Neale, 1990, p. 147; Polanyi, 2001, p. 169). For instance, Polanyi (2001, pp. 139, 162) argues that both the feudal aristocracy and the rising industrial proletariat called for regulatory measures that would "defend the social fabric." But different classes had different visions of this "social fabric." For the landed gentry, it entailed the preservation of feudal rural life. For workers it meant a collectivist urban industrial life, as inspired by the English social reformer Owen. These class-based differences in conceptions of "the social fabric" matter, even though both aristocrats and workers wanted to avoid the replacement of dense social networks by competitive market forces. Polanyi's conception of "protective" regulation lacks clarity, also due to this neglect of class-based interest politics (Dale, 2012, p. 9).

Polanyi's discussion of interest politics is further limited in that he focuses on the political consequences, rather than the political causes of regulatory regimes. For instance, he considers the Speenhamland law as a prime example of the double-movement driven by society. It involves the development of social protection at the same time that markets are expanding (Ebner, 2008, p. 299). He focuses on Speenhamland law's political consequences by arguing that it strengthened the influence of the landed aristocracy over the village poor, while weakening the rural middle class, who resented having to finance this social security scheme through their rate payments (Polanyi, 2001, p. 101). Most importantly, Polanyi (2001, p. 103) points out that the Speenhamland law prevented workers from developing into an economic class that would pose political demands for participation in government and for influence over its working conditions. Instead, the Speenhamland law created an "underclass" of impoverished and demoralized laborers who were "psychologically" trapped through their dependency on poor law relief. Once the Speenhamland law was abolished and national free labor markets developed a modern working class emerged (Polanyi, 2001, p. 105). While this neglect of specific interest politics as drivers of regulation in Polanyi's work is noteworthy, the following parts of the article will focus on discussing how the first two challenges that Polanyi's work poses for contemporary regulation researchers may be tackled. I start with the second challenge that calls for social norms informing the operation of law to be brought into sharper relief. I suggest that building on literature about responsive law and regulation is an important starting point.

DEVELOPING A POLANYIAN CONCEPTION OF SOCIALIZED LEGAL REGULATION

Why Build on Responsive Law and Regulation?

Contemporary accounts of responsive law and regulation can develop Polanyi's underspecified concept of "socialized" legal regulation because they explore how regulation is shaped by its openness to social norms, such as those generated within regulatory and regulated organizations. For instance, how state legal regulation is implemented is also informed by the organizational norms of regulatory agencies. "Risk regulation" can be such an organizational norm. A particular section of the regulated population becomes labeled as posing the most serious threat to regulatory objectives, which therefore should become subject to particularly intense regulatory scrutiny. So, how can the idea that state legal regulation becomes open to social norms be further developed? Below I identify three main dimensions of socializing legal regulation that build on key findings from the literature on responsive law and regulation.

Three Dimensions of Socializing Legal Regulation

First, "participatory citizenship" is a key aspect of responsive law and regulation for a number of authors (Ayres & Braithwaite, 1992; Baldwin & Black, 2007; Nonet & Selznick, 2001; Vincent-Jones, 1998). Nonet and Selznick (2001, pp. 95, 100) define participation widely, referring to citizens' involvement in "making and interpreting legal policy." This entails considerable reliance on civil society actors and "communities" more widely in order to promote compliance of corporate actors with legal provisions (Ayres & Braithwaite, 1992, p. 17). For instance, public interest groups may engage in strategic litigation or naming and shaming media campaigns. Nonet and Selznick (2001, p. 101) as well as Ayres and Braithwaite (1992, p. 18) address the problem that public participation may be dominated by articulate and well-organized interests by advocating state intervention in order to strengthen weaker and more diffuse civil society interests. Civil society actors are central to Ayres' and Braithwaite's conception of "responsive regulation" because it is through negotiation between them, regulated firms, and state regulators that the level of cooperation or punitiveness of enforcement will be determined (Ayres & Braithwaite, 1992, p. 161).

In contrast to Nonet and Selznick, Ayres and Braithwaite perceive economic actors, such as industry associations and self-regulating firms, as key civil society actors in responsive regulation. Ayres and Braithwaite attribute significant regulatory capacity to regulated firms, by suggesting that they may also exercise influence over firms unregulated by the state. For instance, in terms of health and safety or general working conditions, regulated firms are likely to be more attractive to employers and thus can induce unregulated firms to ratchet up their own standards in order to attract employees. Moreover, various private independent professionals, such as financial auditors, insolvency practitioners, and environmental engineers can facilitate responsive regulation (Ayres & Braithwaite, 1992, p. 158). Hence, in developing participatory citizenship as a dimension of socialized legal regulation, it becomes important to critically reflect upon various definitions of a "social" sphere that is being enrolled in regulation. Polanyi (1944, 2001, p. 268) defined a "social sphere" as civil society, more specifically as a moral community of citizens. But this assumption of a social group, homogeneous in normative perspective, if not in actual social composition, has been abandoned in contemporary accounts of responsive law and regulation. For instance, post-structuralists understand a "social sphere" in fluid terms, as an "insistent and unremitting transgression of boundaries of identity and community" (Golder & Fitzpatrick, 2009, p. 110). Similarly, Nonet and Selznick recognize that definitions of "the public interest" underpinning contemporary regulation are contested, and thus cannot be equated with the purposes of an easily assumed communal morality. They argue that multiple interests can be accommodated by making negotiation rather than imposition of order central to socialized legal regulation (Nonet & Selznick, 2001, p. 94).

Second, socializing legal regulation entails becoming responsive to social norms by responding to the attitudes and behaviors of the regulated when implementing enforcement strategies. Ayres and Braithwaite (1992) argue that regulators should not choose between either a punitive, sanctioning, or an informal, cooperative, negotiated approach to enforcement. Instead regulators should move up and down an "enforcement pyramid," also in response to industry structure as well as the motivations of specific regulated companies (Ayres & Braithwaite, 1992, p. 52). The base of the pyramid reflects the default position: regulators engage cooperatively most of the time with those regulated organizations that have every intention to comply with the law. In case of a less compliant attitude by the regulated, the regulator will escalate its enforcement response up the pyramid, culminating finally in prosecution and the imposition of sanctions. The option of "the big stick" of serious sanctions, located at the top of the pyramid, enables the regulator – in a majority of cases – to carry out its work by "speaking softly" (Ayres & Braithwaite, 1992, p. 6). Different interpretations of this type of "responsive" regulation are possible. First, regulators may engage in a "tit-for-tat" game, where they communicate to the regulated in formal terms right from the beginning of the regulatory relationship that they have the power to escalate up the "pyramid." Quantitative empirical research in the context of Australian federal competition and consumer protection laws has shown that in practice such an interpretation yields limited improvement in *attitudes* toward compliance among the regulated, but may, under certain circumstances, change *behavior* in relation to compliance management (Nielsen & Parker, 2009, pp. 382, 396). In contrast to this, a "restorative justice" interpretation of responsive regulation involves regulators seeking to cooperate with the regulated at all times. This also entails to leave the threat of the "big stick" of sanctions in the background and to portray this as a threat imposed by the formal legal system (Nielsen & Parker, 2009, p. 382). Such a "restorative justice" interpretation of responsive regulation has been shown to have some effect, in inducing legal compliance-oriented attitudes among the regulated, but not necessarily a change in behavior in relation to compliance management (Nielsen & Parker, 2009, p. 396).

Baldwin and Black (2007, 2010) go beyond Ayres' and Braithwaite's focus on enforcement and thus broaden the scope of regulatory activity which should be rendered responsive. For instance, they suggest that "really responsive" regulation also becomes responsive to the regulatory logic and philosophy that underpins "regulatory tools and strategies" (Baldwin & Black, 2007, p. 1). They also argue that regulators need to become responsive not only to the attitudes and behaviors of regulated firms or entire industries, but also to changes in these. They, therefore, advocate regulators becoming attuned to "the operating and cognitive frameworks of the regulated firm" and "the institutional environment and performance of the regulatory regime" itself (Baldwin & Black, 2007, p. 1). They suggest that in really responsive *risk*-based regulation, regulatory agencies should focus on the nature and severity of the risks posed by the operating practices of the regulated, rather than on formal legal rules (Black & Baldwin, 2010, p. 184). According to Baldwin and Black, these extra dimensions of responsiveness should be considered during each of the five steps of enforcement such as, first, detecting undesirable and noncompliant behavior; second, choosing tools and strategies for responding to that behavior; third, "enforcing those tools and strategies"; fourth, "assessing their success and failure"; and fifth, "modifying the tools accordingly" (Baldwin & Black, 2007, p. 1). Finally, the very idea of social norms informing responsive regulatory strategies has been further developed through detailed analysis of the *types of relationships* between regulators and regulated and the values that underpin them. Five different ideal-types of interactions can be identified, such as legality, solidarity, self-interest, authority, and judgment relationships, with each of these built around a core value to which also argumentative styles and behavioral strategies become oriented. For instance, compliance with legal rules becomes central to a legality relationship, the building and maintenance of trust to solidarity relationships, the consideration of resources, in particular gains and costs to relationships framed through self-interest, etc. (Etienne, 2013, pp. 36−37). These relationships become managed through positive and negative signals that are exchanged between regulated and regulators in relation to the core values of the particular type of relationship. For instance, mutual assistance between regulated and regulator will count as a positive signal in a solidarity relationship (Etienne, 2013, p. 38).

Third, the theme of law becoming open to social norms is further developed in Golder's and Fitzpatrick's idea of responsive law. They suggest that law's indeterminacy is another way of recognizing such openness. Here socializing legal regulation involves the explicit recognition that law can change and be different given its fundamental indeterminacy. Golder and Fitzpatrick (2009, p. 100) build in particular on Foucault. They suggest that law is responsive in the sense that it is open to the "ultimate contingency and unpredictability of the future." According to Goulder's and Fitzpatrick's reading of Foucault, this enables law to be at the heart of social bonds (Golder & Fitzpatrick, 2009, p. 110). In this take on responsive legal regulation, law never fully acquires the quality of "rules" and is therefore not the source of enduring social orders (Piška, 2011, p. 254). It simply oscillates between sometimes being closed while at other times remaining open (Golder & Fitzpatrick, 2009, p. 53). To summarize, these three main dimensions of socializing legal regulation, through participatory citizenship, responsiveness to the attitudes and behaviors of regulated organizations, and recognition of law's indeterminacy help to develop a Polanyian conception of legal regulation that considers society−economy interactions to be at the core of regulatory processes. Socialized legal regulation explores how legal regulation becomes opened up to social norms that inform the operation of law, and social norms that inform business behavior. It retains a distinct conception of legal regulation, separate from the regulatory force of social norms. For instance, in Golder's and Fitzpatrick's terminology (2009, p. 100) the point is made in the following way: Foucault's conception of responsive law opens it up to powers outside it, but at the same time law remains "resistant to" and "uncontainable" by these powers. Similarly Nonet and Selznick (2001, p. 80) suggest that regulatory law's reliance on "concepts, doctrines, maxims, and principles" render it open to its social contexts, but also maintains its distinct identity. For example, legal principles, such as proportionality or intergenerational justice, are open-textured but also link back to a whole corpus of administrative law and legal values, such as the rule of law. Baldwin and Black (2007, p. 16) also argue that law adapts only selectively to its environment and maintains its own internal institutional integrity because it reconstructs the social norms it encounters in the light of a wider public interest. Among such social norms are "indigenous social ordering," based on "shared experience" and "shared sentiments, sustained by practical needs," developed in "firms, schools, families, and religious organizations" (Baldwin & Black, 2007, p. 16).

In developing a conception of socialized regulation, accounts of responsive law and regulation also start to transcend clear demarcations between economy and society, a key challenge for contemporary regulation researchers as outlined in Section One above. For instance, Ayres and Braithwaite consider regulation of business actors to emerge from combined economic and social regulatory forces:

> market forces for social improvement are unleashed by a combination of professional leadership, PIG [Public Interest Group] activism, and responsiveness by regulators and industry associations. (Ayres & Braithwaite, 1992, p. 161)

They advocate tripartite regulatory communities, which combine, first, governance by markets and market actors, second, state regulators, and third, civil society actors beyond market actors, such as individual citizens and nongovernmental organizations.

Other responsive regulation accounts, however, still operate with a clearer distinction between economy and society and the distinct values and objectives that are perceived to inform these two spheres of social action. For instance, in order to characterize the goals of legal regulation of contracting out UK local government services in the 1980s, Vincent-Jones (1998, p. 369) distinguishes between the "social goals" of equity, fairness, nondiscrimination, and the "economic" goal of efficiency, with "social" goals considered also as "political issues" best decided by local councils and citizens. The next section suggests that post-structuralist social theory, and in particular Laclau's and Mouffe's ideas about discourse, enables one to see economy and society as closely interrelated and thus to go further in understanding the legal regulation of business actors.

ECONOMY AND SOCIETY AS PERFORMED THROUGH OPEN AND RELATIONALLY CONSTRUCTED DISCOURSES

Introducing the Idea of Relationally Constructed Discourses

Post-structuralism questions Polanyi's understanding of economy and society as *conceptually* distinct, discrete spheres. It instead perceives economy and society as performed by open discourses, which are relationally constructed. The idea of discourse suggests that ways of thinking and talking about economy and society do not simply *reflect* the social world but play an active role in *constituting* and *changing* it (Phillips & Jørgensen, 2002, p. 1). Discourses are historically contingent fields of knowledge, expressed through any medium of communication, such as images, audio signals, as well as talk and text. They regulate what can be imagined, talked, and written about in relation to a particular topic (Torfing, 1999, p. 90, referring to Foucault, 1991, pp. 59–60).

The idea that discourses, such as "economy" and "society," are constructed in relation to each other flows from core assumptions in discourse theory. Post-structuralists, like structuralists, not only suggest that a linguistic sign acquires meaning because it is distinguished from other linguistic signs. They also argue that linguistic signs can change in accordance with the context in which they are used. Hence, interrelationships between different linguistic signs become less fixed, given that signs can also change (Phillips & Jørgensen, 2002, p. 11). Moreover, post-structuralists apply this analysis not just to elements of speech but to any system of social signification, including bodies of expert knowledge, such as economics and sociology.

Open Discourses

A number of discourse theorists consider discourses as relatively open. For instance, Fairclough's (2010, pp. 420–421) concept of "intertextuality" suggests that discourses embodied in texts usually draw on elements of discourses enshrined in other texts (Phillips & Jørgensen, 2002, p. 6). Hence, change within a discourse can be explained through interrelationships between different texts. One of the clearest expressions of the idea of relationally constructed open discourses can be found in Laclau's and Mouffe's work on political discourses and hegemony (Laclau & Mouffe, 1985, pp. 111,113). They consider language as fundamentally instable and meaning as never fixed. They define discourse as an "articulation of linguistic and nonlinguistic elements in "a differential and structured system of positions" (Laclau & Mouffe, 1985, p. 108). They therefore consider discursive structures to be not merely cognitive, but to be "articulatory practices which constitute and organize social relations" (Laclau & Mouffe, 1985, p. 96). Like Foucault they consider discursive formations as mere "regularities in dispersion" and thus as not very coherent. Discursive formations are not very unified, because they are not necessarily grouped around the same object, nor do they share a common style of producing statements (Laclau & Mouffe, 1985, p. 105). Moreover, Laclau and Mouffe extend to all social relationships Saussure's structuralist idea that meaning is established referentially through language. Saussure had suggested that the meaning of the term "mother" becomes only established through its difference to the term "father," "daughter," "son," etc. Laclau and Mouffe therefore argue that the differential construction of all objects, lends discourses a quality of "openness." But they also recognize that meaning within a discourse can become at least partially fixed, in particular through what they call "nodal points" and "knots of definitive meanings" (Laclau & Mouffe, 1985, p. 112; Torfing, 1999, p. 97). These operate like metaphors and link signifiers that circulate within a discourse. Nodal points can thus be master signifiers that partially fix the meaning of the different signifiers they draw together (Laclau & Mouffe, 1985, p. 113). To conclude, Laclau's and Mouffe's conception of relationally constructed and open discourses thus helps to think in new ways about economy and society interactions. It transcends Polanyi's idea that economy and society have distinct core rationalities that turn economy and society into distinct fields of social action. The next section illustrates how these discourse ideas can capture what appear to be blurred conceptual boundaries between "economy" and "society," in the actual operation of a specific regulatory regime, here EU authorizations for trade in risky, transgenic agricultural products.

Tracing Socialized Legal Regulation in the Context of EU GMO Regulation

Focusing on a specific regime of *legal* regulation foregrounds law, and thus directs attention to how legal frameworks generate their own conceptions of "economy" and "society." This section discusses two points. First, whether EU authorizations[3] of transgenic agricultural products can be considered as an example of socialized legal regulation. Do the public participation provisions in this regime and the way it frames economic and social regulatory objectives turn this into an example of socialized legal regulation? Second, this section suggests that the EU regulatory regime for transgenic agricultural products can be better understood if we conceive of "economy" and "society" as open and relationally constructed discourses.

The EU Regulatory Regime for Trade in Transgenic Agricultural Products

Directive 2001/18/EC and Regulation 1829/2003/EC require prior authorization before transgenic agricultural products can be lawfully imported, traded, or released into the environment in the EU. Directive 2001/18/EC seeks to prevent, minimize, or contain a range of potential also transnational risks that may harm human health and/or the environment generated by genetically modified (GM) plants, seeds, animal feed, and food (Arts. 1 and 4). Regulation 1829/2003/EC also pursues these objectives, but adds the protection of plant and animal health and welfare (Art. 5), as well as the economic aims of protecting the interests of consumers and the functioning of the EU internal market (Art. 1). In practice most authorizations are granted under Regulation 1829/2003/EC. Central to the authorization procedure is a scientific risk assessment provided by the public- or private-sector applicant, involved in the genetic manipulation of agricultural products. These scientific risk assessments are evaluated by the national competent authority in the case of authorizations under Directive 2001/18/EC. Under Regulation 1829/2003/EC the risk assessment is more centralized because the GMO panel of the European Food Safety Authority (EFSA) oversees the evaluation of the risk assessment. So, how can the fact that transgenic agriculture raises fundamental questions about economy and society interactions be captured and further analyzed through the idea of "socialized legal regulation"?

A Limited Role for Public Participation in EU GMO Authorizations

EU authorizations for transgenic agricultural products can only be described to a limited extent as socialized legal regulation, on the grounds of their provisions for public participation, because formal legal provisions for public participation as well as their practical application are weak. The legally nonbinding preamble 46 to Directive 2001/18/EC suggests that EU citizens' comments should be taken into account when the Commission proposes a draft decision on the GMO application to the Comitology committee. Regulation 1829/2003/EC does not even spell out how EU citizens' comments, for instance on EFSA's scientific opinion should be taken into account in Commission draft decisions. Art. 7 (1) of the Regulation enables the Commission to consider "any other legitimate factors relevant to the matter under consideration."[4] This may well include EU citizens' comments, but the Regulation does not impose a duty to do so.

EU Member States are obliged to transpose the provisions of Directive 2001/18/EC into national law, including Art. 9 which requires Member States to provide for national public consultation procedures, that include reasonable time-periods for the provision of comments, and can extend "where appropriate" to the consultation of groups (Cardwell, 2010, p. 19). Citizens, for instance, in the United Kingdom, the Netherlands, and Germany can comment on summaries of authorization applications placed on a national public register. But usually national legislation only requires the national competent authority to take citizens' comments into account when drafting a national assessment report for the Genetically Modified Organism (GMO). National competent authorities are not bound by citizens' comments. Moreover, in practice, meaningful public participation is further hampered by the fact that only few citizens submit comments in the EU wide consultation phase. There is also limited communication between participants in EU authorizations because views expressed during the public consultation phase often reflect entrenched institutional positions and seem to be formulated in some isolation from the perspectives of other participants.[5] Genuine, open dialogue appears to be limited. For instance, EU citizens' comments on EFSA opinions or applicants' environmental risk assessments are sometimes simply stock responses. Exactly the same arguments are made for different GM products, such as GM maize BT 11 and GM maize 1507. Sometimes different environmental nongovernmental organizations (NGOs) provide identical submissions when commenting on EFSA's scientific opinions (GHK Interim Report, 2009, p. 8). But not just in relation to public participation provisions, but also when considering the relationship between economic and social regulatory objectives, EU authorizations of transgenic agricultural products are only to a limited extent an example of socialized legal regulation. Economic objectives are not subordinated to social ones.

Limited Subordination of Economic to Social Objectives

EU GMO authorizations score low in relation to another indicator of "socialized" legal regulation, the subordination of economic to social aims, for two reasons. First, the EU authorization system is embedded in an international legal framework that restricts the EU's legal powers to limit international trade in GMO agricultural products for the pursuit of "social objectives." Three World Trade Organization (WTO) Agreements, the Sanitary and Phyto-Sanitary Agreement (SPS), the Agreement about Technical Barriers to Trade (the TBT Agreement), and the General Agreement on Tariffs and Trade (GATT) shape powers of EU supranational institutions to regulate GMO agricultural products. Social objectives, pursued through measures adopted by signatory states in order to protect human, animal, or plant life or health, spelt out in Art. XX (b) of the GATT, are defined narrowly as general *exceptions* to free trade. Moreover, in the *EC-Biotech* case,[6] the WTO panel established that the SPS Agreement requires the EU to justify limitations of free trade in transgenic agricultural products on scientific grounds (Scott, 2007, 137–138).

Second, also the case law of the ECJ foregrounds economic objectives of the regulatory regime. In accordance with current EU primary and secondary law the court has construed narrowly EU Member States' powers to limit through unilateral national measures the circulation of transgenic agricultural products once they have been granted EU authorization. For instance, a Polish national law that closed off the Polish market to GM seeds because of – inter alia – religious objections to GM agriculture, was held by the ECJ to be in breach of Arts. 22 and 23 of Directive 2001/18/EC and Articles 4 (4) and 16 of Directive 2002/53/EC (the Directive on the common catalogue of agricultural plants species) (Commission v Poland, Case 165/08). Austria failed to show, as required by Art. 95 (5) ECT (now Art. 114 TFEU), that there were scientific grounds specific to the particular region of Upper Austria in order to justify measures restricting the circulation of transgenic agricultural products for the purposes of environmental protection. When one examines more closely, however, what counts as an economic and a social issue in this regulatory regime, a clear-cut distinction between "economy" and "society" as different fields of social action seems to vanish. Some Member States and farmers, for instance, have argued that when deciding whether to grant an authorization *socioeconomic* considerations should be taken into account. Art. 7 (2) of the Food and Feed Regulation 1829/2003/EC enables the Commission to consider "other legitimate factors" in its GM authorization decisions, socioeconomic considerations being potentially one type of such "other legitimate factors." Moreover, the proposed reform of Directive 2001/18/EC will enable Member States to restrict the cultivation of GM crops on their territory on the grounds of socioeconomic impacts of transgenic agricultural products. This blurring of boundaries between "social" and "economic" aspects of trade in transgenic agricultural products can best be captured by understanding "society" and "economy" as discursively performed.

Why Discourse?

Knowledge about economic and social impacts of transgenic agricultural products is historically specific, socially constructed, contested, and in flux, and therefore has a discursive quality. While the Commission is seeking to develop separate indicators of the social and economic impacts of GMOs, and while it refers to distinct "economic" and "society" actors (European Commission, 2011, p. 6), there are few fixed points that tie down the meaning of socioeconomic impacts. The legally nonbinding Recital (62) of Directive 2001/18/EC defines socioeconomic implications in very general terms as the "socioeconomic advantages and disadvantages" of each category of GMO placed on the market "which takes due account of the interests of farmers and consumers." Moreover, participants in debates about the socioeconomic impacts of transgenic agricultural products explicitly refer to the ideational, rather than just factual nature of their statements. Views about socioeconomic impacts are not based on data derived from actual experience with cultivating GM crops, but on constructions of what those impacts may be, sometimes based on the experience of third countries with GM cultivation (European Commission, 2011, p. 3). 74% of the Member States who participated in the Commission's questionnaire that solicited views about the socioeconomic impact of GMOs currently do not cultivate GMO crops. Most commercial cultivation of GM crops is focused on animal feed, such as GM soy and occurs mainly in Spain (European Commission, 2011, p. 21). Moreover knowledge claims about the economic or social impacts of transgenic agricultural products are instable, also because scientific peer-reviewed studies about their environmental and public health consequences are inconclusive or have not yet been conducted (e.g., studies on the effect of Bacillus Thuringis (BT) maize (European Commission, 2011, p. 38; Committee of the Environment, Public Health and Food Safety, 2011a, pp. 16–17). In addition, the economic discourse is patchy (Committee on the Environment, Public Health and Food Safety,

2011b, p. 23). Few studies have looked at the macro-economic consequences of GMO cultivation, and those that have, have reported varying results. Most studies are concerned with economic impacts at the individual farm level (European Commission, 2011, pp. 5, 20).

While being open-textured and patchy, the knowledge claims about economic and social impacts of GMOs do amount to discourses because they cluster around key themes, or "nodal points," in Laclau's and Mouffe's terminology, which form part of the regularities of these discourses. The next section further develops this point by mapping key elements of the discourses of "economy" and "society" in the context of EU GMO authorizations.

Key Elements of the Discourses of "Economy" and "Society" in the Context of EU GMO Authorizations

The discourses of "economy" and "society" are constructed not just in relation to each other, but also in distinction from the scientific risk assessment, referred to above as central to EU GMO authorizations (see also Lange, 2012).[7] The discourse of "economy," however, is significant in debates about GMO authorizations (Report of the Belgian Workshop, 2010, p. 5).[8] In its strongest version it suggests that socioeconomic impacts of GMO authorizations should not be considered by public regulators within EU GMO legal authorizations. Such impacts should only matter indirectly, to the extent that through the play of market forces they affect whether market actors supply and buy transgenic agricultural products in relevant food and feed markets (European Commission, 2011, p. 53). The discourse of economy is concerned with the costs of and financial gains for various actors involved in transgenic agricultural production. Costs to private economic actors, such as conventional, organic, and GM farmers, feed producers and those storing, handling, and transporting agricultural products are assessed. Also costs to the public administration are considered. These can be caused by additional testing and assessment procedures for GM agricultural products, including the labeling of GM products. Extra costs for the public administration can also arise from monitoring GM field trials and from extra controls for conventional seeds, in order to avoid contamination of non-GM agricultural products with GM material. It is suggested that such increased costs may be of particular significance to small- and medium-sized enterprises, or even prohibit their investment in biotechnology, given also uncertainty in the outcome of authorization procedures (European Commission, 2011, pp. 61, 63). On a macro-economic level, the economic discourse addresses how the competitiveness of different EU Member States is affected by costs imposed by GM agriculture. For instance, higher prices for non-GM feed may disadvantage livestock producers from those EU countries that are opposed to GM agriculture in international competition.

In contrast to a discourse of "economy," a discourse of "society" constructs agricultural production as anchored into specific social relationships. It emphasizes that in some EU Member States small-hold farming is tied into family relationships and close cooperative links between different farmers in a local community, who, for instance, share expensive farming machinery (European Commission, 2011, pp. 46, 59). The discourse of society thematizes the potential threat of GM agriculture, not just to conventional and organic agriculture, but also to these social relationships underpinning farming. Small-hold farming is perceived to be particularly unsuitable to accommodate both GM and non-GM agriculture due to the significant risk of cross-pollination. Moreover, a discourse of society turns into a topic the ethical, religious and philosophical consequences of GM agriculture, through its attempt to push the boundaries of human mastery over the natural world. Poland, for instance, has grounded its objections[9] to GM agriculture in ethical principles, specifically:[10]

> A Christian and Humanist conception of progress and development which urges respect for creation and a quest for harmony between Man and Nature; and, lastly, Christian and Humanist social principles, the reduction of living organisms to the level of products for purely commercial ends being likely, inter alia, to undermine the foundations of society. (Case 165/08, para. 31)

The discourse of "society" thus turns into a legitimate topic the impact of GM agriculture on local communities, in particular their cultural identity (European Commission, 2011, p. 83).

Finally, the discourse of "society" develops a specific language for thinking about the consequences of GM agriculture that goes beyond cost considerations. It raises the question whether GM agriculture detracts from national food security and whether it can contribute to the reduction of food shortages in the developing world also in order to meet Millennium Development goals (European Commission, 2011, p. 42). It resists the language of costs in order to capture the potentially negative environmental impacts of GM agriculture, such as the risks GMO agriculture poses to biodiversity in case herbicide resistant, dominant weeds develop and in case GM mono-cultures are planted. Hungary, for instance, explicitly suggests that potential losses to biodiversity cannot be expressed in economic terms

(European Commission, 2011, p. 51). While key statements around which a discourse of "economy" and "society" cluster can be identified, some of the main knowledge claims of these discourses are contested and thus render them open.

Contested Knowledge Claims Open up a Discourse of "Economy"

The potential hegemony of a discourse of "economy" is undermined due to the instability of its own internal knowledge claims, and this instability starts to open this discourse up, also to a discourse of society. For instance, the discourse of economy addresses the question of "who economically benefits to what extent from GM agriculture." Finding answers to this question is also complicated by the fact that there is no insurance currently available for the risk of environmental and public health damage caused by GM transgenic agricultural products. Moreover, very different claims about who benefits from GM agriculture have been advanced. While some consider farmers to benefit due to an increase in yields, because GM crops are considered to have greater pest resistance, others suggest that farmers will only gain minimally, also due to the development of resistance among pests to insecticides expressed by GM plants (European Commission, 2011, p. 26). The economic discourse is also open because there is no systematic consideration of various economic benefits and losses in order to assess the overall economic impact of the cultivation of transgenic agricultural crops. For instance, there are claims that GM seeds are more expensive than non-GM seeds, but this is not quantified (European Commission, 2011, p. 70). There is also no determination of the level of cost at which GM seed would reduce farmers' profit margins, and could no longer be passed on to consumers. Moreover, higher costs of GM seeds, arising from the fact that these seeds are patented and thus cannot be used as saved farm seed in successive years of cultivation, are not off-set against potential economic gains, due to potentially less need for insecticides and less intensive tillage being required for weed clearing when herbicide resistant GM crops are grown (European Commission, 2011, p. 25).

But these discourses are not static, they are in flux. Those Member States with the greatest interest in transgenic agriculture seek to stabilize and reinforce a discourse of economy also by closing it. For instance, Spain has suggested that under high pest pressure, the GM maize variety MON810 can increase yield by 11%, and that BT-cotton would save 15,8 l/ha of insecticide and increase yield by 12% in comparison to conventional cotton production in Spain under 1998 conditions (European Commission, 2011, p. 39). To summarize, contested knowledge claims render the discourse of economy open. This also facilitates the production of a link between "economic" and "social" considerations, for instance through a national political economy approach to socioeconomic impacts of GMOs.

Linking Economy and Society Through a National Political Economy Approach

The discourse of economy tends to rely on abstract, universal economic categories, such as the market in order to address what costs and benefits GM agriculture generates. A national political economy approach anchors market activity into specific national political interests and conditions. Here economic interests of an EU Member State are defined with reference to specific patterns of agricultural production that have developed due to a particular social organization of agricultural work, such as family or large industrial-scale farming, and specific, local environmental factors, such as climate and soil conditions, as well as pest pressures[11] (European Commission, 2011, p. 44). For instance, some EU Member States, including Austria, Hungary, and Greece, ground their objection to GM agriculture in the central role that small-scale farming plays in maintaining national agricultural production and food security, as well as the significant revenue that is generated for these countries through exports of conventional and organic agricultural products (European Commission, 2011, p. 53). In future this national political economy approach is set to gain further salience when the draft Regulation (European Commission, 2011, p. 375) is adopted which will revert back legal powers to EU Member States to restrict the cultivation of GM crops which have received EU wide authorization on their territory on "socioeconomic" grounds, but not on the basis of disagreement with the EU wide scientific risk assessment. To summarize, while the EU internal market in transgenic agricultural products could be considered as a key example of "disembedded economic relationships," the actual discourses that are generated during the operation of this regime show that for key actors "economy" and "society" become opened up to each other and linked. This section has therefore argued that while Polanyi's clear demarcation of "economy" and "society" that underpins his embeddedness metaphor has analytical and rhetorical appeal on a macro-sociological level, it may have limited analytical purchase for understanding the operation of specific regulatory regimes on a small-scale level.

The analysis in this article has drawn on economic sociology literature on interactions between "economy" and "society," in order to tease out the implications of this literature for understanding regulation. It has also drawn on an inductive small-scale analysis of the discourses of "economy" and "society" that are actually invoked in EU public policy documents about the socioeconomic impacts of transgenic agricultural products. The detail of the discourses of "economy" and "society" discussed here are specific to EU regulation of transgenic agricultural products. But the wider themes in these discourses, such as the competitiveness of national economies and individual companies, as well as citizens' moral concerns, also in the light of scientific uncertainty about the environmental and public health risks posed, are likely to be relevant also in other regimes for transnational risk regulation. Whether and how "social" and "economic" impacts of products should be considered is also an issue in administrative authorizations for pharmaceuticals, nano-technological products, deep water oil exploration, and shale oil mining.

But discourse analysis of transnational risk regulation regimes also comes with its own challenges. First, what criteria should govern the selection of sites for the production of discourse, of which there are many in the case of transnational risk regulation? For instance, in the case of GMO regulation discourses produced by the applicant biotech companies themselves also matter, as well as the discourses of "economy" and "society" produced by academic writing in the field (Diez, 1999, p. 604). Second, the very notion of an overarching "discourse" may have to be qualified, in light of the fact that we often observe the coexistence of globalized discourses of "economy" and "society" with nationally or regionally specific discourses of "economy" and "society" produced by national or regional language communities.[12] Do national or regional discourses of "economy" and "society" limit the effects of power of seemingly transnational discourses of "economy" and "society"? Moreover, from a Foucauldian perspective discourses are produced by particular rules (Howarth, 2000, p. 53). If these rules are specific to language communities, not just the content, but also the normative practices that give rise to discourses may be subject to cultural variation.

CONCLUSION

This article has suggested that Polanyi's ideas about regulation imply a conception of socialized legal regulation that needs to be further fleshed out, also through reference to contemporary scholarship on responsive law and regulation. More centrally the article suggested that the linguistic turn in social theory and in particular attention to how language performs the social world can help to address a key question that Polanyi's work raises for contemporary regulation researchers: Is it really possible to distinguish in the context of a specific regulatory regime between an "economic" and a "social" sphere in order to understand how law contributes to the embedding of economic in social relationships? Discourse theory enables to analyze how "economy" and "society" become discursively performed and opened up to each other. This captures what seem in practice often blurred boundaries around "economy" and "society'. Last but not least, Polanyi's work prompts not only interesting analytical, but also normative reflection about regulation. He considered regulation as central to ensuring citizens' freedom, in contrast to popular, contemporary images of regulation as "red tape" and restriction of the entrepreneurial spirit. Contrary to Adam Smith and Ricardo, he started from the assumption of the "primacy of society" and thus was intrigued by the question how social actors can be free in spite of the dense social relationships that make up society. He considered freedom to flow from the discharge of individuals' moral obligations toward each other, and this, in turn, he thought would be facilitated by regulation (Polanyi-Levitt, 1990, p. 119). The challenge for contemporary regulation researchers then is to develop detailed accounts that can help to flesh out a Polanyian vision of socialized regulation.

NOTES

1. During mercantilism, the commodification of labor had been limited, for instance through the 1662 Act of Settlement, but rural labor markets existed before restrictions on the movement of labor were abolished at the end of the 18th century (Dale, 2010a, pp. 80–81, 85). Similarly, markets in money and credit started to develop during mercantilism. Trade in land was still fairly restricted because most land was still owned by the Monarch, church, and aristocracy (Dale, 2010a, p. 51).

2. Given limitations of space this chapter focuses on addressing the first and second challenges raided by Polanyi's work.

3. The sources for this examination are the EU legal framework itself, academic commentary on it, and key European Commission policy documents: European Commission (2011), Report of the Belgian Workshop (2010), Committee on the Environment, Public Health and Food Safety, Draft Report (2011a), and Committee on the Environment, Public Health and Food Safety, Report (2011b).

4. Art. 7 (1) of Regulation 1829/2003/EC applies as *lex specialis* to GMO authorizations. In addition Art. 3 (12) of Regulation 178/2002/EC (the General

Food Law Regulation) specifies that risk management involves a consideration not just of the risk assessment but also of "other legitimate factors," without providing a definition of such factors. Member States have invoked traditional methods of food production and maintaining diversity of food products in the EU internal market as "other legitimate factors" when seeking to justify national measures in food law cases before the ECJ (Szajkowska, 2011, p. 536).

5. See citizens' comments as part of GMO authorization dossiers listed on the GMO compass website: http://www.gmo-SECpass.org/eng/home/

6. EC – Biotech (measures affecting the approval and marketing of biotech products, DS 291, 292, 293, 29 Sept. 2006.

7. In practice socioeconomic considerations are currently marginalized in EU GMO authorizations (Lee, 2008, Chapter 2; interview with member of staff from Directorate General for Health and Consumers in the European Commission (DG Sanco)). Most applications for authorization under Regulation 1829/2003/EC are granted by the Commission subsequently to EFSA's positive scientific opinion. Moreover, some Member States have explicitly stated that in national public participation phases scientific comments rather than socioeconomic considerations by citizens are given the most consideration.

8. Upon request of the Council the Commission issued a report to the European Parliament and the Council on socioeconomic implications of GMO cultivation (European Commission, 2011). This extensive report is based on information solicited through a questionnaire issued to Member States. Member States, in turn, obtained input into answering the questionnaire from national ministries, regional authorities, professional federations, companies, nongovernmental organizations, research centers, and individual experts in the field (European Commission, 2011, p. 2). The contributions of these various stakeholders are, in turn, informed by a wide range of sources, such as peer-reviewed studies, opinion polls, field trials, and scenario analysis (European Commission, 2011, p. 2).

9. The ECJ rejected Poland's argument that it could rely on these grounds in order to justify a derogation from the free movement of goods principle under Art. 36 TFEU (old Art. 30 ECT) because it accepted the Commission's argument that the consideration of ethical issues had been sufficiently harmonized at EU level through Directive 2001/18/EC. This preempted powers for Member States to derogate from the provisions of the Directive.

10. The Commission questioned whether Poland's decision was really motivated by these ethical considerations, or whether they were a disguise for a protectionist trade measure, also in light of the fact that Poland had not relied upon these considerations in the pre-litigation phase (Case 165/08, para. 35). This illustrates again difficulties of disentangling "economic" from "social" objections to GMO agriculture.

11. For instance, late blight potato disease is specific to some Member States, such as Ireland, so that GM crops specifically engineered to address this disease are only relevant for some EU Member States (European Commission, 2011, p. 54). Similarly the corn borer only affects some regions in the EU, only for these is BT maize of interest (European Commission, 2011, p. 51).

12. For instance, Diez (1999, p. 602) points out that European integration was discussed in Britain in the 1960s through reference to the "common market," while in Germany the term "Europäische Gemeinschaft" (European Community) was used. Hence in Britain the accent was on economic integration, while German

terminology foregrounded political and social integration. This generated specific effects of power, for example by structuring the UK debate about entry into the then – in legal terminology – European Economic Community – in terms that legitimized supranational governance in the economic realm.

REFERENCES

Ayres, I., & Braithwaite, J. (1992). *Responsive regulation: Transcending the deregulation debate*. Oxford: Oxford University Press.

Baldwin, R., & Black, J. (2007). *Really responsive regulation, law, society and economy*. Working Paper No. 15/2007. Law Department, London School of Economics and Political Science, London. Retrieved from www.lse.ac.uk/collections/law/wps/wps.htm

Black, J., & Baldwin, R. (2010). Really responsive risk-based regulation. *Law and Policy*, *32*(2), 181–213.

Block, F. (2001). Introduction to the great transformation. In K. Polanyi (Ed.), *The great transformation (1944, 2001)*. Richmond, VA: Beacon Press.

Bognár, J. (1990). Opening address. In K. Polanyi-Levitt (Ed.), *The life and work of Karl Polanyi* (pp. 13–17). Montreal: Black Rose Books.

Cardwell, M. (2010). Public participation in the regulation of genetically modified organisms: A matter of substance or form? *Environmental Law Review*, *12*(1), 12–25.

Committee on the Environment, Public Health and Food Safety. (2011a). Draft report on the proposal for a regulation of the European Parliament and of the Council amending Directive 2001/18/EC as regards the possibility for the Member States to restrict or prohibit the cultivation of GMOs in their territory (COM(2010)0375 – C7-0178/2010 – 2010/0208 (COD)), 27.1.2011a, Rapporteur, Corinne Lepage.

Committee on the Environment, Public Health and Food Safety. (2011b). Report on the proposal for a regulation of the European Parliament and of the Council amending Directive 2001/18/EC as regards the possibility for the Member States to restrict or prohibit the cultivation of GMOs in their territory (COM(2010)0375 – C7-0178/2010 – 2010/0208(COD)), 20.4.2011b, Rapporteur, Corinne Lepage.

Dale, G. (2010a). *Karl Polanyi: The limits of the market*. Cambridge: Polity Press.

Dale, G. (2010b). Social democracy, embeddedness and decommodification: On the conceptual innovations and intellectual affiliations of Karl Polanyi. *New Political Economy*, *15*(3), 369–393.

Dale, G. (2011). Lineages of embeddedness: On the antecedents and successors of a polanyian concept. *American Journal of Economics and Sociology*, *70*(2), 306–339.

Dale, G. (2012). Double movements and pendular forces: Polanyian perspectives on the neoliberal age. *Current Sociology*, *60*(3), 3–27.

Diez, T. (1999). Speaking "Europe": The politics of integration discourse. *Journal of European Public Policy*, *6*(4), 598–613.

Ebner, K. (2008). Institutional evolution and the political economy of governance. In K. Ebner & N. Beck (Eds.), *The institutions of the market: Organizations, social systems and governance* (pp. 287–308). Oxford: Oxford University Press.

Etienne, J. (2013). Ambiguity and relational signals in regulator–regulatee relationships. *Regulation & Governance*, *7*, 30–47.

European Commission. (2011). *Accompanying document to the report from the commission to the European Parliament and the council on socio-economic implications of GMO cultivation on the basis of member state contributions, as requested by the conclusions of the environment council of December 2008*. Staff Working Paper, Brussels.

Fairclough, N. (2010). *Critical discourse analysis: The critical study of language* (2nd ed.), Harlow: Longman.

Foucault, M. (1991). Politics and the study of discourse. In G. Burchell & P. Miller (Eds.), *The foucault effect* (pp. 53–72). London: Harvester.

GHK Interim Report. (2009). Evaluation of the EU Legislative Framework in the Field of Cultivation of GMOs under Directive 2001/18/EC and Regulation (EC) 1829/2003, November 2009.

Golder, B., & Fitzpatrick, P. (2009). *Foucault's law*. Abingdon: Routledge.

Haines, F. (2011). *The paradox of regulation*. Cheltenham: Edward Elgar.

Hann, C., & Hart, K. (2011). *Economic anthropology: History, ethnography, critique*. Cambridge: Polity Press.

Hawkins, K. (1984). *Environment and enforcement: The social definition of pollution*. Oxford: Oxford University Press.

Hawkins, K. (2003). *Law as a last resort*. Oxford: Oxford University Press.

Howarth, D. (2000). *Discourse*. Buckingham: Open University Press.

Jessop, B. (2002). The social embeddedness of the economy and its implications for economic governance. In F. Adaman & P. Devine (Eds.), *Economy and society: Money, capitalism and transition* (pp. 192–222). London: Black Rose Books.

Laclau, E., & Mouffe, C. (1985). *Hegemony and socialist strategy: Towards a radical democratic politics* (2nd ed.), London: Verso.

Lange, B. (2012). Getting to yes: Structuring and disciplining arguments for and against transgenic agricultural products in European Union (EU) authorisations. In B. Jessup & K. Rubinstein (Eds.), *Environmental discourses* (pp. 143–169). Cambridge: Cambridge University Press.

Lee, M. (2008). *EU regulation of GMOs: Law, decision-making and new technology*. Cheltenham: Edward Elgar.

Neale, W. (1990). Karl Polanyi and American institutionalism: A strange case of convergence. In K. Polanyi-Levitt (Ed.), *The life and work of Karl Polanyi* (pp. 145–151). Montreal: Black Rose Books.

Nielsen, V., & Parker, C. (2009). Testing responsive regulation in regulatory enforcement. *Regulation and Governance*, *3*, 376–399.

Nonet, P., & Selznick, P. (2001). *Law and society in transition: Toward responsive law*. New Brunswick, NJ: Transaction Publishers.

Phillips, L., & Jørgensen, M. (2002). *Discourse analysis as theory and method*. London: Sage.

Piška, N., (2011). Radical legal theory today, or how to make Foucault and law disappear completely. Review of Foucault's Law (Routledge, 2009) by Golder, B. and Fitzpatrick, P., *Feminist Legal Studies*, *19*(3), 251–263.

Polanyi, K. (1944, 2001). *The great transformation: The political and economic origins of our time*. Boston, BA: Beacon Press.

Polanyi-Levitt, K. (1990). The origins and significance of the great transformation. In K. Polanyi-Levitt (Ed.). *The life and work of Karl Polanyi* (pp. 111–124). Montreal: Black Rose Books.

Reichman, N. (1998). Moving backstage: Uncovering the role of compliance practices in shaping regulatory policy. In R. Baldwin, C. Scott, & C. Hood (Eds.), *A reader on regulation* (pp. 325–346). Oxford: Oxford University Press.

Report of the Belgian Workshop. (2010). Views on the assessment of the socio-economic impact of genetically modified organisms (GMOs) in food, Brussels, 29 March 2010, Federal Public Service, Health, Food Chain Safety and Environment.

Rotstein, A. (1990). The reality of society: Karl Polanyi's philosophical perspective. In K. Polanyi-Levitt (Ed.), *The life and work of Karl Polanyi* (pp. 98–110).

Salsano, A. (1990). The great transformation in the Oeuvre of Karl Polanyi. In K. Polanyi-Levitt (Ed.), *The life and work of Karl Polanyi* (pp. 139–144).

Scott, J. (2007). *The TWO agreement on sanitary and phytosanitary measures: A commentary*. Oxford: Oxford University Press.

Somers, M. (1990). Karl Polanyi's intellectual legacy. In K. Polanyi-Levitt (Ed.), *The life and work of Karl Polanyi* (pp. 152–158). Montreal: Black Rose Books.

Szajkowska, A. (2011). Different actors, different factors–science and other legitimate factors in the EU and National Food Safety Regulation. *European Journal of Risk Regulation*, (4), 523–539.

Torfing, J. (1999). *New theories of discourse: Laclau, Mouffe and Žižek*. Chichester: John Wiley & Sons.

Vincent-Jones, P. (1998). Responsive law and governance in public services provision: A future for the local contracting state. *Modern Law Review*, *61*(3), 362–381.

Waller, W., & Jennings, A. (1991, June). A feminist institutionalist reconsideration of Karl Polanyi. *Journal of Economic Issues*, *XXV*(2), 485–497.

PART II
APPLYING AND DEVELOPING POLANYIAN IDEAS

THEME 1
REGULATING THROUGH EMBEDDING SOVEREIGN DEBT DEFAULT

HOW MARKETS WORK: THE LAWYER'S VERSION☆

W. Mark C. Weidemaier and Mitu Gulati

ABSTRACT

This article combines two sources of data to shed light on the nature of transactional legal work. The first consists of stories about contracts that circulate among elite transactional lawyers. The stories portray lawyers as ineffective market actors who are uninterested in designing superior contracts, who follow rather than lead industry standards, and who depend on governments and other outside actors to spur innovation and correct mistakes. We juxtapose these stories against a dataset of sovereign bond contracts produced by these same lawyers. While the stories suggest that lawyers do not compete or design innovative contracts, their contracts suggest the contrary. The contracts, in fact, are consistent with a market narrative in which lawyers engage in substantial innovation despite constraints inherent in sovereign debt legal work. Why would

☆W. Mark C. Weidemaier and Mitu Gulati are on the faculties of the University of North Carolina Law School and Duke University Law School, respectively. An earlier version of this article was presented at the conference on Socializing Economic Relationships: New Perspectives and Methods for Transnational Risk Regulation, at the Centre for Socio-Legal Studies at the University of Oxford. We thank Bettina Lange, Dania Thomas, and conference participants for comments on the article.

From Economy to Society? Perspectives on Transnational Risk Regulation
Studies in Law, Politics, and Society, Volume 62, 107–133

ISSN: 1059-4337/doi:10.1108/S1059-4337(2013)0000062005

lawyers favor stories that paint them in a negative light and deny them a potent role as market actors? We conclude with some conjectures as to why this might be so.

Keywords: Sovereign debt; international finance; lawyers; contracts

INTRODUCTION

Lawyers are integral players in the world of international finance, and contracts are the primary tools of their trade. We focus on one group of these lawyers, those who structure loans to governments, and we explore their relationship to their primary legal product: sovereign bond contracts. Our inquiry stems from a conference on the relevance of Karl Polanyi's work to the current global financial crisis. As we write, in December 2011, fear of sovereign default in the Eurozone and anger over bailouts given to distressed countries have prompted intense debate over how to avoid future crises. To a degree, this is a debate about contracts. Eurozone politicians, for example, seem to believe that sovereign borrowers and their lenders can avert future crisis by adopting the right contract terms. In particular, they have proposed that all future sovereign bond contracts include terms called Collective Action Clauses (CACs).

It may seem far-fetched to suggest that a contract term can prevent global financial crisis or make future bailouts unnecessary. (It seems so to us.) But this is not the first time CACs have been touted as the solution to such problems. Nor is it new for CACs to be the subject of discussion among participants in the sovereign debt markets. CACs occupy a prominent place in what one might call the modern mythology of sovereign debt. Lawyers, policymakers, and academics tell stories about the origins of these clauses, speculate as to how they have evolved over many decades, and assign CACs near-talismanic power to ward off financial collapse. We begin this article by recounting these stories. We do so not because they are true. Our primary empirical finding is that the stories do *not* match reality. But this does not deprive them of meaning. Stories are not necessarily – and certainly not only – empirical propositions. The stories people tell shed light on how they make sense of their everyday experience. We use stories about the origin and evolution of CACs to shed light on how lawyers view their role in sovereign lending transactions.

In the process, we reveal a tension. Sovereign debt lawyers occupy high-status positions in prestigious law firms, and their transactions occupy the front pages of the financial newspapers. They are quintessential market actors, and one might expect them to situate their stories within a broader market narrative that emphasizes the virtues of competition and implies that elite lawyers distinguish themselves through superior skill and ability to innovate. But in fact, sovereign debt lawyers routinely tell stories that portray them as reluctant competitors who depend on governments or other third parties to spur innovation. The stories imply that lawyers are uninterested in producing superior contracts, reluctant to innovate, eager to portray any changes they do make as following (as opposed to leading) industry standards, and skeptical of the market's ability to recognize or value higher-quality contracts. Many of the stories imply that sovereign debt work consists primarily of photocopying, even when the documents being copied contain mistakes.

If the stories were true, they would describe a case of serious market failure and agency costs. The stories imply that lawyers do not try to design optimal or even second-best terms for their clients; they cannot even be bothered to correct obvious mistakes. If this were so, we would struggle to explain why lawyers do not compete or innovate and why finance ministers continue to spend their government's money on prestigious law firms that provide such little value. The stories, however, do not seem to match how lawyers behave. In the second part of the article, we use a dataset of sovereign bonds to explore actual contracting practices with respect to CACs. While the stories suggest that lawyers do not compete or design innovative contracts, the data on their contracts suggest the contrary. The contracts, in fact, are consistent with a market narrative in which lawyers engage in substantial innovation despite constraints inherent in sovereign debt legal work.

The disjuncture between the stories and the contracts raises a different puzzle: Why would lawyers favor stories that paint them in a negative light and deny them a potent role as market actors? We take up this question in the final section, when we return to the organizing theme of this conference. To a degree, our findings challenge a common understanding of Polanyi's conception of markets: as autonomous spheres "disembedded" from social institutions and relations. The stories told by sovereign debt lawyers very clearly reflect the social and institutional context in which they operate. That context imposes significant and no-doubt unwelcome constraints on lawyers' ability to innovate. We speculate that one function of the stories is to provide a form of cover, creating space in which innovation can occur without disrupting the widely held belief that sovereign bond contracts are standardized.

COLLECTIVE MYTHS ABOUT COLLECTIVE ACTION

Infinite Variety... At Least in Theory: An Introduction to CACs

Sovereign issuers and bondholders face a problem common to lending relationships. If the issuer encounters financial difficulty, all parties might be better off agreeing to reduce or restructure its repayment obligations and thereby hasten its return to financial health. Yet bondholders are many and dispersed, and this results in familiar coordination problems that can block an otherwise beneficial restructuring (Sachs, 1984). Unlike corporate debt, moreover, no sovereign bankruptcy regime exists to impose restructuring terms on a recalcitrant minority of holdout creditors (Bratton, 2004; Skeel, 2003). As a result, issuers who wish to provide for the possibility of a future restructuring must turn to the institution of contract.

At least in theory, an issuer could include a wide range of restructuring-related terms in its bonds. Here, we focus on the subset of terms commonly labeled CACs. Reading the sovereign debt literature, and listening to the pronouncements of public officials, one sometimes gets the sense that CACs have near-magical properties. Over the past two decades they have twice been touted as the solution to global financial crisis. The first time was in the aftermath of the Tequila crisis and Asian financial crisis in the mid to late 1990s. As we have noted, the second time is now, when Eurozone public officials have placed CACs at the center of a proposed mechanism for resolving future sovereign defaults (Flanders, 2011; Oakley, 2011).

CACs are intended to solve coordination problems among holders of sovereign bonds. In the absence of a sovereign bankruptcy mechanism, a financially distressed country that wants to restructure its payment obligations must obtain the assent of its bondholders. But the sheer number and geographic dispersion of bondholders makes it nearly impossible even to locate them all. Moreover, an effective restructuring requires a mechanism by which bondholders can make an orderly *and collective* decision that will bind them all. Otherwise, some bondholders may withhold their assent hoping to extract a side payment from those who favor the plan or to be paid in full if there is an Official Sector (i.e., taxpayer) bailout. And the prospect that such "holdouts" may receive a better deal may deter participation in the restructuring, or even derail it altogether.

In theory, CACs solve these problems by enabling bondholder coordination. Broadly speaking, CACs come in four varieties.

Modification Clauses: Modification clauses provide that every bondholder is bound by a change in contract terms approved by a defined percentage of the group. The clauses also establish procedures for obtaining bondholders' assent to the change, and these procedures can vary significantly. For example, one clause might require that any vote to change the issuer's payment obligations occur at a meeting at which a specified percentage of bondholders will constitute a quorum. A different clause might allow the issuer to solicit bondholders' written assent to the change. These are not trivial differences. Bonds that require a meeting, for example, create a forum in which unhappy creditors can meet and possibly organize against a restructuring proposal (Gelpern & Gulati, 2008).

Modification clauses are recent innovations in sovereign bonds. They began to appear in the 1980s, primarily in bonds governed by English law. A typical clause allowed terms related to the issuer's payment obligations to be modified by a supermajority (usually 75%) vote and nonpayment terms to be modified by a lesser vote. Any vote on a proposed restructuring had to occur at a physical meeting of the bondholders. Significantly, the requirements for conducting a meeting often operated to reduce the vote needed to approve a restructuring. Despite the supermajority requirement, in fact, holders of as little as 18.75% in aggregate amount of the outstanding debt could in theory approve a restructuring.

A different practice prevailed in bonds governed by New York law. These bonds allowed a majority of bondholders to approve a change to nonpayment terms but required bondholders unanimously to approve changes to payment terms. Given the coordination difficulties noted above, this unanimity requirement was essentially unattainable. Beginning in 2003, however, bonds governed by New York law began to incorporate modification clauses (without the requirement of a physical meeting of the holders), and these soon became ubiquitous (Bradley & Gulati, 2011). The story of how New York–law bonds evolved to include modification clauses – which we recount below – occupies a central place in sovereign debt contracts lore.

Creditor Committee Clauses: A financially distressed issuer may wish to negotiate over the terms of a restructuring, but with whom should it negotiate? In the 19th and early 20th centuries, major capital exporting countries established representative committees to negotiate with sovereign borrowers on behalf of dispersed bondholders (Eichengreen & Portes, 1995). Creditor committee clauses seek to revive this practice by contract. A typical clause might allow bondholders to establish a committee empowered to negotiate on their behalf, specify the circumstances under which such a committee may be appointed, identify powers that may be assigned to the committee, and even require the issuer to pay the expenses of any professionals hired to assist the committee (Richards, 2010).

Trustee Clauses: A variety of administrative and ministerial tasks must be performed in connection with the issuance of sovereign bonds. The agent that performs these tasks (often a Fiscal Agent) owes duties to the borrower and not to the bondholders. Some bond contracts, however, provide for a trustee that owes specified duties directly to bondholders. For example, a trustee clause might empower the trustee to institute litigation against the borrower in response to a default. Because the trustee owes duties to the bondholders as a group, and not to any bondholder in particular, the presence of a trustee may offer some protection against bondholders whose self-interested behavior may harm the group (Bradley & Gulati, 2011; Richards, 2010).

Nonacceleration Provisions: Most sovereign bonds require the issuer to make periodic small payments to bondholders. For obvious reasons, bondholders may interpret the failure to make one of these payments as a sign of financial distress. One response to such a signal is for the bondholder to accelerate their loan – i.e., to demand full payment of the principal. Until at least the mid-1990s, sovereign bonds often allowed each bondholder to decide whether to accelerate their loan in response to the issuer's default in making a small payment (Bradley & Gulati, 2011). Individual creditors, however, often are quick to accelerate, in part because they fear other creditors will beat them to it and deplete the issuer's remaining assets. And in the aggregate, these individual decisions to accelerate can have disastrous consequences for the issuer's ability to meet its obligations. As a result, some modern bonds take the decision to accelerate out of the hands of individual bondholders. Instead, these bonds require acceleration to be approved by a specified percentage of bondholders (typically 25%). They also allow a defined percentage of bondholders (often 50%) to reverse the decision to accelerate.

A Mistake, Compounded: The Mythology of CACs

Sovereign bonds issued under New York and English law observed different drafting conventions before 2003. English-law bonds included modification clauses that allowed for modifications with a vote as low as 18.75%, while New York–law bonds required unanimous approval to change payment terms. This difference rapidly disappeared after 2003, when Mexico became the first major issuer of New York–law bonds to include CACs. Other issuers quickly followed suit, and modification clauses became standard in bonds issued under both laws.

Sovereign debt lawyers tell a number of stories about this evolution. These stories have circulated widely and assumed a prominent place in current and past debates about resolving global financial crises.[1] We report the stories because we believe they can shed light on the work that lawyers do, although we are aware that stories do not always match reality (Mather, McEwin, & Maiman, 2001, p. 199). Indeed, one reason we find the stories interesting is that they often *do not* match reality (Weidemaier, Scott, & Gulati, 2013). The stories purport to explain a significant evolution in modern contracting practices. They do so, first, by communicating an origin myth that locates the divergence between New York- and English-law contracts in a mistake made nearly a century ago. The stories also provide an explanation for why this divergence persisted for so long. And, they explain how New York–law bonds finally came to adopt CACs and provide reason to believe that sovereign bonds are now largely standardized.

As we show later, these stories are largely inaccurate. Like other terms in sovereign bonds (Gelpern & Gulati, 2008; Weidemaier, 2009), CACs exhibit a great deal more variance than the stories allow. But this does not deprive the stories of meaning. Storytelling is a common social activity. And although stories are often framed as representing a widely shared experience (Briggs, 1996), they do not simply recount some objective reality (Bauman, 1986). Origin myths, for example, need not be viewed as empirical propositions. In a sense, their truth is unimportant; adherents to such myths view them as self-evident explanations for prevailing cultural or social practices (Engle, 1993; O'Barr & Conley, 1992). For that reason, stories can provide insight into how people make sense of their everyday experience. We use these myths about the origin and evolution of CACs – and their doppelganger, the unanimity requirement – to shed light on how lawyers view their role in sovereign lending transactions.

The first story purports to explain how New York – and English-law bonds adopted different drafting conventions nearly a century ago and adhered to these separate practices until 2003. It begins with a mistake.

How Lawyers Learned to Stop Worrying and Love the CAC

As noted, bonds issued under New York and English law observed different drafting conventions until around 2003. The difference was a matter of common knowledge but engendered little discussion. Bonds issued under the different laws were, well, different. It didn't really matter why.

That began to change after a series of financial crises and defaults beginning with the Mexican Tequila crisis in the mid-1990s and culminating in Argentina's default in 2001 (Roubini & Setser, 2004). The former resulted in a politically unpopular bailout and the latter in a lengthy and contentious restructuring. Neither outcome was desirable, and public officials felt pressured to give assurances that future defaults would be resolved quickly and without taxpayer-funded bailouts. (A similar saga unfolds in the Eurozone as we write this.) Key policy actors, including prominent economists and lawyers, identified CACs as the solution (Buchheit & Gulati, 2002; Eichengreen & Mody, 2000a, 2000b; Quarles, 2010). Much of the relevant debt had been issued under New York law, where the unanimity requirement made restructuring difficult. In theory, the problem could be solved by creating a mechanism to facilitate future restructurings. One possibility was to create a sovereign bankruptcy regime that could impose restructuring terms on bondholders. The other was to convince the New York market to emulate English drafting conventions and to adopt CACs (Eichengreen, 2003).

Many public officials favored CACs as the solution, including policymakers within the US treasury (Gelpern & Gulati, 2006; Quarles, 2010). But there was a problem. Participants in international capital markets tend to have some faith in the market (at least the bankers). And a significant part of the market for sovereign debt seemingly had voted against CACs. For years, countries had issued and investors had happily bought New York–law sovereign bonds whose payment terms could not be amended without unanimous assent. True, no one seemed to know just *why* these bonds required unanimity, but it was not hard to posit a rational explanation: The unanimity requirement functioned as a commitment device. Viewed ex post from the perspective of a distressed sovereign and its creditors, the requirement seems hard to justify. By exacerbating bondholder coordination problems, the requirement can delay a beneficial restructuring that will allow a genuinely distressed sovereign to resume debt service (Eichengreen, 2003). But viewed ex ante, the unanimity requirement arguably makes more sense. By committing to an expensive and cumbersome restructuring process, issuers who adopt the requirement can send a credible signal that default is unlikely. Because lenders cannot completely verify the sovereign's intent and ability to repay at the time they make the loan, they may value that signal and agree to lend on more favorable terms (Weinschelbaum & Wynne, 2005).

Despite these arguments in favor of current practices, public officials continued to view CACs as a substantial improvement over terms requiring unanimity. But how to convince the market to adopt them? Part of the solution was to tell a story designed to show that the unanimity requirement had no rational purpose – that it was, in fact, nothing but a historical mistake that had somehow persisted in modern contracts. In this story, the unanimity requirement emerged from the Trust Indenture Act (TIA) of 1939 (Olivares-Caminal, 2009; Quarles, 2010; Raffer, 2010). Part of a package of Depression-era reform legislation, the TIA forbade the use of CACs in publicly issued corporate debt (Roe, 1987). This unanimity requirement may have made sense in the context of corporate bonds, since corporate entities can always restructure their debt through bankruptcy (Skeel, 2001, pp. 121–122). But without recourse to bankruptcy, sovereign issuers can only restructure their debt with creditor consent. In that context, the unanimity requirement imposes a nearly insuperable barrier to restructuring and, indeed, the TIA does not impose the requirement on sovereign bonds (Buchheit & Gulati, 2002).

According to the story, lawyers drafting sovereign bonds began with corporate bonds as their template. They imported the unanimity requirement from these bonds, either because they mistakenly believed the TIA required them to do so or because they did not bother to read the documents they copied. In most versions, the mistake happened shortly after the TIA's enactment in 1939 (Gray, 2003a; Quarles, 2010).[2] But whenever the mistake occurred, it persisted, as lawyers copied the mistake over and over in new sovereign issuances. The unanimity requirement, though originally a mistake, had become boilerplate in bonds governed by New York law. By contrast, English-law bonds did not incorporate the unanimity requirement. This was because English law did not require unanimity for corporate bonds, and there was a long-standing English practice of including CACs in corporate debt. Thus, whether by design or because English lawyers, too, simply copied a corporate form, English-law sovereign debt allowed a supermajority to amend payment-related terms.

This story does not flatter the lawyers. It begins by positing that the initial adopters of the unanimity requirement were ignorant of the law as it relates to sovereign debt or too lazy to read the corporate forms they used as templates. Nor is the story much kinder to modern lawyers, for it suggests they repeatedly failed to correct the mistake even though CACs would be an improvement for both country borrowers and their lenders. Under the circumstances, one might expect modern lawyers to resist the story and to offer functional explanations, along the lines we outlined above, for the unanimity requirement. The different standards, they might suggest, exist to satisfy different investor preferences. Investors who want some assurance against default buy New York–law bonds, while those who value ease of restructuring buy bonds governed by English law.

The lawyers, however, seem to like the story just fine. In a related study, Gelpern and Gulati (2006) spoke to over 100 bankers and lawyers (mostly lawyers) about the adoption of CACs in the New York market. Almost no one suggested that the unanimity requirement served any rational purpose. Indeed, a number explained that the story about the irrational origins of the unanimity provision helped overcome lawyers' ingrained resistance to changing established contracting practices. In effect, the lawyers welcomed the story as a necessary antidote to their path dependency. The implication is that, although the unanimity requirement served no purpose, lawyers never would have gotten around to removing it if the Official Sector hadn't explained that it was all just a mistake.

Competition? Who Needs Competition?

Once they had been convinced that the unanimity requirement made no sense, sovereign debt lawyers were free to adopt CACs. But what kind of CACs? The story as we have related it thus far suggests an answer: English-style CACs. If all lawyers do is copy existing forms, then they presumably would have copied recent English-law bonds. After all, many of them worked at global law firms with offices in London, where CACs were standard. In these firms, lawyers could have imported English-style CACs into new bonds with the push of a button. If the copying story holds true, the existing model of CACs would have migrated into bonds governed by New York law. For example, just like English-law bonds, bonds governed by New York law would require any vote to amend payment terms to take place at a meeting of bondholders.

Note, again, that this story does not assign much significance to the work that lawyers do or portray lawyers as potent market actors. A market story might describe contracts as products sold by competing law firms that may differ in quality and price. A superior CAC, for example, would somehow manage to ensure a smooth restructuring in cases of genuine financial distress without tempting issuers to default when they can afford to repay their debts. Because it is not obvious what such a CAC would look like, or that the same clause would be right for every issuer, a market story might posit that lawyers will compete to design the best clause and that the market will supply pricing information about their efforts. By 2003, in fact, a number of studies had been conducted examining whether issuers would suffer a pricing penalty by adopting CACs. The best known of these studies, by Barry Eichengreen and Ashoka Mody (2004), suggested that CACs could affect issuers in different ways. They found that CACs lowered borrowing costs for credit-worthy issuers, who were not likely to default if they could avoid doing so, but increased borrowing costs for higher-risk issuers, for whom CACs arguably exacerbated moral hazard problems.[3] In a market-oriented story, one would expect law firms to find data like this relevant to their efforts to design new clauses and advise issuers about what kind of CAC (if any) to adopt.

Once again, however, the lawyers describe their work primarily as copying standard forms, rather than competing to design a superior CAC. Copying stories are rampant in the sovereign debt world, seemingly invoked whenever lawyers encounter unexpected variance in contract terms (Gulati & Scott, 2012; Weidemaier et al., 2013). For example, most participants in the sovereign debt markets believed that Mexico's 2003 issuance was the first to include CACs in bonds governed by New York law. Only it wasn't. Two economists discovered that a number of less prominent issuers had included CACs in their New York–law bonds as early as 1997 (Gugiatti & Richards, 2004). Was this under-the-radar innovation? Not according to a prominent story, which attributed these early CACs to blind copying. The lawyers involved, the story explained, probably began with an English-style form and thus inadvertently imported CACs into bonds governed by New York law (Gugiatti & Richards, 2004).

This is just one example. In other work, Gulati and Scott (2012) and Weidemaier et al. (2013) report many instances in which sovereign debt lawyers attribute variance in bond contracts to blind copying – often of a mistake made by a junior lawyer. The assumption underlying these stories is that bond contracts are supposed to be standardized. Across a range of contexts, sovereign debt lawyers attribute variance to carelessness, not competition.

Stories about the change in New York drafting practices post-2003 are consistent with this general theme. For example, supporters of the switch to CACs in both public and private sectors invested substantial time and energy making the case that issuers could switch to the English model without suffering a pricing penalty (Gelpern & Gulati, 2006; Gray, 2003b). But from the stories sovereign debt lawyers tell, they needn't have bothered. In two separate interview studies, Gelpern and Gulati (2006) and Gulati and Scott (2012) report that sovereign debt lawyers deny that bond prices are sensitive to anything but the most dramatic changes to contract terms and routinely dismiss academic studies purporting to show the contrary. A related story is that investors do not wish to buy anything but standardized CACs. For them, the story goes, the only thing worse than a world in which CACs affected bond prices is a world in which CACs actually "became a source of competition" (Gray, 2004).

We have retold these stories in a somewhat stylized fashion. Put simply, the story of how CACs originated and evolved is a story of a mistake compounded by years of rote copying. Lawyers in New York and London supposedly imported corporate drafting conventions into sovereign bonds, either without bothering to read the forms they copied or because they were ignorant of the different legal regimes applicable to corporate and sovereign borrowers. These different drafting conventions persisted until the Official Sector helped lawyers to understand that the unanimity requirement made no sense for sovereign issuers. None of the stories so much as hint that the market valued these different drafting conventions differently. Nor do the stories suggest that the move away from unanimity in New York–law bonds created any space for innovation or competition. Instead, the stories imply that the move simply freed lawyers to copy a different set of forms – presumably those based on English law.

Fig. 1 depicts what bond contracts would look like if this stylized story were true. It suggests that bonds governed by New York law incorporated the unanimity requirement sometime after the enactment of the TIA in 1939, while English-law bonds incorporated CACs at some earlier date, when lawyers first copied terms from corporate bonds. Fig. 1 also shows the post-2003 convergence, when New York – and English-style drafting conventions merged. In the next section, we demonstrate that this story does not begin to capture actual drafting practices. We also consider some more nuanced, though also inaccurate, stories about sovereign bonds. As we shall see, all posit a degree of standardization – and thus a lack of innovation – that does not map onto the contracts themselves.

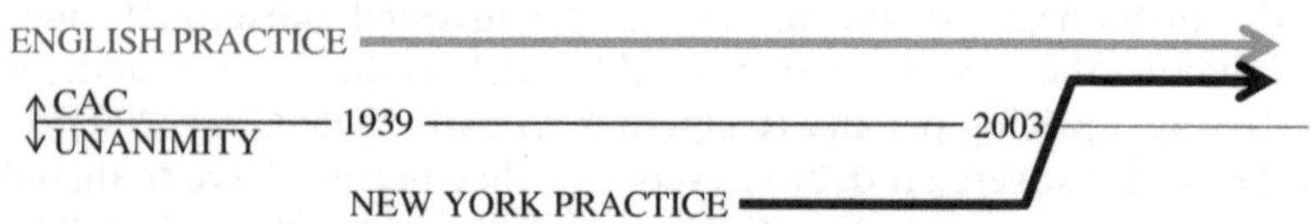

Fig. 1. Stylized Diagram of the Perceived Evolution of CACs: 1900s to 2011.

MESSY REALITY: A STORY OF VARIANCE AND (MAYBE?) INNOVATION

In this section, we contrast the stories against a dataset of sovereign bond contracts. The dataset consists of over 1,300 contracts and disclosure documents for sovereign bonds issued between 1823 and 2010. To our knowledge, this is the most extensive and comprehensive available dataset of sovereign bond contracts. We provide details about the dataset in Weidemaier et al. (2013).

Pre-2003: The Origins of Separate English and New York Drafting Conventions

The stories generate at least two predictions about the origin of the different drafting conventions under New York and English law. One is that majority amendment clauses have appeared in English-law sovereign bonds for over 100 years (Liu, 2002). There were many sovereign issuances in the 19th and early 20th centuries, and the majority amendment clause was available to be copied from English corporate forms by the 1870s (Buchheit & Gulati, 2002). A second prediction is that sovereign bonds governed by New York law began to require unanimous assent to modify payment terms not long after the 1939 enactment of the TIA. The sovereign bond markets were not active in the ensuing decades, but there were issuances, and these could have copied the unanimity requirement from corporate documents.

Our dataset, however, supports neither prediction. The earliest CACs that we have found appeared simultaneously in London and New York in a 1922 Czechoslovakian bond issuance. These clauses allowed holders of a majority of the outstanding bonds to approve "any proposal" by the issuer – language seemingly broad enough to include a restructuring proposal.[4] With that exception, however, none of the bonds issued before 1976 specified the vote required to amend payment terms, or for that matter any other terms. By remaining silent on the subject, these bonds effectively required that bondholders unanimously agree to any change. This was true of both New York – and English-law bonds, meaning that sovereign bonds issued under English law did not conform to corporate drafting conventions that prevailed at the time. Our data suggest that amendment terms first began to appear in the mid-1970s but gained acceptance only slowly.

A relatively sudden shift begins in the mid-1980s. Up to that point, few bonds had addressed whether and how bondholders could amend bond terms. Beginning around 1985, a significant portion of the bonds began explicitly to address this subject and did so in a manner that was largely, but not completely, consistent with corporate drafting practices. Thus, most English-law bonds adopted terms that allowed a supermajority of bondholders to amend payment terms at a meeting. And most New York–law bonds adopted terms that allowed a majority of bondholders to amend some terms but explicitly required unanimous assent to modify payment-related terms.

The pre-2003 difference between New York and English drafting conventions is thus of recent vintage. The unanimity requirement in New York, moreover, did not result from lawyers blindly copying corporate bonds in the wake of the 1939 enactment of the TIA. In our sample, the first New York–law bond to adopt an explicit unanimity requirement was issued in 1981, over 40 years after the passage of the TIA. Nor do English-law bonds reveal a long-standing practice of copying from corporate bonds. English-law sovereign and corporate bonds observed different drafting conventions until the mid-1980s.

Our data do not explain why these different drafting conventions emerged or why sovereign bonds began to adopt explicit modification provisions in the 1980s. A summary of the history of these markets may help provide some context for this shift. Although sovereign bond markets were robust throughout the 19th and early 20th centuries, a wave of Depression-era defaults dramatically reduced this form of sovereign lending. Sovereigns continued to issue bonds after World War II, but for several decades sovereign lending was dominated by multilateral lenders such as the World Bank or by commercial banks. The bond markets did not begin to revive in earnest until the late-1980s (Gelpern & Gulati, 2008), which is around the time the different New York and English drafting conventions emerged. Thus, our data is consistent with a story of copying spurred by the revival of the sovereign bond markets. Perhaps lawyers at the time, suddenly pressed to do a large volume of sovereign bond transactions, borrowed some terms from corporate bonds issued under the relevant legal regime (Ahdieh, 2004; Buchheit & Gulati, 2002; Eichengreen, 2003). But even if this story is true, it hardly follows that lawyers blindly or unthinkingly copied corporate bond documents.

To the contrary, there are at least three other (we think, plausible) explanations why different conventions might have emerged in London and New York. One possibility is that investors already were familiar with the different drafting conventions for New York – and English-law corporate bonds, and lawyers did not want to adopt unfamiliar practices for their increasing volume of sovereign issuances.

A second possibility is that some investors preferred bonds that included terms that made restructuring more difficult. Financial institutions within the United States, for example, arguably had been more seriously affected by a wave of sovereign defaults that immediately preceded the adoption of amendment terms in the 1980s. These institutions may have been averse to the risk of default and may have preferred sovereign bonds that were relatively hard to restructure. Perhaps bonds issued under New York law attempted to satisfy this preference by requiring unanimous assent to any proposed restructuring. In addition, there is some reason to believe that institutional investors dominated the New York market for sovereign bonds, whereas dispersed retail investors played a larger role in European markets. Because large institutional investors can more easily coordinate their response to a sovereign default than can a group of dispersed and small retail investors, there may have been less need for majority amendment terms in the New York market.

A third possibility stems from differences between the two legal regimes. By the early 1980s, in the midst of the Latin American debt crisis, lawyers would have known that holdout creditors could derail a sovereign restructuring. Syndicated loans dominated sovereign lending in the 1970s, and they typically required syndicate members unanimously to approve any modification to payment terms (Buchheit, 1991). By this time, US corporate lawyers also had developed a technique to bypass the TIA's unanimity requirement: the exit exchange. This technique capitalized on the fact that US corporate bonds allowed a majority of bondholders to modify some *non*payment terms. In an exit exchange, a majority of bondholders could restructure the loan by exchanging old bonds for new ones, in the process voting to modify key nonpayment terms in the old bonds. Holdouts were not bound by the restructuring, but they would be left with old bonds that had been modified in ways that made them less attractive, and this threat encouraged participation in the restructuring. By the late 1980s, important US courts had approved of this arguably coercive technique (Coffee & Klein, 1991). We know of no similar development under English law.

In the sovereign context, these developments imply that the different standards that existed in New York and London until 2003 arose by design rather than accident. Lawyers who drafted New York–law bonds could adopt the unanimity requirement for payment-related terms while still leaving open the possibility of a restructuring through an exit exchange. By contrast, lawyers who drafted English-law bonds had no reason to believe the exit exchange technique would work. Because the unanimity requirement might pose an impossibly high barrier to restructuring, they may have chosen to allow a supermajority of bondholders to modify payment terms.

The point is that it is entirely possible that the different drafting conventions emerged in response to market demand and reflect different functional approaches to sovereign lending. We raise this as possibility, not fact, since the data do not rule out the blind copying story. It is striking, however, that lawyers choose to describe their work in terms that make lawyers seem ineffective or outright incompetent when there are equally plausible, and more flattering, characterizations available. Simply put, if the lawyers had explained that the different drafting conventions existed for a *reason*, we would have been inclined to agree, and nothing in our data would suggest otherwise. Yet time after time, lawyers explain sovereign bond contracts as the product of a rote and essentially unthinking copying process.[5]

So what caused the shift in 2003, when sovereign bonds governed by New York law finally moved away from the TIA model? This is a complex question explored in detail in Gelpern and Gulati (2006). For present purposes, what matters is that the stories often attribute the switch to the Official Sector's successful effort to disabuse issuers and their lawyers of the errant but long-standing belief that the TIA applied to sovereign bonds. We cannot disprove that sovereign issuers and their advisors held this belief, but we think it exceedingly unlikely. For one thing, the statute explicitly exempts from its scope "any note, bond, debenture, or evidence of indebtedness issued or guaranteed by a foreign government" (15 U.S.C. 77ddd(a)(6)). It does not take a $1,000-an-hour lawyer to understand what this means. For another, while lawyers may attribute *to others* the mistaken belief that the TIA applied to sovereign bonds, we have yet to meet the lawyer who professes to have held this belief himself.

Variance (and Innovation?) after 2003

Stories of copying extend into the post-2003 era. The simplest story is that, when New York–law bonds began to adopt CACs, they simply borrowed the English model. If this version of the story were true, then the amendment provisions in New York – and English-law bonds would look alike after 2003. Other versions of the story allow for some continuing differences. For example, bonds governed by New York law sometimes are described as conforming to a model promulgated by the G-10 Working Group on Contractual Clauses, an eminent group of lawyers who drafted model clauses at the behest of governments comprising the Group of Ten (Galvis & Saad, 2004, 2005).[6] Likewise, bonds governed by English law sometimes are described as following a model clause promulgated by the International Capital Market Association (ICMA), an industry trade group (Yianni & Malek, 2010).[7] But even these more nuanced stories tend to assume a high degree of standardization within the New York and English markets.

Our point is not that the lawyers deny the existence of variation in sovereign bonds; they do not (Koch, 2004; Richards, 2010). Rather, it is that the lawyers emphasize standardization and, when they do acknowledge variation, almost never take credit for it. For example, in two separate studies, Gelpern and Gulati (2006) and Gulati and Scott (2012) interviewed lawyers they knew to be directly responsible for recent innovations in sovereign bond contracts. Time and again, the lawyers declined to characterize their work as creative or innovative. In the same vein, stories about CACs inevitably explain contract variance by attributing it to a mistake or to some authoritative external source: a statute (the TIA), a government-sanctioned drafting committee (the G-10 standard), or an important industry group (the ICMA standard). The stories do not attribute variance to lawyer ingenuity or competition.

Our data from the post-2003 era, however, reveal variation that is difficult to attribute to mistakes or to thoughtless adoption of model clauses. Beginning with bonds governed by New York law, our data reveal what at first appears to be a sudden shift from one standard to another. Before 2003, the vast majority of New York–law bonds required unanimous approval to change payment-related terms. After Mexico's 2003 adoption, almost all New York–law bonds have included modification clauses permitting changes to payment-related terms with the approval of the holders of at least 75% in aggregate principal amount of outstanding bonds.

Fig. 2 depicts this shift by focusing on one variable: the minimum possible vote needed to amend payment-related terms.[8] To understand the figure, bear in mind that a number of factors potentially influence the required vote. The most obvious is the voting threshold itself – here, 75%. But there are other important factors. For example, assume that a bond contract permits or requires the vote to occur at a meeting. The loan documents will specify the quorum for that meeting (typically 75%) and also may specify a lower quorum (say, 25%) for any postponed meeting. Now

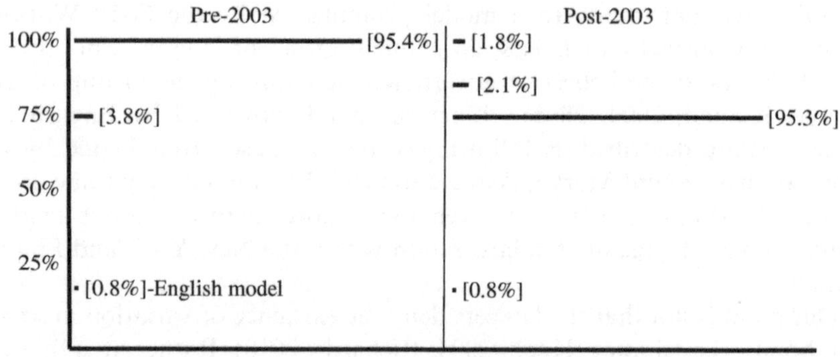

Fig. 2. Minimum Vote Required to Change Payment Terms; New York–Law Bonds, Pre- and Post-2003.

assume the modification clause requires the approval of "holders of 75 percent in aggregate principal amount of outstanding bonds *represented at the meeting*." This is the standard English-law CAC before 2003, and it in theory allows restructuring with the approval of holders of only 18.75% in aggregate principal amount of the outstanding bonds.[9] A different (and purely hypothetical) bond might explicitly require the approval of "holders of 18.75 percent of aggregate principal amount of outstanding bonds," whether approval was solicited at a meeting or in writing. This bond, too, would permit amendment upon a favorable vote by holders of 18.75% of the debt.[10]

For simplicity, Fig. 2 collapses these potential differences and reports only the minimum possible vote sufficient to modify payment terms. Fig. 2 depicts a sudden shift from unanimity to collective action beginning in 2003. The figure makes clear, however, that the shift in New York–law bonds was not modeled on English forms. As noted above, bonds governed by English law typically allowed restructuring with a vote as low as 18.75%. Post-2003 bonds issued under New York law, by contrast, typically do not contemplate a meeting and require the approval of holders of at least 75% in aggregate principal amount of the outstanding debt.

At first glance, Fig. 2 seems consistent with a story of blind copying in two respects. First, the fact that the vast majority of issuances adopt the same voting threshold is consistent with a story in which later issuers simply adopt forms used by earlier ones. Second, the 75% voting threshold matches that recommended by the G-10 working group in its model clause.

After noting concerns that the English model made restructuring too easy and thus too tempting for sovereign borrowers, the working group adopted 75% as a "reasonable threshold" (Group of Ten, 2002).

There is, however, additional variance in the New York–law bonds that undermines these copying stories. The G-10 working group, for example, recommended that sovereign bonds appoint a trustee or other permanent representative of bondholder interests. But only a small minority (10.8%) of post-2003 issuances adopts the trust structure, and only two issuers of New York–law bonds explicitly provide for the appointment of a committee to represent bondholders, even on a temporary and limited basis. The G-10 working group, moreover, recommended that all bonds issued under New York law contain provisions requiring a 25% vote to accelerate the loan after a default. Despite this recommendation, there remains significant variance in New York. Nineteen issuers have continued to allow individual bondholders to accelerate their loans, and even those issuers who have limited the right to accelerate often depart from the G-10's recommended 25% threshold.[11]

But the variance in bonds governed by New York law is trivial compared with the post-2003 variance under English law. In fact, it is as if the switch from unanimity to majority amendment terms in New York created a space in which issuers of English-law bonds could experiment. To put this in context, experimentation is not exactly the norm with boilerplate sovereign bond contracts. Fig. 3 depicts a rather dramatic change in English-law bonds, again focusing on the minimum possible vote to change payment terms. Recall that, before 2003, holders of as little as 18.75% of

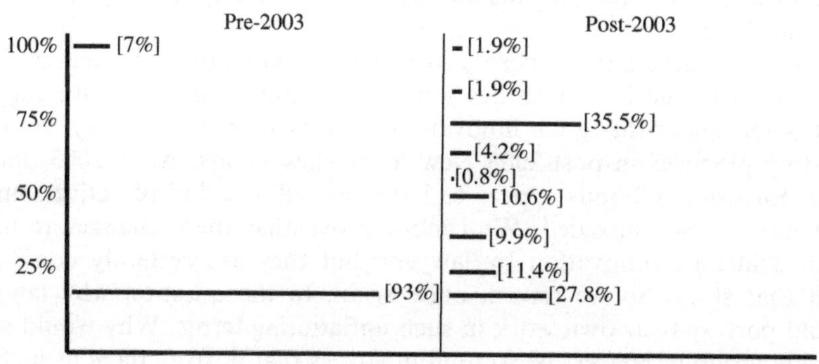

Fig. 3. Minimum Vote Required to Change Payment Terms; English-Law Bonds, Pre- and Post-2003.

the aggregate principal amount of outstanding bonds could vote to modify payment terms. Ninety-three percent of pre-2003 English-law issuances conformed to this standard. After 2003, English-law bonds have adopted a dizzying array of approaches. Nearly 30% adhere to the former English standard. Approximately one-third have adopted the New York model and now require a vote of at least 75% to amend payment terms. The rest adopt a range of voting thresholds that do not match any bonds previously issued under New York or English law and that do not conform to either the G-10 or ICMA models.

This variance does not square with any version of the copying story. And there is additional variance, not fully captured by Fig. 3, across a range of collective action terms. A minority of post-2003 issuances, for example, have selectively adopted some aspects of the ICMA model clause, such as the term permitting bondholders to appoint a committee to represent them in negotiations with the issuer (5.9% versus 0% pre-2003). A much larger percentage have adopted terms preventing individual bondholders from accelerating their loans – another ICMA recommendation (68% versus 48% pre-2003). In addition, some English-law issuances (14.6%) have introduced another ICMA recommendation: a new term requiring unanimous approval to change a select few terms unrelated to the issuer's payment obligations, such as choice of law clauses. In each of these cases, the issuer appears to have selectively adopted parts of the ICMA model clause, sometimes pairing these borrowed terms with completely new provisions. One issuer, for example, adopted two of the ICMA recommendations but permitted amendment to payment terms upon a vote of only 37.5% of the aggregate principal amount of outstanding bonds – an apparently novel voting threshold.

Thus, the picture that emerges from actual contracting practices is more complex than the lawyer stories imply. At a minimum, our data suggest that some under-the-radar innovation persists despite relatively uniform drafting practices in post-2003 New York–law bonds. After 2003, moreover, English-law bonds appear to have entered a period of active foment that has not yet subsided. We cannot prove that these changes resulted from deliberate innovation by lawyers, but they are certainly consistent with that story. So we return, once again, to the question why lawyers would portray their own work in such unflattering terms. Why would such an elite group of lawyers be so fond of stories that portray them as ineffective and impotent market actors, when the data is consistent with a much more flattering story?

STORIES AS A WINDOW INTO LEGAL PRACTICE

Sovereign debt lawyers have been talking about CACs for at least a decade. In doing so, they also have been talking about themselves – communicating information about their work and their main claim to expertise: designing sophisticated contracts for complex transactions. Why would they speak in such negative terms? We do not believe there is a straightforward answer to this question, but we offer some tentative suggestions.

They Don't Think; They Just Do

In at least one respect, it is not surprising that lawyers tell inaccurate stories about contracts. As some of our colleagues have pointed out, some CEOs might deny that their companies raise or lower prices in response to changes in supply and demand. Instead, they might claim that their prices are driven by other concerns, such as the desire to produce the best quality product. (Henry Ford famously claimed he only wanted to provide the public with affordable cars, even while producing spectacular profits.) To take another example, pool players employ the laws of physics quite nicely, even if they cannot describe them. So perhaps we should not expect sovereign debt lawyers to wrap their own stories in some broader market narrative – explaining, say, that bond terms evolve in response to market demand for more or less protection against restructuring. After all, they are busy and may not have time to formulate cogent explanations for their work. Perhaps they just do the work.

We are inclined to agree with this sentiment, but we do not think it fully responds to the questions raised by the stories. It may be no surprise that lawyers do not know the origin of boilerplate terms or the reasons why those terms have evolved over time. After all, the same boilerplate form may persist for generations of lawyers, gathering contract terms like "barnacles" along the way (Wood, 2009). It is more surprising, however, that lawyers *care* about origins enough to devise stories to explain the provenance of contract terms (Weidemaier et al., 2013). And it is more surprising still that such an elite group of lawyers has devised such an unflattering set of stories.

The CEOs posited by our economist colleagues describe their actions in self-congratulatory terms – as motivated by concern for the customer, desire to produce the best product, etc. But our lawyers tell stories that make them look bad. They describe sovereign debt lawyers as largely uninterested in the quality of their contracts and as engaged primarily in rote copying. True, the stories tend to blame *other* lawyers for the most egregious errors, such as mistakenly believing the TIA applies to sovereign bonds. But the stories implicate all lawyers in the mindless copying that supposedly characterizes sovereign debt work. Because our contracts data suggest that something other than mindless copying is going on, we think the larger puzzle is why these elite lawyers do not seem to embrace the philosophy of the market in which they plainly operate.

Back to Polanyi

A better explanation might attempt to situate these stories in the broader context of sovereign debt legal work. A useful starting point would be to contrast our findings with Polanyi's conception of markets – at least as that conception is often understood. Polanyi has sometimes been read to assert that markets are "disembedded" from social and cultural institutions (Barber, 1995; Lie, 1991). Markets are distinct realms coordinated by market prices alone and populated by individuals whose sole motivation is gain (Polanyi, 1957, p. 68). Because contracts are the primary instrument of market transactions, we might expect lawyers – as producers of these contracts – to behave accordingly. Yet the stories we have recounted are hardly what one might expect to hear from idealized market actors devoted solely to maximizing their own gain.

This understanding of Polanyi has been criticized as failing to recognize that Polanyi did not draw such sharp distinctions between market and non-market societies (Block, 2003; Krippner, 2001). For our purposes, however, it usefully highlights the oddity of an elite set of market actors engaging in such seemingly irrational behavior. Instead of publicizing their innovations to enhance their status and profits, lawyers routinely disclaim credit for innovations and instead portray their services as highly routine and prone to error. If true, the stories would paint a picture of seemingly irrational behavior: sophisticated transactional lawyers copying suboptimal forms rather than designing contracts that would maximize value for their clients.

Of course, our contracts data suggest that lawyers are *not* engaged in blind copying; this is just how their stories portray sovereign debt legal work. And although we remain puzzled by their popularity, we suspect that these stories may serve an important function, one that can be understood in light of the constraints under which lawyers in these markets operate.

We suspect that most participants in the sovereign debt markets assume that bond contracts are standardized, at least in material respects. To an extent, that assumption is self-serving: bond contracts are lengthy, and what investor wants to scrutinize dozens of pages of boilerplate looking for slight changes in wording that might distinguish two bonds?

Sovereign debt lawyers may be accustomed to encouraging this view, even if doing so causes some insult to their professional status. This is because – paradoxically – the assumption of standardization may create space in which lawyers can actually do their work. We have little doubt that sovereign debt lawyers see themselves as elite practitioners whose status derives, at least in part, from their ability to design contracts. Yet sovereign lending transactions are driven by bankers and finance officials who are likely to resist making changes to contract boilerplate. Perhaps by cultivating stories of standardization, lawyers deflect attention from the fact that they do make frequent, albeit modest, changes to contract templates. Likewise, stories that (wrongly) attribute changes to some approved source – such as model clauses promulgated by ICMA or the G-10 drafting committee – suggest that some external authority has vetted the change to assure that market participants will not react unfavorably.

We are speculating, of course. Our aim is to find some rational explanation for why even senior sovereign debt lawyers routinely fail to characterize themselves as potent market actors (Weidemaier et al., 2013). We are skeptical that these lawyers are content to run the copy machine – or that their clients are content to pay $1,000 or more an hour for that service – and we think our contracts data show that a good deal more is going on. Lawyers are constrained, it is true, and we think it fair to say that most innovation in sovereign debt contracts occurs at the margin. But innovation occurs nonetheless. It is at least possible that the stories create some space for this to occur.

CONCLUSION: CACS IN THE EUROZONE

We write this in December 2011, and CACs are back in the news. Senior Eurozone officials have stated that they want all Eurozone sovereigns to adopt identical CACs in future issuances, and multiple drafting committees are busy designing the template for the new clauses (Buchheit & Gulati, 2011). To date, this project has drawn no serious objections from sovereign debt lawyers. In other contexts, the lack of resistance would be unusual.

After all, the politicians are proposing that governments, not lawyers and not markets, should fix contract terms.

In the context of sovereign lending, the lack of resistance is less surprising. Judging by their stories, sovereign debt lawyers do not characterize their own work in market terms. Instead, they emphasize that they mainly copy old forms, and they attribute contract change to the beneficent intervention of outside actors, such as public officials who explain that sovereigns need not observe statutory requirements applicable only to corporate issuers, or working groups that design new model clauses for lawyers to copy instead of their existing forms. Yet these stories are hard to square with the contracts themselves, which appear to reveal a good deal of innovation. It remains to be seen whether a new, government-created "model" will suppress that innovation for long.

NOTES

1. The stories we recount circulated widely in print, but we also rely on extensive interviews with sovereign debt lawyers. Methodological and other detail on these interviews is provided in Gelpern and Gulati (2006). To a lesser extent, we also draw on stories explored in Gulati and Scott (2012) and Weidemaier et al. (2013).

2. The economic historian Barry Eichengreen (2003), however, located the split in the 1990s, when robust sovereign bond markets revived after decades of Depression-induced dormancy.

3. Unpublished versions of this paper were in wide circulation as early as 2000 (see Eichengreen & Mody, 2000a, 2000b).

4. We cannot identify exactly why the bonds included CACs, but the impetus may have come from the Financial Committee of the League of Nations, which was involved in arranging reconstruction loans to some European borrowers.

5. In no instance did any lawyer explicitly acknowledge engaging in blind copying. The stories purport to describe general practices in the industry. At least implicitly, however, the stories implicate all lawyers.

6. The report and model clauses are available at http://www.bis.org/publ/gten08.pdf (Group of Ten, 2002).

7. International Primary Market Association, 2004.

8. The figure only includes bonds that address the subject of modification.

9. This would be the voting threshold at a postponed meeting with a 25% quorum (.75 × .25 = .1875).

10. The previous example, by contrast, would permit amendment with a vote of 18.75%, but only in one limited scenario: a postponed meeting. Other scenarios would require a higher vote.

11. For example, four issuers allow acceleration on a vote of holders of 10% of the aggregate principal amount of outstanding bonds, while two more allow acceleration after a 33% vote.

REFERENCES

Ahdieh, R. (2004). Between mandate and market: Contract transition in the shadow of the international order. *Emory Law Journal*, *53*, 691–762.

Barber, B. (1995). All economies are "embedded": The career of a concept and beyond. *Social Research*, *62*, 387–413.

Bauman, R. (1986). *Story, performance, and event: Contextual studies of oral narrative*. Cambridge: Cambridge University Press.

Block, F. (2003). Karl Polanyi and the writing of 'The great transformation'. *Theory and Society*, *32*, 275–306.

Bradley, M., & Gulati, M. (2011). *Collective action clauses for the Eurozone: An empirical analysis*. Retrieved from http://papers.ssrn.com/sol3/papers.cfm?abstract_id=1948534

Bratton, W. W. (2004). Pari Passu and a distressed sovereign's rational choices. *Emory Law Journal*, *53*, 823–868.

Briggs, C. L. (1996). Introduction. In C. Briggs (Ed.), *Disorderly discourse: Narrative, conflict, and inequality* (pp. 3–40). Oxford: Oxford University Press.

Buchheit, L. C. (1991). Exchanging places. *International Financial Law Review*, *10*, 13–14.

Buchheit, L. C., & Gulati, M. (2002). Sovereign bonds and the collective will. *Emory Law Journal*, *51*, 1317–1364.

Buchheit, L. C., & Gulati, M. (2011). Drafting a model collective action clause for Eurozone sovereign bonds. *Capital Markets Law Journal*, *6*, 317–325.

Coffee, J. C. Jr., & Klein, W. A. (1991). Bondholder coercion: The problem of constrained choice in debt tender offers and recapitalizations. *University of Chicago Law Review*, *58*, 1207–1273.

Eichengreen, B. (2003). Restructuring sovereign debt. *Journal of Economic Perspectives*, *7*, 75–98.

Eichengreen, B., & Mody A. (2000a). *Would collective action clauses raise borrowing costs? An update and additional results*. World Bank Policy Research Paper Working Series, No. 2363.

Eichengreen, B., & Mody A. (2000b). *Would collective action clauses raise borrowing costs?* NBER Working Paper Series, No. 7458.

Eichengreen, B., & Mody, A. (2004). Do collective action clauses raise borrowing costs? *The Economic Journal*, *114*, 247–264.

Eichengreen, B., & Portes, R. (1995). *Crisis? What crisis? Orderly workouts for sovereign debtors*. London: Centre for Economic Policy Research.

Engle, D. M. (1993). Origin myths: Narratives of authority, resistance, disability, and law. *Law & Society Review*, *27*, 785–826.

Flanders, S. (2011). Mrs Merkel's intriguing concession. *BBC News* (*Business*). Retrieved from http://www.bbc.co.uk/news/business-16042730

Galvis, S., & Saad, A. (2004). Collective action clauses: Recent progress and challenges. *Georgetown Journal of International Law*, *35*, 713–729.

Galvis, S., & Saad, A. (2005). Sovereign exchange offers in 2010. *Chicago Journal of International Law*, *6*, 219–229.

Gelpern, A., & Gulati, M. (2006). Public symbol in private contract: A case study. *Washington University Law Review*, *84*, 1627–1715.

Gelpern, A., & Gulati, M. (2008). Innovation after the revolution: Foreign sovereign bond contracts since 2003. *Capital Markets Law Journal*, *4*, 85–103.

Gray, R. B. (2003a). *Collective action clauses: Remarks prepared for delivery at UNCTAD Fourth Inter-Regional Debt Management Conference in Geneva*. Retrieved from http://www.icmagroup.org

Gray, R. B. (2003b). Crisis resolution: A market-based approach. In S. Griffith-Jones, A. Bhattacharya & A. Antoniou (Eds.), *Enhancing private capital flows to developing countries* (pp. 33–38). London: Commonwealth Secretariat.

Gray, R. B. (2004). Collective action clauses: Theory and practice. *Georgetown Journal of International Law*, *35*, 693–711.

Group of Ten. (2002). *Report of the G-10 Working Group on Contractual Clauses*. Retrieved from http://www.bis.org/publ/gten08.pdf

Gugiatti, M., & Richards, A. (2004). The use of collective action clauses in New York law bonds of sovereign borrowers. *Georgetown Journal of International Law*, *35*, 815–835.

Gulati, M., & Scott, R. (2012). *The three and a half minute transaction: Boilerplate and the limits of contract design*. Unpublished manuscript.

International Primary Market Association. (2004). *Standard collective action clauses for the terms and conditions of sovereign notes: English law, fiscal agent structure*.

Koch, E. B. (2004). Collective action clauses: The way forward. *Georgetown Journal of International Law*, *35*, 665–691.

Krippner, G. (2001). The elusive market: Embeddedness and the paradigm of economic sociology. *Theory and Society*, *30*, 775–810.

Lie, J. M. (1991). Embedding Polanyi's market society. *Sociological Perspectives*, *34*, 219–235.

Liu, Y. (2002). *Collective action clauses in international sovereign bonds*. Retrieved from http://www.imf.org/external/np/leg/sem/2002/cdmfl/eng/liu.pdf

Mather, L., McEwin, C., & Maiman, R. (2001). *Divorce lawyers at work: Varieties of professionalism in practice*. Oxford: Oxford University Press.

Oakley, D. (2011). Bond dealers skeptical about Eurozone plans. *Financial Times*. Retrieved from http://www.ft.com/cms/s/0/d1d45e36-5a33-11e0-86d3-00144feab49a.html#axzz

O'Barr, W. M., & Conley, J. M. (1992). *Fortune and folly: The wealth and power of institutional investing*. Homewood, IL: Business One Irwin.

Olivares-Caminal, R. (2009). To rank pari passu or not to rank pari passu: That is the question in sovereign bonds after the latest episode of the Argentine saga. *Law and Business Review of the Americas*, *15*, 745–779.

Polanyi, K. (1957). *The great transformation*. Boston, MA: Beacon Press.

Quarles, R. (2010). Herding cats: Collective action clauses in sovereign debt – The genesis of the project to change market practice in 2001 through 2003. *Law & Contemporary Problems*, *73*, 29–38.

Raffer, K. (2010). *Debt management for development*. Cheltenham: Edward Elgar Publishing.

Richards, M. B. (2010). The Republic of Congo's debt restructuring: Are sovereign creditors getting their voice back? *Law and Contemporary Problems*, *73*, 273–299.

Roe, M. J. (1987). The voting prohibition in bond workouts. *Yale Law Journal*, *97*, 232–279.

Roubini, N., & Setser, B. (2004). *Bailouts or bail-ins? Responding to financial crises in emerging economies*. Washington, DC: Institute for International Economics.

Sachs, J. (1984). Theoretical issues in international borrowing. *Princeton studies in international finance* (p. 54). Princeton, NJ: Princeton University Press.

Skeel, D. A. Jr. (2001). *Debt's dominion: A history of bankruptcy law in America*. Princeton, NJ: Princeton University Press.

Skeel, D. A. Jr. (2003). Can majority voting provisions do it all? *Emory Law Journal, 52*, 417–426.

Weidemaier, M. (2009). Disputing boilerplate. *Temple Law Review, 82*, 1–54.

Weidemaier, M., Scott R. R., & Gulati, M. (2013). Contracts, origin myths, and the hunt for pari passu. *Law and Social Inquiry 78*, 72–105.

Weinschelbaum, F., & Wynne, J. (2005). Renegotiation, collective action clauses and sovereign debt markets. *Journal of International Economics, 67*, 47–72.

Wood, P. R. (2009). *Life after Lehman: Allen & Overy analysis of changes in market practice*. London: Allen & Overy.

Yianni, A., & Malek, L. (2010). Seychelles debt restructuring: Restoring the viability of public finances. *Journal of International Banking Law and Regulation, 25*, 330–336.

SOVEREIGN DEBT RESTRUCTURING IN THE EUROZONE: A POLANYIAN READING OF PRIVATE LAW ENFORCEMENT

Dania Thomas

ABSTRACT

The social protests on the streets of indebted sovereigns in crises across the Eurozone have made debt restructuring an imperative. Further delay in achieving this expeditiously and equitably significantly exacerbates the social costs of crises from which current and future generations will struggle to recover. This article examines the feasibility of the drastic and widespread debt restructuring needed to resolve the problem in the face of existing private law sanctions that protect individual creditor rights. It relies on an analysis of US policy in the transition to a securitized market and of key sovereign debt cases to reveal the historical contingency of private law protections. It concludes by showing that the effectiveness of private law protections have always been constrained by the overriding imperative to achieve debt sustainability with negotiated

From Economy to Society? Perspectives on Transnational Risk Regulation
Studies in Law, Politics, and Society, Volume 62, 135–159

ISSN: 1059-4337/doi:10.1108/S1059-4337(2013)0000062006

and consensual workouts. This can be achieved in the Eurozone with statutory constraints on enforcement action pending the settlement of debt workouts as suggested in a recent proposal.

Keywords: Polanyi; sovereign bond contracts; US debt litigation; Eurozone debt crisis; securitization

Over the past couple of years, protestors on the streets of Athens, Spain, Cyprus, and Portugal have been the face of a social resistance to continuing austerity and recession. The protests have made the sovereigns concerned and the rest of Europe realize that the current, unsustainable levels of debt make debt restructuring an urgent policy issue (Buchheit & Gulati, 2012; IMF, 2013; Gulati, 2012). This urgency is reflected in an evolving consensus among policymakers, debtor sovereigns, practitioners, and the official sector, that due to the absence of expeditious action, the existing debt overhang combined with austerity, will in the short term significantly and irrevocably exacerbate the social costs of the ongoing Eurozone sovereign debt crisis (*ibid.*). This article examines the feasibility of the drastic and widespread debt restructuring needed to resolve the ongoing Eurozone in the face of existing private law sanctions that protect individual creditor rights against defaulting debtors.

It is a matter of historical record that "serial default on external debt remains the norm throughout every region in the world including Asia and Europe" as Carmen Reinhart and Kenneth Rogoff (2009, p. 87) conclude in their quantitative study of sovereign debt default spanning eight centuries. Successful debt restructuring relies on a negotiated agreement between a sovereign and a majority of its creditors. The latter voluntarily limiting their individual rights to enforce a sovereign's outstanding debt obligations. The creditors who prefer to enforce their claims against the debtor for the face value of their debt (holdouts) are in a position to prolong a crisis by delaying a debt restructuring until such time as their claims are satisfied. This conflict between individual creditors asserting their rights and the majority willing to write down their outstanding claims defines post-default negotiations in the informal, market-driven framework that regulates the sovereign debt market. This market is sustained as debt restructuring or debt workouts have similarly become the norm. This raises the question of whether creditor rights to enforce a sovereign's debt obligations in full should be protected at whatever cost? Should the social costs of an ongoing crisis be seen as an imperative that necessitates debt workouts even at a cost to private law enforcement?

The possibility that private law enforcement can give way to the attempts to resolve a ongoing crisis questions the assumption made by scholars like Reinhart and Rogoff who attribute serial sovereign default to what they identify to be "the most fundamental 'imperfection' of international capital markets, *the lack of a supernational legal framework for enforcing debt contracts across borders*" (2009, p. 53, emphasis added). In fact as suggested, timely debt restructuring in the Eurozone on the scale required is possible only if holdout claims are not enforced against debtors pending resolution of crisis. The authors recognize legal institutions matter, contrary to mainstream economic reasoning focused on market mechanisms of restraint, such as the reputational sanctions that operate to exclude "wilfully" defaulting sovereigns from international capital markets (such as Argentina has been since 2001) (Eaton & Gersovitz, 1981). However, by stressing the necessity of private law sanctions, they overlook the inevitability of debt workouts or indeed that sovereign bonds have themselves evolved to account for the political risk of constrains on private law protections to achieve debt sustainability (Choi, Gulati, & Posner, 2012).

In contrast to the view taken by Reinhart and Rogoff, it is argued here that recent developments in sovereign debt offerings reflect the inevitability of debt restructuring. Bond contracts now constructed to offer creditors much more than judicial enforcement on default. A development overlooked by scholars that focus on the absence of enforcement as a flaw of sovereign debt markets rather than an integral aspect of sovereign lending itself. For instance, the widespread adoption of different forms of collective action clauses (CACs) in debt contracts is specifically structured to factor in the risk of sovereign default. CACs offer creditors a legal mechanism to collectively restructure their debt *independent of* contract enforcement through the courts. Similarly, the securities market has responded to the reality of sovereign default with their offering of innovative credit default swaps which were successfully redeemed in the aftermath of the Greek default (Morgenson, 2011).

To explore the issue further, this article examines the extent to which enforcement of creditor claims in full is historically contingent on the wider impact that unsustainable levels of sovereign debt has on society. The question is whether the current social backlash against austerity in countries across the Eurozone reflects a threshold at which debt restructuring has become inevitable at the cost of contract enforcement. Or is it the case that the sovereign debt market is sustained by a balance between debt restructuring and the enforcement of private rights against a defaulting debtor.

An examination of the possibility that private law enforcement in sovereign debt litigation is historically contingent interrogates the persistent faith of policymakers and academics in judicial enforcement. The article avoids a detailed discussion of the highly polarized policy debate on sovereign debt regulation in US markets that followed the Argentine debt default in 2001. Briefly, at the time, markets strongly resisted the statutory initiative proposed by the International Monetary Fund (IMF). The IMF took the view that crises were endemic to sovereign bond markets and sought to impose statutory changes to ensure speedy and orderly debt workouts. Accordingly, the IMF and later a committee under the aegis of the United Nations (UN) (the chairmanship of Joseph Stiglitz) proposed new legal and institutional frameworks – along the lines of corporate and municipal bankruptcy proceedings – to regulate sovereign debt markets (Krueger, 2002; UN Report, 2009). The IMF suggested alternative fell through not least on account of the conflicting roles it would play as official creditor and de facto sovereign bankruptcy court (Miller, 2002). The UN proposal remains marginal to policy debates. This raises questions independent of those raised in this article, for example, whether the statutory initiative is better than the market-driven framework that regulate both the Eurozone and the US sovereign debt markets.

This article begins by clarifying the theoretical justifications that underpin the belief in effective private law enforcement. It proceeds to develop a Polanyian reading to examine the possibility that the effectiveness of private law enforcement can be historically contingent and ideologically informed. The third section examines whether this was the case when policymakers in the US relied on private law sanctions to incentivize private creditors to take on the increased risk of sovereign lending in the transition to a securitized sovereign debt market in the 1980s. The fourth section analyzes a sample of key sovereign debt cases and asks the same question in relation to the policy imperatives that influence the often contradictory ways in which US courts respond to the conflicting demands of a majority-led debt workout and minority holdouts. A subsection examines the recently concluded Greek debt workout that relied on the retrospective modification of domestic law bonds and the satisfaction of foreign holdout claims in full to settle. The latter, further indebting the country, but leading to further proposals that suggested debt restructuring on the scale required in the Eurozone needed to rely on a statutory intervention that limits private law enforcement pending a workout. It also highlights the historical contingency of private law enforcement.

PRIVATE LAW ENFORCEMENT: A POLANYIAN READING

This section develops a Polanyian reading to reveal the assumptions that underpin a widespread belief that the protection of private law claims is necessary for the functioning of markets and must therefore be enforced at whatever cost to society. As far as sovereign debt markets are concerned, the high social costs of crisis make this assumption problematic. This especially so in the face of evidence, that enforcement of individual claims stymie debt workouts and exacerbate debt crises.

Contemporary debates on how best policymakers should respond to the global credit crisis of 2007 provides a flavor of the theoretical justifications that inform the faith that private law enforcement is necessary to sustain markets. As far as sovereign debt restructuring is concerned, there is an obvious issue of fit as contemporary debates are a response to a distinct but intersecting problem. The global credit crisis revealed the failure of bank regulation. In the Eurozone, undercapitalised banks tipped already indebted sovereigns into crises (De Grauwe, 2011). The intersecting nature of the ongoing crisis is informed by contemporary regulatory debates. Raghuram Rajan, an influential economist and one of a handful who predicted the housing crisis in US markets, lays the blame for the credit crisis on political intervention in markets. He identifies this to be one of several "fault lines" that predisposed credit markets in the US to fail. His main regulatory proposal: the prevention of "distortions that emerge when governments want to push markets and market prices in particular directions" (Rajan, 2010, p. 231). The distortions he argues were evidenced when political pressure was put on markets to provide cheap credit and redress rising social inequality in the US Rajan's solution: markets are self-regulating and should remain so. As far as sovereign debt markets are concerned, this resonates with the policy choice made by European policymakers to adopt the informal, market-driven framework to regulate sovereign debt crises. They have not opted for statutory initiatives of the kind mentioned above on the understanding that markets prefer sovereign debt markets to remain self-regulating with limited or no political intervention.

For Rajan, market failures – the endemic problem in self-regulating markets – are best redressed by its inherent system of checks and balances. This system he argues is essentially sound in "competitive financial systems in countries like the United States and the United Kingdom, [which] include an accent on transparency and *easy enforceability of contracts through the legal system* … Financiers gain confidence because of their ability to obtain publically available information and understand the borrowers' operations and *they know that their claims will be protected and enforced by the courts.* As a result, they are willing to hold long-term claims … such as … long-term debt, and to finance the final user directly rather than going through intermediaries like banks" (Rajan, 2010, p. 12, emphasis added). Admittedly, his conclusions are made in relation to the situation in the US economy. However, it is clear that private law enforcement is fundamental to his vision of self-regulating markets. This raises the question about whether the same reasoning can be relied on by Eurozone policymakers dealing with the ongoing sovereign debt crises. It appears that once a policy decision was made that sovereign bond markets would remain self-regulating, private law enforcement became the preferred backstop by default. The market would rely on their inherent checks and balances available in English law for instance, to enforce debtor obligations and thereby deal with the problem of recurring debt crises. This choice obviates political intervention in sovereign debt markets despite evidence that market instruments such as bonds and derivatives are structured in part to facilitate workouts and in part to limit the political risk of default.

Rajan does not provide any evidence that the private law enforcement works in the way suggested. In his case, the assumption that it will is an article of faith. Following on from the discussion above, it can be argued that his faith in private law enforcement is informed by an ideological position that resists political intervention in markets. Similarly, in the absence of a debate on whether or not the statutory alternative should be adopted, the Eurozone policy choice is underpinned by an ideological position aimed to appease markets. However, the widespread social discontent with austerity, negative growth, and continuing recession makes this ideological stance politically short-lived as will be discussed later. This section proceeds to unpack the assumptions that inform a disdain of political intervention as an ideological position and how this may need to change with a view to facilitate successful debt restructuring.

When compared to Rajan, Joseph Stiglitz occupies the other end of the regulatory spectrum in this debate. He offers a different assessment of the credit crisis of 2008. He argues that the credit crisis that originated in deregulated US capital markets was systemic. It "uncovered fundamental flaws in the peculiar version of capitalism that emerged in the latter part of the twentieth century in the United States" (Stiglitz, 2010, p.xxi). Like Rajan, Stiglitz accounts for how flawed political interventions predispose markets to crises. However, markets are to be blamed too. Independent of flawed political intervention, market players, namely banks "created risk, misallocated capital, and encouraged excessive indebtedness while imposing high transaction costs" (Stiglitz, 2010, p.7). This explains why the "drive for short-term returns led banks to focus on how best to generate more fees – and in some cases, how to circumvent accounting and financial regulations ... there was little or no effective 'quality control' exercised by markets or by regulators" (Stiglitz, 2010, p. 13). Further, bankers were not expected to give any thought to externalities or the effects that the realization of their short-term interests would have on the rest of society. He stresses that their "short-term returns" mentality was a response to incentives offered in a historically specific regulatory environment. Thus for Stiglitz, the markets inherent system of checks and balances – private law enforcement for instance had failed. In his modified version of capitalism, market actors should be incentivized by the state to "perform their essential social functions of managing risk, allocating capital, and mobilizing savings while keeping transaction costs low" (Stiglitz, 2010, p.7). Thus unlike Rajan, Stiglitz argues for a reassessment of the modes of political intervention in markets. This debate between two influential economists has far-reaching implications on responses to the sovereign debt crises in the Eurozone as elaborated below.

As far as sovereign debt regulation is concerned, Stiglitiz's systemic view opens up the possibility that the regulatory environment in which private law enforcement is relied on exclusively to incentivize market actors is one mode of political intervention. Thus its efficacy is historically contingent. This reading of Stiglitz's interventionism is a limited concession to his preference for structural change through the statutory initiative he proposed for regulating sovereign debt markets as mentioned above. On closer examination, the differing regulatory prescriptions Rajan and Stiglitz offer arise from the distinct ways in which they conceptualize the interface between the state and markets. Their assumptions are examined to reflect the basis of the faith that policymakers have in private law enforcement.

For Rajan, effective regulation must assume that markets and nonmarket constituencies such as the state (the key driver of political intervention) coexist as separate domains. It follows then that for regulatory purposes, the state has no role in markets. Markets in turn are sufficiently constrained by market forces (competition) and a well-defined and historically established (and thus by definition essentially unchanging) system of private law enforcement. His belief in self-regulation is premised on a necessarily efficacious system of private law. This ideological position engenders the view that private law enforcement works independent of political intervention as self-regulation and nonintervention are two sides of the same coin.

For Stiglitz, in contrast, the specific structure of each capital market is itself a function of political intervention and therefore can only be constrained by the latter. Incentives can change market behavior, so, by definition, states have to be responsive to markets. Conceptually, the boundaries between the state and markets are diffused and imprecise. The assumptions that underpin their distinct views lead to different policy prescriptions. So, for instance, the need to constrain private law enforcement to facilitate a debt workout is excessive political intervention in Rajan's framework. In contrast, for Stiglitz this must be the norm in main to limit the social costs of an ongoing and unresolved sovereign debt crisis. His framework is not restrained by the "self-regulating market" ideological straightjacket that ossifies the boundaries between markets and the state. In the fluctuating and self-reinforcing interface between markets and the state, private law protections must be limited by the overriding imperative to resolve crises and thereby reduce its social costs. As far as sovereign debt restructuring is concerned, the social backlash against austerity is potentially a tipping point at which private law enforcement must give way to debt restructuring. The possibility that the effectiveness of private law enforcement is historically contingent revives the contribution of Karl Polanyi to this regulatory debate. The relevance of his work is discussed in more detail in the rest of this section.

Karl Polanyi's *The Great Transformation* offers the classic textbook justification for political intervention in markets (2001). His views often form the starting point for mainstream scholarship theorizing the impact of financial crises on society and markets (Abolafia, 2001; Block, 2003; Ebner, 2010). Specifically, the institutional and ideological factors that predispose markets to crisis and the necessity of political intervention to limit the inevitable social costs that follow. In his foreward to the latest reprint of the book (Polanyi, 2001) Joseph Stiglitz, for instance, identifies key Polanyian theses. They include "the idea that self-regulating markets never work; their deficiencies not only in their internal workings but also in their consequences (e.g., for the poor) are so great that government intervention becomes necessary..." (Polanyi, 2001, p. vii). The following discussion develops a Polanyian reading that offers a conceptual and theoretical justification for imposing constraints on private law enforcement to facilitate debt restructuring in the Eurozone. The relevance of his work is brought to the fore by the social response across the Eurozone to ongoing recession and austerity.

Polanyi's main interests lay in the "institutional arrangements that *coordinated* the commodity production and exchange in modern capitalism" (Polanyi, 2001, p. 76). He defined commodities as things produced for exchange in markets. Laissez-faire capitalism, he argued, was sustained by institutions that viewed nature, money supplied by governments, and the activity of human beings as commodity fictions, namely property (including intellectual property), credit, and labor, respectively. Commodity fictions were recognized as such by legal institutions that marked them as distinct from the real commodities in which they were grounded. For instance, in markets that developed to satisfy the demands of industrial production, laissez-faire laws recognized labor to be a commodity fiction devoid of "real magnitudes" (Polanyi, 2001, p. 76). In other words, the welfare of the human beings whose activities were commodified as labor was deemed not to be the concern of markets. This view combined with the valorization of the price mechanism as the central organizing (and regulating) principle of markets came to define laissez-faire capitalism.

The view of policymakers that labor was an abstract commodity fiction to be regulated only by the price mechanism also obviated the need for political intervention in markets. For example, labor welfare laws would change the price of labor and thus "endanger the self-regulation of the system" (*ibid.*). Polanyi showed that laissez-faire capitalism was sustained by a clear demarcation between the state, markets (and society). Institutions informed by the ideology of self-regulation were required to maintain this delineation. He found evidence of this in English Parliamentary legislation in the early part of the 19th century (Polanyi, 2001, p. 146). Polanyi also identified this delineation to be the central problem with laissez-faire capitalism: its oversight of what were the inevitable social costs of economic crises. As mentioned, Stiglitz would later argue that this inevitability was consistent with modern theories of market failure (Stiglitz, 2001).

However, this oversight Polanyi argued was what also undid the laissez-faire project. This was in part as the social costs of laissez-faire capitalism reached a tipping point after which the certainties that informed policy-making in the early part of 19th century could no longer be relied on. He records the legislative changes in the latter half of the 19th century as evidence of active political intervention in markets, such as an amendment of the Mines Act, "making it penal to employ boys under twelve not attending schools and unable to read or write" (Polanyi, 2001, p. 152). He reveals the changes to be spontaneous and arising from society responding to limit the costs of laissez-faire markets. Polanyi's main contribution lies in the recognition that the institutions that sustained both laissez-faire capitalism and the countermovement in the latter part of the 19th century were historically contingent, ideologically defined, and arose spontaneously. To sum up, the legal institutions that specified commodity fictions as such were neither timeless, abstract nor unchanging but historically contingent and ideologically defined. Can the same be said of private law enforcement in sovereign debt regulation?

The Polanyian reading developed in this section reveals the possibility that the effectiveness of private law enforcement as the central backstop in sovereign debt regulation may be historically contingent and ideologically informed. It also opens up the possibility that the current unrest among the populace of heavily indebted sovereigns could be a tipping point at which private law constraints become inevitable to facilitate debt workouts. The following section is a case study of securitization to reveal whether the effectiveness of substantive private law (property, contract law) protections to regulate sovereign debt markets is historically contingent.

SECURITIZATION OF SOVEREIGN DEBT: A POLITICAL PROJECT

The securitization of US sovereign debt markets is described here as a historically specific, political project. Accordingly, this section focuses on the financial and legal incentives offered to key market players to realize this project. The focus of this examination is on the private law enforcement of individual creditor claims against defaulting debtors. This examination is different from mainstream technical discussions that explore issues such as whether the legal changes that underpinned this change were an efficient way to extract payment from a sovereign debtor or whether litigation initiated before or after default is better for debt workouts (Sturzenegger & Zettelmeyer, 2006, pp. 31–81). Prior to the 1980s, the ideological imperatives of the cold war laid the ground for securitization. Legislative changes at the time had adopted a very restrictive interpretation of sovereign immunity protections in international law. This was a necessary precursor to private law enforcement actions contractually being made available to creditors taking on the risk of lending to sovereign debtors. As mentioned, this was the period in which US investors and other market actors were being actively incentivized to transition to a securitized debt market by the US state.

In any event, the economic conditions were right for securitization. In the 1970s, a handful of US commercial banks dominated international sovereign lending in a context where sovereign defaults (and financial crises) were and remained frequent (Reinhart & Rogoff, 2009). The predisposition of this system of official lending to crises exposed the US economy to what were then perceived to be unhealthy levels of uncertainty and investor risk. Further, in the aftermath of the Mexican moratorium on its debt repayment in the early 1980s, almost all commercial bank lending ceased and most loans were rescheduled (Power, 1996, p. 2701). This reduced the gains to be made from sovereign lending even though private sector (nonbank) lending during this period had not ceased completely (Buchheit, 1988, p. 226). The high demand for debt evidenced by the "rapid growth of the secondary market ... underscored the depth of investor interest in sovereign debt instruments paying high rates of return" (*ibid.*). The central regulatory goals at the time, to minimize the impact that the crisis-prone system of official lending posed to the US economy, reduced the risk to US banks and the creation of a significantly larger market to meet the demands of mainly US investors for new sources of wealth. The Brady Plan (Plan) was formulated to achieve them.

US investors, banks, and sovereign debtors were offered strong financial incentives to accept the Plan (Hayter & Watson, 1985, pp. 26–27). For instance, it was made easier for already indebted sovereigns to borrow fresh capital by exchanging their outstanding debt for bonds. The latter were offered at a discount and their maturity was set typically for 30 years (a period considerably shorter than the longer maturity of outstanding bank loans). This was extremely beneficial for debtors as their debt overhang was curtailed on favorable terms. The incentives for the banks to accept the transition, lay in the opportunity it afforded them to erase their exposure to sovereign debt from their books (Buchheit, 1988). Further, the Plan allowed payments due on emerging market sovereign debt to be made in tandem with the refinancing of existing debt. This two-pronged strategy was preferred by sovereigns, investors, and the official sector (the US administration and international financial institutions) at the time (*ibid.*). It formally redressed the continuing debtor demand for capital and took advantage of the "short-term" memory of private lenders who were willing to overlook debt defaults in the early 1930s in their quest for new sources of wealth. Thus securitization was entrenched by a political consensus structured to placate two key constituencies who would be most affected by the change: the official sector banks and mainly private US investors.

The significantly increased size of the market and the windfall gains that were to be made with securitization also increased the political risk of default and private investors had to be incentivized to accept the Plan. It was clear to the market and policymakers at the time that existing private law sanctions in United States were necessary but not sufficient to resolve three structural problems. Since then US courts have continually been faced with issues that have arisen on account of varying impacts on creditor rights. First, the Plan was framed in a context where sovereigns still had established defences against private suit in international law, such as International Comity and the Act of State Doctrine. Both are discussed briefly in the next section. In addition, the enforcement of US judgments that would entail the attachment of the tangible and intangible property of a defaulting foreign state was another problem that neither the private law sanctions, nor the restrictive interpretation of sovereign immunity has successfully remedied. Sovereigns could (and still do) exercise their residual sovereign powers in international law to remove attachable assets from the territorial jurisdiction of US courts to avoid enforcement. It has been argued that the absence of effective debtor sanctions increases the incidence of opportunistic debtor default (Porzecanski, 2005). It has also been argued that private law protections skewed regulation in favor of creditors to counter this problem (Gathii, 2006). Both views overlook the larger geopolitical context that necessitated this transition and why a belief in the effectiveness of private law enforcement was a crucial feature.

The second structural problem exacerbates sovereign debt crises as the expeditious adoption of the Plan was facilitated by a trans-Atlantic ideological consensus between the Reagan and Thatcher administrations. This consensus saw no role for political intervention in debt markets. The ideological tenor of this consensus is evidenced in the recognition that US sovereign debt markets would remain self-regulating and thus necessarily reliant on private law enforcement. The third structural problem was that the private law protections were offered to all creditors in the face of significant changes in the number and identity of investors. The adoption of the Plan eventually entailed the consolidation and repackaging of bank loans owed by debtors. This was then offered to private creditors as bonds. In a debt crisis, the availability of this protection exacerbates the conflicting demands of individual private law claims and the collective interests of the market. As discussed in the following section, this conflict would eventually lead to situations where minority creditors would be denied private law protections without legal justification. More often individual creditors rely on them to delay debt workouts and thereby give debtors no choice but to satisfy their claims in full. In the process, prolonging debt crises and increasing the associated social costs despite the collective will of the majority to participate in a debt workout. The structural problems that existed at the time of securitization still define the issues that dominate regulatory concerns (Dixon & Wall, 2000; Sturzenegger & Zettelmeyer, 2006, pp. 63–64). This is evidenced in the cases analyzed in the following section.

In time, the unresolved structural problems discussed above would expose the flaws of the informal market-driven framework backstopped by private law sanctions in the face of entrenched international law protections for sovereigns. This would lead to calls for a multilaterally negotiated statutory framework to resolve debt crisis of the kind proposed by the IMF and the UN, as discussed above.

SOVEREIGN DEBT LITIGATION IN US COURTS: A SNAPSHOT

Following from the discussion in the preceding section that highlights the structural problems that define the resolution of sovereign debt crisis, this section examines how US courts respond. Sovereign debt litigation is marked by judicial attempts to resolve what a problem endemic to sovereign debt markets is in general: the conflicting demands of minority creditors seeking to enforce their individual private law claims and the collective interests of a majority wishing to restructure their debt. The discussion in this section is limited by constraints of space to a case study of two batches of cases, selected as each was decided in very distinct political environments.

The first batch of cases was decided in the context of a market transitioning to securitization and the other in a securitized market. This selection is not exhaustive and is open to the criticism of a self-selection bias. Suffice to say here that the decision to use the two sets of cases is to reveal the historically contingency of the effectiveness of private law sanctions against defaulting debtors. The discussion here is not intended to either be an overview of US sovereign debt litigation (Gathii, 2006;

Sturzenegger & Zettelmeyer, 2006) or to provide a comparative litigation analysis of the US and UK jurisdictions.

The Costa Rican Debt Litigation (1980)

Allied Bank International, a US chartered bank ("Allied Bank"), was an agent of a syndicate of 39 lending banks that had advanced credit to 3 Costa Rican government-owned banks in 1979. Under the terms of the indenture on the promissory notes issued by the Costa Rican banks, the debt was payable in New York in US dollars and under the jurisdiction of US law. The banks defaulted in 1981 under directions of the Costa Rican government (Gathii, 2006, p. 270). In response, Allied Bank sought a summary judgment against Costa Rica to recover on the promissory notes payable to the syndicate. Costa Rica countered this suit by claiming inter alia sovereign immunity and the act of state Doctrine (Doctrine) – two sovereign defences against private suits entrenched in international law and binding US courts. By consenting to submit to US law, Costa Rica had accepted the restrictive interpretation of sovereign immunity. In the first instance, Judge Griesa of the Southern District Court of New York (SDNY) dismissed Allied Bank's motion for summary judgment (*Allied I*).[1]

The question – as the court saw it – was whether the governmental acts preventing payment of the notes fell within the purview of the Doctrine. The judge found that it did. He also recognized this as a situation in which the court was being invited "to judge a foreign government's conduct under ambiguous principles of international law" (*ibid.*). At the time the case was decided, it was clear that US courts had no jurisdiction to enquire into takings of property owned by US citizens abroad. At the time, precedents on the applicability of the Doctrine to situations involving intangible property were unclear.[2] The judge was constrained by this and the absence of jurisprudence to deal with "permissible appropriations of intangible property in international financial transactions" (Gathii, 2006, p. 271). To complicate matters, the judge was vested with sole jurisdiction to enforce creditor suits. As discussed in the preceding section, there existed no formal or official mechanisms to ensure Costa Rica fulfilled its debt obligations as the political consensus at the time was committed to the ideological position that debt markets would remain self-regulating. This decision effectively left Allied Bank with no option but to accept a settlement on terms favorable to Costa Rica. It appealed to set it aside.

While the appeal was pending in the Second Circuit, 38 of the 39 banks (a majority) in the syndicate decided to accept the debtors offer and participate in a workout. They consented to withdraw their cases accordingly. The Second Circuit (*Allied II*)[3] did not decide the validity of the lower court's interpretation of the Doctrine in *Allied I.* It dismissed Allied's appeal on the ground of Comity – another established sovereign defence in international law.[4] The order reflected the courts concern that the ongoing debt restructuring negotiations between Costa Rica and its 38 creditors would be jeopardized by a ruling in favor of fidelity, the lone holdout creditor. This was an early example of the conflicting demands of holdouts asserting their private law rights through enforcement litigation to seek the repayment of the face value of their debt and the majority willing to participate in restructuring the outstanding debt. However, the denial of minority claims increased uncertainty as this precedent would potentially render the individual rights of all other market actors unenforceable. Thus, *Allied II* was strongly disapproved by the market. A campaign to set aside both decisions was initiated by creditor banks, the business press, and organizations, such as the National Foreign Trade Council,[5] the Rule of Law Committee,[6] and the New York Clearing House (NYCH).[7] This campaign formed the basis of a further appeal by Allied Bank to the Second Circuit to rehear *Allied II.*

The US Department of Justice (DOJ), as amicus curiae intervened in the proceedings to question both the judicial interpretation of the Doctrine and the relevance of Comity to Allied Banks enforcement actions. The Second Circuit's finding of Comity as a defence in Costa Rica's favor reflected what the DOJ represented to be the US debt restructuring policy (US policy) at the time. In accordance with this policy, the court was asked to set aside the interpretation of the Doctrine in *Allied I* on the following ground. The Doctrine was available only where a taking or confiscation took place exclusively within the territory of a foreign state. This interpretation was backed up by a situs analysis carried out by the DOJ. They found the promissory notes were payable in New York and in US dollars. Costa Rican decrees affecting contract rights outside Costa Rica territory could not benefit from the protection that judicial abstention under the Doctrine would give the sovereign. Reflecting market expectations, the DOJ argued that this "strictly territorialist" requirement was appropriate in the context of "the globalised nature of international financial lending" (Gathii, 2006, p. 274). As mentioned, this intervention was historically contingent. It was defined by the context in which creditors were being actively incentivized to transition to a securitized market.

The DOJ also argued the court had misconstrued US policy on two grounds. First, that US leadership and involvement in the cooperative rescheduling of debt was through the Paris Club and through federal assistance under statute (Power, 1996). According to this policy, *Allied II* had wrongly applied the notion of cooperative debt adjustment to debt borrowed privately while it was only designed to apply to borrowing between sovereigns. Second, *Allied II* had misconstrued US support for cooperative debt adjustment as a basis to undermine the rights of private creditors to obtain effective remedies, including due process safeguards against expropriation of their property through enforcement litigation. In accordance with US policy, this misunderstanding left creditors with the undesirable remedy of collective workouts, wholly at the mercy of indebted sovereigns and international organizations. It left individual creditors who choose to opt out of them without any avenues for judicial redress. This interpretation was without precedent as it relied on jurisprudence developed in relation to tangible property. This interpretation also by-passed an established international law sovereign defence against private suits (Gathii, 2006, p. 276).

The US policy stated was affirmed by the market. In its amicus brief, Bank of America (the coordinating agent for the ongoing refinancing and a member of the Rule of Law Committee) favored an early if not preferential pay-out for Fidelity through litigation. Ten members of the NYCH who accepted the refinancing now supported Fidelity's effort to collect. Their support was justified on the ground that while they disagreed with Fidelity's enforcement action (and preferred to refinance their debt), they nevertheless "believed it to be of overriding importance to the conduct of their business – and to the interests of New York and the United States – that Fidelity's legal right to a judgement *that upheld the inviolability of its right to repayment be recognised and upheld in unequivocal terms*" (*ibid.*, emphasis added). US policy was in effect underpinning the effectiveness of the private law sanctions Fidelity was seeking to enforce against Costa Rica. In the absence of this intervention the private law sanctions would be ineffective against a defaulting debtor. The efficacy of private law sanctions reliant on state intervention is therefore not abstract or unchanging but historically contingent and ideologically informed.

Allied I and *Allied II* were both eventually overturned by a three judge panel of the Second Circuit (*Allied III*)[8] in accordance with US policy. Eventually, in a further intervention, Costa Rica avoided repaying Fidelity in full and reduced its claim to the extent accepted by the other 38 creditors. The next batch of enforcement litigation had a different outcome.

They were decided in a securitized debt market where debt restructuring rather than individual creditor enforcement action would define the policy imperative. This counterexample highlights the historical contingency of private law sanctions.

The Argentine Default Cases (2001 to the present)

In 2001, Argentina defaulted on its foreign debt in what was then the largest debt default in the history of sovereign lending.[9] It was also the "most protracted taking almost three and a half years between the default and the closing of the restructuring deal" (Sturzenegger & Zettelmeyer, 2006, p. 165). The delay was attributable in part to the failure of creditor coordination through the formation of creditor committees and in part to the flawed intervention of the IMF (2013).This debt crisis "extracted by far the highest economic cost, with output collapsing between the first quarter of 2001 and the first quarter of 2002 by a staggering 16.3 percent" (*ibid.*). It is now widely accepted that the roots of the 2001 crisis can be traced to the Convertibility Plan under which "the Argentine peso was pegged to the US dollar at 1:1, and the Central Bank of the Republic of Argentina (BCRA) was required to back at least two-thirds of its monetary base with hard currency reserves" (*ibid.*). In addition, Argentina underwent "significant structural reforms (deregulation, trade liberalization and privatization) as well as the reopening of its access to capital markets after the signing of the [Plan] in April 1992" (*ibid.*).

In September 2005, Argentina's debt was eventually restructured after more than 36 months. Creditor coordination had become an intractable problem and the requisite majority for a debt workout to be binding could not be reached. The problem lay in the distinct interests of majorities (willing to participate) and minorities (refusing to participate and seeking instead to enforce their claims to the face value of their debt). A majority of 76.15 percent of its creditors finally accepted Argentina's offer. They included foreign, domestic bondholders, both institutional investors and private bondholders. A key factor that increased the participation of foreign bondholders for the workout to settle was the passing of what has been referred to as the "Padlock" law by Argentina (Sturzenegger & Zettelmeyer, 2006, p. 193). This domestic statute prohibits the Argentine government from reaching a settlement with the minority holdouts who had refused to participate in the workout – The latter holding out from the debt restructuring to enforce their individual private law claims against Argentina. The political intervention of the debtor was a crucial factor in the success of this workout. However, this intervention was – as the ongoing litigation indicates – at a cost to holdout enforcement action.

In *NML Capital Ltd.* (*NML Capital*), a holdout suit for repayment, the SDNY ordered an attachment of $7 billion worth of Argentine bonds. However, instead of supporting *NML Capital* – the holdout – as was the case in the *Allied* batch of cases, the NYCH now weighed in on behalf of Argentina. This shift was supported by the US policy, that now found that isolating the holdouts was necessary to protect the market, and contain the potentially systemic effects of a continuing crisis. As far as Argentina was concerned; this shift in US policy diminished the private law sanctions available to the holdouts. This was in contrast to the pre-securitization cases discussed above. Further, markets accepted this diminution, as necessary, to resolve what had by now become an endemic problem: the conflicting demands of holdout creditors and the collective interests of the majority. In response, the court reversed its original decision and vacated its attachment orders.

On appeal, the Second Circuit agreed. It found that it was within the lower court's jurisdiction to vacate the attachment orders because doing so would avoid "a substantial risk to Argentina's debt restructuring" and the restructuring was "of critical importance to the economic health of a nation" (*NML Capital*). Thus allowing the attachments to proceed would undermine the well-established "consensual, good-faith process leading to a restructuring of debt" and would "damage ... settle market expectations" (*ibid.*). The workout eventually settled on account of the court's refusal to enforce private law claims against Argentina.

In a second successful debt restructuring in 2010, Argentina swapped some 12.6 billion US dollars in defaulted bonds for new debt. The holdouts rejected the second workout and are still suing to recover the full value of their defaulted bonds. Argentine assets still subject to the threat of seizure as holdouts try to enforce multibillion-dollar court judgments against the country. The presiding District Court Judge Griesa has granted several billion dollars in court judgments to them. So far they have not been able to enforce the entirety of their outstanding debt in the face of US sovereign immunity laws that protect sovereign assets. The holdouts are currently seeking to enforce their contractual claims with a particular interpretation of pari passu – a contractual term that mandates equal treatment between creditors. In an order accepting their arguments, the SDNY Judge Griesa has opened the Padlock law by offering holdouts the right to the face value of their debt and recurring interest on par with creditors who participated in the debt workout (February 23, 2012). This decision contravenes Argentine law. It also overrides the actions of a sovereign state (Pearson, 2012; Russo, 2012a). Finally, this increases uncertainty as it opens up the 2005 workout, by potentially offering the holdouts a better deal than those offered to the majority creditors who had consented to accept a debt write-down and the possibility of technical default (Russo, 2012b).

The holdout interpretation of pari passu is contested (Buchheit & Pam, 2004). By accepting this interpretation, the court is attempting (unsuccessfully so far) to enforce private law claims against the defaulting debtor. This is contrary to market expectations.The US administration has also indicated that it will side Argentina in the pending appeal against this decision. Their support justified on the ground that the orders issued by the court are both "impermissibly broad" and "harmful to US foreign relations" (Hurtado & Benson, 2012; IMF, 2013). As far as the author is aware, this decision is pending appeal at the time of writing. It is arguably the case that the context in which the first decisions were made that constrained enforcement action by the same holdouts for the debt workout to settle has changed significantly. The country has since recovered from the crisis achieving high GDP growth notwithstanding its exclusion from capital markets. In this case, the markedly differing contexts in which creditor claims are being adjudicated may still define the effectiveness of private law enforcement action.

Successful debt workouts rely on the consensual diminution of private law sanctions and the satisfaction in full of minority holdout claims at the margins. This ad hoc strategy developed for each sovereign in distress is customized to deal with the specificities of the country's debt profile has nonetheless kept the problem of holdout creditors real. They continue to use their private law protections to delay debt workouts, prolong crises and exacerbate the associated social costs as evidenced in the cases analyzed in this section. The policy response of Eurozone countries to the holdout problem is discussed in the following subsection and includes an analysis of the Greek debt workout.

The Policy Response to the Eurozone Debt Crises

When drawing lessons from the US experience, it is important to recognize the significant differences in the political contexts that will inform the resolution of sovereign debt crises in the Eurozone. The Eurozone cases will be informed by English law which has been more amenable to collective resolution and the restriction of holdout claims.[10] The workouts would have to negotiate different constitutions, domestic laws, treaty obligations, concessions, and official sector policymakers belonging to the European Central Bank, the IMF, and the European Stability Mechanism (ESM).

In October 2011, the European Council agreed on the need to set up the ESM) a permanent crisis mechanism to safeguard the financial stability of the euro area as a whole. The ESM will provide financial assistance packages to euro area Member States under strict conditionality. The ESM will "complement the new framework of reinforced economic governance, aiming at an effective and rigorous economic surveillance, which will focus on prevention and will substantially reduce the probability of a crisis arising in the future" (ESM Treaty, 2012). In the event of insolvency, the Member State will have to negotiate a comprehensive restructuring plan with its private sector creditors, in line with IMF practices. This intervention is made with a view to restoring debt sustainability. The restoration of debt sustainability relies on the market-driven initiative rather than statutory change.

The market-driven initiative was bolstered with the inclusion of "standardized and identical collective action clauses"[11] (CACs) into all new euro area government bonds starting in January 2013. CACs would enable the creditors to pass a qualified majority decision agreeing a legally binding change to the terms of payment in the event that the debtor is unable to pay. CACs introduce a participation threshold which could vary in different bond issues. Once this threshold is reached, the holdouts are tied into accepting the wishes of the majority. However, reaching this threshold may take time that a distressed sovereign does not have. Further, this change does not apply to the existing stick of debt that is currently the concern of policymakers.

In March and April 2012, Greece restructured approximately $199 billion in government and government guaranteed debt in what has become the largest workout in the history of sovereign lending (Financial Stability Council, 2012, p. 48). Greece's privately held debt was reduced by over 50 percent. Creditors participating in the workout received bonds with lower interest and longer maturities. Holders of bonds denominated in Greek law suffered losses estimated at 75–80 percent of their net present value. Holders of debt denominated in foreign law were paid out in full (Zettelmeyer, Trebesch, & Gulati, 2012). The workout was necessary for Greece to achieve "sustainable debt dynamics" – a precondition for official lenders such as the IMF to disburse funds to the country under a second official sector aid program.[12] It was certainly not sufficient as it marks the likelihood of default, increasing austerity, more bailouts and possibly exit from the Eurozone. Prior to the workout, Greece retrospectively modified its domestic bond contracts to include CACs. The workout involved "90 percent or more" of debt governed by Greek law, thus the retrospective modification was possible as a sovereign act. As far as this workout is concerned, the litigation risk was eliminated as holdouts with foreign law denominated debt were paid in full.

This was necessary as they held majority stakes in their bond issues. They refused to participate in the workout and demanded the repayment of the face value of their bonds. This meant that the Greek workout would potentially be delayed indefinitely by holdout litigation. Thus though the changes have been positive, the holdout problem remains. This will continue to potentially delay workouts and exacerbate the social costs of a crisis. One solution recently proposed by influential scholars would be to constrain creditor enforcement action pending a debt workout if the widespread restructuring required to return distressed sovereigns to debt sustainability in the Eurozone is to be achieved (Buchheit, Gulati & Tiredo, 2013).

The recently concluded Greek debt workout relied on a similar ad hoc strategy customized to reflect its particular debt profile. This gave policymakers innovative options such as the retrospective modification of its domestic law debt to achieve the required majority for the debt to settle. However, the holdout problem remains and mandatory contract modification does not entirely solve this. As discussed, the differences are however quite marked in that the structural impediments to debt workouts in US law have been addressed to a limited degree by new policy changes in the Eurozone as discussed in this section (Choi, Posner, & Gulati, 2011). This discussion highlights the need for more ways to reign in holdouts. On possibility is a politically negotiated Eurozone wide debt restructuring initiative similar to the Brady Plan discussed above to reduce the impact of obstructive private law sanctions that will continue to stymie debt workouts in the future.

CONCLUSIONS

Debt restructuring is a central plank of any initiative to resolve the ongoing sovereign debt crises in the Eurozone. The central impediment to achieving this is holdout enforcement litigation. Here holdouts seek to enforce their private law claims against debtors engaged in workout negotiations. This article reviews private law enforcement actions in US markets from the period when the sovereign debt markets were securitized in the 1980s to the ongoing pari passu litigation in US courts. The debt market is sustained by a balance between the policy imperative to achieve debt workouts and the protection of creditor rights. Private law protections are not immutable.

In the current informal market driven framework, the effectiveness of private law protections have been historically contingent on the imperatives that face policymakers in a crises. This queries the dominant belief that debt markets are sustained by timeless, unchanging, and abstract private law sanctions. It also indicates that the increasing social costs of the ongoing sovereign debt crisis in the Eurozone (as evidenced in widespread anti-austerity protests) is an imperative that justifies constraints on private law protections pending debt workouts to expeditiously resolve the problem.

Methodology

The Polanyian reading in this article is premised on the insight that the boundaries between markets, society, and the state are fluid and constantly in flux. The legal institutions developed to delineate these boundaries are seen to be historically contingent and ideologically informed. The regulation of sovereign debt markets relies on a similar delineation. This was however not evidenced in the policy leading up to the securitization of the sovereign debt market in the 1980s and in sovereign debt litigation in US law. It is clearly the case that the debt market is itself sustained by a balance between the competing claims of individual creditors and the debtor's interest in a debt workout to resolve an ongoing sovereign debt crisis. It is this balance that reveals the historical contingency of private law protections. This has special significance for the Eurozone where the threat of holdout claims is viewed as the main obstacle to achieving debt workouts.

NOTES

1. *Allied Bank Int'l v Banco Credito de Agricola* 566 F. Supp at 1442 (*'Allied I'*)
2. The precedents on the issue were contested and remain so. *French v Banco Nacional de Cuba*, 242 N.E.2D 704, 712 (N.Y. 1968); *Hunt v. Coastal States Gas*

Producing Co. 583 S.W. 2d. 322, 325-36 (Tex, 1079) (Holding that the right to explore for and extract oil is not property right).

3. *Allied Bank Int'l v. Banco Creditor Agricola de Cartago* 733 F. 2d 23,27 (2d. cir. 1984) (*Allied II*).

4. Comity refers to "the recognition which one nation allows within its territory to the legislative, executive or judicial acts of another nation." *Hilton v. Guyot* 159 US 113, 164 (1895).

5. The National Foreign Trade Council is a private US-based group that lobbies on behalf of US companies and for free trade.

6. Also referred to as the Committee for the Rule of Law is to ensure the legal system is strictly accountable to the people and to the law. It deals with the accountability of the adjudication process.

7. The New York Clearing House Association is the oldest US bank clearing house that plays a key role in supporting the development of the banking system.

8. 757 F.2d. 516 (2d. Cir. 1985) (*Allied III*).

9. The Argentina default was at one point the largest debt default in the history of sovereign lending. It involved more than $100 billion of privately held and official bilateral debt on loans worth $81 billion.

10. The promulgation of the recently introduced anti-vulture legislation *The Debt Relief (Developing Countries) Act 2010* in UK law is a case in point.

11. The version of CACs used in the Eurozone was proposed by Report of the G-10 Working Group on Contractual Clauses (http://www.bis.org/publ/gten08.htm).

12. The first aid was disbursed in May 2010.

REFERENCES

Abolafia, M. Y. (2001). *Making markets: Opportunism and restraint on wall street*. Cambridge, MA: Harvard University Press.

Benson, D. (2012, March 15). *What Greece can learn from Argentina's default*. http://www.businessweek.com/articles/2012-03-15/what-greece-can-learn-from-argentinas-default. Accessed on April 13, 2012.

Block, F. (2003). Karl Polanyi and the writing of the great transformation. *Theory and Society, 32*(3), 275–306.

Buchheit, L. (1988). The capitalization of sovereign debt: An introduction. *University of Illinois Law Review, 401*, 401.

Buchheit, L. C., & Gulati, G. M. (2012, October 8). *The Eurozone debt crisis – The options now*. Retrieved from http://ssrn.com/abstract=2158850 or http://dx.doi.org/10.2139/ssrn.2158850

Buchheit, L., Gulati, M., & Tirado, I. (2013). *The problem of holdout creditors in Eurozone sovereign debt restructurings*. Retrieved from http://ssrn.com/abstract=2205704

Buchheit, L., & Pam, J. (2004). The pari passu clause in sovereign debt instruments. *Emory Law Journal, 53*, 869.

Choi, S., Gulati, M., & Posner, E. (2012). The evolution of contractual terms in sovereign bonds. *Journal of Legal Analysis, 4*(1), 131–179.

Choi, S., Gulati, M., & Posner, E. (2011). *Pricing terms in sovereign debt contracts: A Greece case study with implications for the European crisis resolution mechanism*. Olin Working Paper No. 541, University of Chicago Law & Economics. Retrieved from http://ssrn.com/abstract=1713914

De Grauwe, P. (2011). *The European central bank: Lender of last resort in the government bond market*. CESifo Working Paper No. 3569. Retrieved from http://www.cesifo-group.de/ifoHome/publications/working-papers/CESifoWP/CESifoWPdetails?wp_num=3569

Dixon, L., & Wall, D. (2000). Collective action problems and collective action clauses. *Bank of England Financial Stability Review*, *8*, 142–151.

Eaton, J., & Gersovitz, M. (1981). Debt with potential repudiation: Theory and estimation. *Review of Economic Studies*, *48*(2), 289–309.

Ebner, A. (2010). Transnational markets and the Polanyi problem. In C. Joerges & J. Falke (Eds.), *Karl Polanyi, globalisation and the potential of the law in transnational markets* (pp. 19–44). Oxford: Hart.

ESM Treaty. (2012). *European stability mechanism treaty*. Retrieved from http://eurozone.europa.eu/esm-treaty-signature. Accessed on August 25.

Financial Stability Council. (2012, August 7). *Annual report*. Retrieved from http://www.treasury.gov/initiatives/fsoc/2012report/2012/Annual Report.pdf

Gathii, J. T. (2006). *The sanctity of sovereign loan contracts and its origins in enforcement litigation. The George Wash. Int'l L. Rev.* [Vol. 38], 251.

Gulati M. G. (2012). *Mitu Gulati: Portugal, Spain and Italy should also restructure their debts' interview with Isabelle Couet*. Retrieved from http://blogs.lesechos.fr/by-les-echos/mitu-gulati-portugal-spain-and-italy-should-also-restructure-their-debts-a10752.html

Hayter, T., & Watson, C. (1985). *Aid: Rhetoric and reality*. London: Pluto Press.

Hurtado, P., & Benson D. (2012, April 5). *US seeks reversal of lower courts Argentine bond rulings*. Retrieved from http://www.bloomberg.com/news/2012-04-05/u-s-seeks-reversal-of-lower-court-argentine-bond-rulings-1-.html

IMF. (2013). *Sovereign debt restructuring–Recent developments and implications for the fund's legal and policy framework*. Retrieved from http://www.imf.org/external/np/pp/eng/2013/042613.pdf

Krueger, A. (2002, August 8). *A new approach to sovereign debt restructuring*. Retrieved from www.imf.org/external/pubs/ft/exrp/sdrm/eng/sdrm.pdf

Miller, M. (2002, April). *Sovereign debt restructuring: New articles, new contracts or no change?* International Economic Policy Brief No. PB02-3. Institute for International Economics, Washington, DC.

Morgenson, D. C. G. (2011). Fair game: Scare tactics in Greece. *The New York Times*. Retrieved from http://www.nytimes.com/2011/11/20/business/credit-default-swaps-as-a-scare-tactic-in-greece.html?_r=1&ref=gretchenmorgenson. Accessed on April 13, 2012.

Pearson, S. (2012, March 6). *Elliot management wins U.S. court ruling over defaulted Argentine bonds*. Retrieved from http://www.bloomberg.com/news/2012-03-06/elliott-management-wins-u-s-court-ruling-over-defaulted-argentina-bonds.html. Accessed on April 13, 2012.

Polanyi, K. (2001). *The great transformation: The political and economic origins of our time*. Boston, MA: Beacon Press.

Porzecanski, A. C. (2005). From rogue creditors to rogue debtors: Implications of Argentina's default. *Chicago Journal of International Law*, *6*(1), 311–326.

Power, P. (1996). Sovereign debt: The rise of the secondary market and its implications for future restructurings. *Fordham Law Review*, *64*, 2701–2720.

Rajan, R. (2010). *Fault line: How hidden fractures threaten the world economy*. Princeton, NJ: Princeton University Press.

Reinhart, C., & Rogoff, K. (2009). *This time is different: Eight centuries of financial folly*. Princeton, NJ: Princeton University Press.

Russo, C. (2012a, March 5). *Argentina ordered to pay interest on defaulted debt, Nacion says*. Retrieved from http://www.bloomberg.com/news/2012-03-05/argentina-ordered-to-pay-interest-on-defaulted-debt-nacion-says.html. Accessed on April 13, 2012.

Russo, C. (2012b, March 7). *U.S. ruling on Argentine bonds raises risk of second default, Citi says*. Retrieved from http://www.bloomberg.com/news/2012-03-06/u-s-ruling-on-argentine-bonds-raises-risk-of-second-default-citi-says.html. Accessed on April 13, 2012.

Stiglitz, J. (2010). *Freefall: America, markets and the sinking of the global economy*. New York, NY: W.W. Norton & Company Inc.

Sturzenegger, F., & Zettelmeyer, J. (2006). *Debt defaults and lessons from a decade of crises*. Cambridge, UK: The MIT Press.

United Nations. (2009). *Report of the Commission of Experts of the President of the United Nations General Assembly on Reforms of the International Monetary and Financial System*. Retrieved from http://www.un.org/ga/econcrisissummit/docs/FinalReport_CoE.pdf

UN Report. (2009). *Final report of the commission of experts of the president of the United Nations General Assembly on reforms of the international monetary and financial system*, September 21. Retrieved from www.un.org/ga/econcrisissummit/docs/FinalReport_CoE.pdf. Accessed on August 8.

Zettelmeyer, J., Trebesch, C., & Gulati M. (2012). The Greek debt exchange: An autopsy. Retrieved from SSRN: http://ssrn.com/abstract = 2144932

THEME 2
MORALIZING MARKETS THROUGH FAIR TRADE AND CORPORATE SOCIAL RESPONSIBILITY

DEFIANCE IN THE SOCIAL SPHERE: THE COMPLEXITY OF RISK REGULATION IN THE CASE OF FAIR TRADE

Anna Hutchens

ABSTRACT

The evolution of the Fair Trade movement offers an apposite case through which to examine the idea of regulating risk through a "social sphere." An analysis of Fair Trade through the lens of "defiance" reveals discrete models and actors of risk regulation that evolve in an iterative fashion. These findings not only add complexity and heterogeneity to the social actors and mechanisms of regulation in the social sphere, but also highlight the challenges this diversity poses for the project of alleviating market risk. In turn, the framework of defiance offers a fertile analytical framework for the study of transnational risk regulation by capturing the dynamic actor and institutional complexities that underpin, and embody challenges for, the regulation of risk through the social sphere. The article begins with an overview of the Fair Trade movement and consideration of Fair Trade's approach to regulating market risk. It then introduces the notion of defiance,

From Economy to Society? Perspectives on Transnational Risk Regulation
Studies in Law, Politics, and Society, Volume 62, 163–187

ISSN: 1059-4337/doi:10.1108/S1059-4337(2013)0000062007

focusing on two of its subtypes: game playing and resistance. Following a short overview of the methodological framework employed to analyze these dynamics, the third section applies these analytical categories of defiance to explore primary data gathered on Fair Trade's evolution. The article shows that the motivational posture of game playing, through its continued experimentation and entrepreneurship in transnational risk regulation, is pregnant with potential to mitigate the risks generated by economic activity.

Keywords: Power; defiance; nongovernment organizations (NGOs); Fair Trade

INTRODUCTION

The evolution of the Fair Trade[1] movement offers an apposite case through which to examine the idea of regulating risk through a "social sphere" or civil society (O'Malley, Rose, & Valverde, 2006; Pavlich & Wickham, 2000). Since the mid-20th century the Fair Trade movement has experimented with regulating the risks faced by small producers and artisans through social norms and institutions to improve the conditions and terms on which they interact with global markets. However, an analysis of Fair Trade through the lens of "defiance" (Braithwaite, 2009) reveals discrete models and actors of risk regulation that evolve in an iterative fashion. These findings not only add complexity and heterogeneity to the social actors and mechanisms of regulation in the social sphere, but also and more importantly highlight the challenges or threats posed by this diversity to the project of alleviating market risk. This highlights the value of defiance as an analytical tool in the study of transnational risk regulation: defiance captures the dynamic actor and institutional complexities that exist within, are produced by, and pose ongoing challenges to regulating risk through, the social sphere.

The article is set out in four parts. The first considers the Fair Trade movement's approach to regulating market risk, defining risk in terms of information asymmetries between producers and traders in global markets. The second section introduces the concept of "defiance" (Braithwaite, 2009), focusing on and then elaborating two particular types of defiance, resistance and game playing, in the regulation of risk through the social sphere. This elaboration explains how the relationship between resistance and game playing makes risk-regulation through civil society an unpredictable and ongoing project. The third section draws on the author's primary field data and existing research to empirically illustrate these types of defiance as discrete models of risk regulation that have driven Fair Trade's development in an iterative fashion and which give expression to the real tensions that challenge the project of mitigating market risk. The fourth section briefly concludes.

REGULATING RISK IN FAIR TRADE

> Fair Trade is a trading partnership, based on dialogue, transparency and respect that seeks greater equity in international trade. It contributes to sustainable development by offering better trading conditions to, and securing the rights of, marginalized producers and workers – especially in the South. Fair Trade organizations (backed by consumers) are engaged actively in supporting producers, awareness raising and in campaigning for changes in the rules and practice of conventional international trade. (WFTO, 2009a)

Since the mid-20th century the Fair Trade movement has experimented with regulating markets with social norms and institutions to mitigate the risks faced by small producers and artisans in engaging with the international trading system. In the sociological literature "risk" is classically defined as "a systematic way of dealing with hazards and insecurities induced and introduced by modernization itself" (Beck, 1992, p. 21).[2] As Giddens (1999, p. 4) goes on to explain, while industrial society was characterized by natural or "external" risk (such as natural disasters), modern society is characterized by "manufactured" risk, which involves human agency in its production and mitigation (such as pollution, crime, exploitation). This article is interested in the agency of actors within the social sphere that have acted (i.e., exercised agency) to redress the risks produced by inequitable power relationships in global markets.[3] Specifically, "risk" in the context of Fair Trade refers to the "risk" of exploitation of small producers by more informed and resourced market actors who capitalize on an unequal power structure in the global market.[4] As Nicholls and Opal (2005, p. 18) describe:

> A fundamental necessity for the functioning of any free market is "perfect information," implying that producers and traders have access to knowledge about market prices. Remote producers with no access to radio, newspapers, or telephones cannot access information about prices, and are at the mercy of the middlemen who come to their often isolated farms.[5]

For example, marginalized producers tend to have limited information or knowledge about market prices and trends, their competitors, who their end-buyers are and the retail prices their goods sell for, in which markets their goods sell, whether they will be paid and how much they will receive, expected quality standards and industry requirements, or future orders or prices. In addition to addressing these sources of uncertainty among producers, the Fair Trade movement tackles the risks faced by weaker market actors which flow from an unequal playing field steeped in specific historical political (and in some cases colonial) relations. The Fair Trade movement has attempted to mitigate the risk of exploitation and marginalization that producers face through principles that both reduce information disequilibria between producers and traders and reallocate risk more evenly across the trading chain. The movement of Fair Trade Organizations (FTOs) has sought to implement and promote several principles in trading and business relations to mitigate this primary source of risk for producers.[6]

Direct Purchasing from Producers

The requirement that traders purchase directly from producer organizations reduces producers' lack of information about buyers and their location, and enables greater communication and information sharing between the producer and trader. Direct relations and communication with the buyer can increase producers' security about, and ability to plan for, future orders while steady buyers can be a source of ongoing and direct information about quality and industry requirements or new market trends. They can also provide valuable feedback from the market to help producers make quality improvements.

Producer Organization into Cooperatives

The requirement for producers to organize into cooperatives can help reduce producers' lack of information about market prices and other market information. Often producers are atomized and have contact with – and access to information about – the market only through exploitative middlemen. Organizing with other producers and gaining awareness of the prices other farmers receive can increase producers' collective bargaining power, and enable them to pool incomes to purchase the resources (phones, faxes, internet, radios, newspapers) to access information on market prices and trends, quality standards and industry requirements, and to purchase for instance storage facilities that enable producers to have greater control over when they sell to buyers (Nicholls & Opal, 2005, pp. 34–45).

Transparent and Long Term Trading Relations

The requirement for importers to commit to transparent relations and long-term trading contracts with producers can help address information asymmetries for producers by locking in prices which in turn gives producers greater income security (Nicholls & Opal, 2005, p. 40). It can also open up the opportunity for producers to diversify into other crops or products if they have greater assurance about long-term relations with a buyer. Greater transparency in the chain can improve producers' knowledge about the end retail price of the products they sell which can increase their bargaining power in price negotiations with other buyers.

Set Minimum Prices

The requirement for agreed or set minimum prices provides producers with the knowledge and certainty to be able to invest in meeting both day-to-day needs for fundamental well-being and in longer term outcomes in relation to business (such as crop/product/service diversification), or to family and community assets such as schools, medical facilities, or roads (WFTO, 2009b, p. 5).

Capacity Building

The requirement for capacity building equips producer organizations with information about market conditions and trends as well as new knowledge and skills that enable producers to exercise greater control over their circumstances (WFTO, 2009b, p. 5). Building producer capacity through sharing information and knowledge aims to overcome the initially unequal and dependent relationship between producers and traders in the Fairtrade system.

As can be seen, these principles of Fair Trade are designed in order to spread or reallocate risk more evenly across the supply chain by reducing the information disequilibria between producers and other market chain actors, primarily buyers. As a way of promoting and exercising these norms or principles for regulating risk, two primary regulatory mechanisms or tools have evolved: the most traditional, an organizational model and the more recent product-based "Fairtrade" product certification and labelling system. These distinct approaches are analyzed below.

Fairtrade Product Certification and Labelling

Fairtrade certification and labelling has emerged to enable "Fairtrade" labelled products to enter and be sold through mainstream distribution and retail channels and by dominant large-scale corporations operating in these circuits. Governed by the Fairtrade Labelling Organizations International (FLO), Fairtrade product certification focuses on "verification and communication of 'Fairtrade' product attributes" (Lockie, 2008, p. 216). Product-based certification involves compliance with codified rules, norms, and expectations associated with more conventional quality-assurance and supply-chain traceability schemes, and compliance is verified by independent third-party auditors. FLO auditors monitor producer organizations that are seeking FLO registration for their compliance with "Fairtrade" requirements set by FLO in the North while trade standards and requirements (ostensibly payment of a Fairtrade minimum price and premium) are audited by FLO staff at the level of the exporter and importer. These requirements include long-term contracts, direct trading relationships, advanced credit, guaranteed minimum prices, and social premiums (Nicholls & Opal, 2005). This model of product verification adheres to rules on standard-setting, auditing, and certification established by supranational bodies such as the International Organization for Standardization (ISO). FLO's system has evolved in a more market-oriented or market-friendly fashion to encourage the participation of conventional corporations in its system such as *Nestle*, *Starbucks*, *Procter & Gamble*, *Cadbury's*, and *Chiquita*, and retailers including *Wal-Mart*, *Tesco's*, the UK's *Co-op* and *Sainsbury's*, and Switzerland's two major national chains *Migros* and *Coop*. These players offer Fairtrade products significant opportunity for mainstream market growth and volume increase.

Fair Trade Organizations

By contrast with FLO's market-oriented model, fair or "alternative" trading networks link producer organizations, traders/wholesalers, committed "world shops" (Fair Trade retailers), activists/volunteers, and consumers which have historically operated on the basis of interpersonal interaction, trust, and a dedication to a "mission," rather than on formal product guarantees. The 300+ organizations that identify with this movement, such as Ten Thousand Villages, SERRV International, GEPA, Oxfam, and Trade Aid, are formally certified as "Fair Trade Organizations" by the World Fair Trade Organization (WFTO, formerly the International Fair Trade Association, or IFTA). Traditionally the credibility of FTO claims have been upheld by strong ties of trust between producers, FTOs, and consumers where Fair Trade was expressed through practices between traders and producers rather than "performance targets" or adherence to formal certification against set criteria for their merchandise (Tallontire, 2002). Lockie (2008, p. 219) suggests these more informal, subjective processes of regulating performance are possible within FTO networks because they are small enough to allow "direct interpersonal relationship building and trust." While less rigorous and transparent than FLO's model its advantage is that it targets poor producers more effectively, is responsive to mutually identified priorities, and increases producer returns by eliminating costs of independent certification (*ibid.*, 2002). In 2004 the WFTO introduced a new three-tiered system for guaranteeing quality including self-assessment, mutual review (second-party conformity assessment), and external verification of performance on the "10 Standards of Fair Trade Organizations," which is recognized by the FTO Mark for use on marketing materials (but not on products).

These two models of Fair Trade reflect distinct approaches to regulating the market risk faced by producers in global markets. They also engage with different actors and use different regulatory tools to do so. Whereas, the FLO system is based on formal, independent, and compliance-oriented auditing and verification, seeks to involve large scale traders of large-volume (primarily food) products, and operates within the dominant production and consumption circuits in which these actors operate, the FTO approach to regulating risk is more trust based – involving informal and subjective mechanisms – and governed by a membership of actors committed philosophically to broader principles of Fair Trade. These actors deal in smaller volumes of primarily craft-type products and through relatively small-scale retail, import, and wholesale circuits.

THE COMPLEXITY OF REGULATING RISK THROUGH THE SOCIAL SPHERE: THE LENS OF DEFIANCE

While the foregoing analysis of the Fair Trade movement's different models, approaches, and principles to regulating risk helps to map the broad contours of the Fair Trade landscape under examination in this article, the lens of "defiance" (Braithwaite, 2009) provides a fertile analytical framework for understanding this picture. This section introduces the concept of "defiance" and elaborates two particular types of defiance, "resistance" and "game playing," as two distinct and iterative approaches to and models of risk regulation. This elaborated theoretical framework (Hutchens, 2009) reveals the challenges and threats posed by this diversity for the project of regulating market risk.

Defiance

Defiance is a term Braithwaite (2009) uses to refer to the psychology of defying institutional and structural constraints. Individuals express defiance through words, actions, or both as a communicative signal of their "unwillingness to follow the authority's prescribed path without question or protest" (Braithwaite, 2009, p. 26). Braithwaite (2009, p. 29) views defiance as a necessary response when "institutions cease to serve citizens well or dominate their lives to the point where they cause distress and destruction" and enables them to "forg[e] a path to institutional change." Recognizing social institutions can be both enabling and constraining, defiance captures how individuals move to preserve their freedom in the context of institutional constraint by creating some degree of "distance" between themselves and the regulator or authority.

The degree of distance individuals seek to put between themselves and the regulatory code differs from person to person, is dynamic, and the modes of distancing are creative:

> Expressions of defiance are wide-ranging and constantly in creation, most obvious in overt oppositional actions to discredit or undermine regulatory authority and practice. Contexts of defiant expression extend from war, protest, mutiny, strike and social movements at the collective level to acts of criminality, deviance, genius, eccentricity and mischief-making at the individual level. (Braithwaite, 2009, p. 34)

As I will explain in the following section, the different degrees of distance that different actors put between themselves and the authority create real tensions and challenges that ultimately threaten the goal of reducing market risk.

To capture or concretize these degrees of distance, Braithwaite develops distinct categories of defiance which she calls "motivational postures." Motivational postures embody "sets of beliefs and attitudes that sum up how individuals feel about and wish to position themselves in relation to another social entity ... Postures are subjective – they bind together the cognitive, emotional and behavioural components of attitude. They provide the narrative within which the authority's message is given meaning. They have coherence for the self and are socially acceptable to significant others" (Braithwaite, 2009, p. 20). In her research on the Australian taxation system, Braithwaite (2009, p. 39) identified the following motivational postures:

1. *Commitment* to the system, represents the degree to which individuals knowingly and willingly embrace the mission of the regulatory institution.
2. Similarly common is *capitulation* to the standards imposed by the regulatory authority, without necessarily engaging with the regulatory code or its purpose.
3. *Resistance* involves outspoken opposition to the way in which an authority uses its powers. Those who resist want to be heard, and they want the system to change for the better.
4. Individuals who *disengage* from or "game" authority appear to be stepping outside or transcending the constraints of the regulatory institution. Disengagement entails psychological dissociation from authority.
5. *Game playing* represents a more imaginative and bold practice for escaping regulatory constraint by moving around or redefining the rules. This response involves keen engagement with the regulatory code, analyzing the system that administers it with disarming acuity and clarity of purpose, and using the code to dismantle or change the meaning of regulations.

Resistance and Game Playing: Models and Dynamics of Risk Regulation

Two postures of defiance are particularly relevant in the case of Fair Trade: resistance and game playing.[7] As Braithwaite's schema describes, "resistance" involves active defiance, and resisters want their criticisms heard and want to play a part in changing the system for the better.

Resisters challenge regulations and regulatory administrators, yet not by creating new norms or rules. Instead resisters inject new or radical ideas of others into the system. In order to do so, they "yield" to the norms and constraints imposed by the existing order. As Braithwaite, Makkai, and Braithwaite (2007, p. 292) describe, "resisters often lose the argument and succumb to become a compliant citizen of the regulatory order over time."

"Game playing" by contrast is a more "imaginative" and "bold" form of defiance. It involves defying or transcending regulatory constraints through "moving around or redefining the rules" of the game. Game players innovate where there is an absence of recognition of authority: they think outside the square rather than acknowledge the confines of convention. The "game player" is a creative and visionary individual seeking transformation of his/her regulatory environment.

Elsewhere I have examined and developed the postures of resistance and game playing in the context of the Fair Trade movement in which the two postures occupy opposite ends of a spectrum of agency – one is conservative, the other radical (though the two are not rigid or homogenous categories). At the same time, they share an iterative existence (see also Braithwaite, 1998; Hutchens, 2007, 2009). In this process, resisters transport the game players' radical model from the periphery to the center to make money out of the propagation or institutionalization of the model. To achieve institutional acceptance of the model, resisters negotiate with and make compromises for institutional actors, leading to resisters' "capture" and the modification of the game players' more radical model. Unlike resisters, game players cannot be captured. Instead they re-innovate in new models when earlier models become captured to enable the evolution in the normative basis of markets to continue. In this regard, game playing holds the potential for agency and empowerment of both self and others by freeing structures from their traditional institutional anchors, producing new structures and institutions (Hutchens, 2009).

Applied to risk regulation, this actor and institutional dynamic creates ongoing challenges to the project of alleviating market risk for vulnerable producers in world markets. On the one hand, game players create innovative models of risk sharing (in the Fair Trade movement's case, "information-sharing") that *redistribute risk more evenly* among all supply chain actors and *reduce risk asymmetries* suffered by weaker actors. On the other hand, resisters seek to institutionalize the model but their approach to doing so (through negotiation, compromise) results in the model's modification and its reduction to minimum elements. While modifying the model enables resisters to attract institutional actors to the model, this process implies reallocating or redistributing risk disproportionately to weaker actors – as well as introducing new sources and sites of risk. In response, game players re-innovate with yet more radical models of information and knowledge sharing designed to advance or ratchet up weaker actors' control over information and knowledge in the trading relationship.

The point of this elaborated framework for the purposes of this article is that it illuminates an ongoing tension between the two types of actor within the social sphere that pose challenges to the prospect of mitigating market risk. Resisters place the project in jeopardy by their approach to institutional engagement while game players seek to recapture and elevate the level of risk-mitigation they seek to create for weaker market actors. The article now turns to the Fair Trade movement where these complex evolutions and dynamics in risk regulation are empirically demonstrable.

METHOD

The data that informed this analysis derive from empirical research conducted as part of a research project on the globalization of the Fair Trade movement (Hutchens, 2007, 2009). The data were collected during April–May and June–July in 2005, and include more than 60 semi-structured interviews (primarily face-to-face and several by phone) with Fair Trade practitioners. Respondents were selected in a snowball fashion, starting with a network of academic colleagues who had links to practitioners within the Fair Trade industry. Subsequent respondents were identified and referred to by those initial interviewees.

This approach to recruitment was informed by the methodological idea of selecting participants for their "competence" or expertise not their "representativeness" to help gain insight into a dense (regulatory) "culture" about which little is known. The notion of investigating *regulatory* fields as anthropological cultures derives from Braithwaite and Drahos' (2000) study of global business regulation in which they perceived themselves as anthropologists and ethnographers of rich "cultures" or communities of global regulation. Recognizing the explanatory limits of micro-micro and macro-macro methods, the authors adopted a micro analysis (of individual perceptions) of macro events (global regulation) to build a micro-macro theory of regulatory globalization.

In the context of addressing my research concerns, this nuanced and novel method for studying the socio-legal phenomenon of global business regulation was apposite, and data collection for my project followed this method. Referrals were obtained for the staff from the international "Fairtrade" product certification body, the FLO and various Labelling Initiative (LIs) in Europe and the United States, FTOs, specialty and "mainstream" coffee companies, and producer representatives in Mexico. Different "cultures" within the movement were identified as were their roles in informing the development of the international Fair Trade systems. The interaction between these cultures and systems was examined in the case of the coffee industry/market in which the strategy of "mainstreaming" Fairtrade products (inserting Fairtrade-labelled products into mainstream distribution channels) was first attempted.

DEFIANCE IN FAIR TRADE

The Fair Trade movement emerged in the context of the post-World War II political economy[8] to promote "trade not aid" and to demonstrate that marginalized producers and artisans in developing countries could realize economic independence and development if the conditions and terms of international trade were changed in their interests. The "Alternative Trade" (now "Fair Trade") Organizations that promoted this vision emerged throughout the 1950s and 1960s, then more consistently in the 1970s and 1980s, across Europe and Northern America. These organizations, many from religious, missionary, or charitable backgrounds, sought to establish and expand a "parallel" trading system for craft and textile products as well as coffee, tea and spices, by selling to ideologically committed consumers through mail-order catalogues, social networks, and church services as well as through nonprofit shops. This system was designed on the idea of providing producers with access to higher returns, Northern consumer markets and technologies, education and credit, and to traders who would treat them with respect and educate consumers in the North about the unfair terms of international trade (Barratt-Brown, 1993; Tallontire, 2000). These organizations subscribe to an expansive set of criteria (see below) that apply to "100 percent" of organizational conduct set out by the WFTO (formerly the International Fair Trade Association, or IFAT), which was established in 1989 to represent and further the mission of FTOs in the North and South (Table 1).

As explained earlier, these expansive principles work to reduce producers' risk through information sharing between producers and traders to

Table 1. 10 Standards for Fair Trade Organizations (FTOs).

1. Creating opportunities for economically disadvantaged producers; supporting the poorest producers.
2. Transparency and accountability; dealing fairly and openly with trading partners.
3. Trading Practices; the trading organization maintains long-term relationships based on solidarity, trust, and mutual respect; provides timely payment of Fair Trade wage; provides interest-free prepayment upon request from suppliers.
4. Payment of a fair price; ensuring that producers receive a fair price for their products.
5. Child Labor and Forced Labor; ensuring that the UN Convention on the Rights of the Child is respected.
6. Nondiscrimination, gender equity, and freedom of association; providing equal pay and opportunities for women and men.
7. Working Conditions; ensuring that producers are working in a healthy and safe place.
8. Capacity building; developing the skills of producers and creating opportunities for trading their products.
9. Promoting Fair Trade; telling as many people as possible about Fair Trade and informing customers where products have come from.
10. The Environment; ensuring that materials used in production and packing do not damage the environment From the "10 Standards of Fair Trade Organizations (FTOs)" (WFTO, 2009c).

www.wfto.com

strengthen producers' position in the trading relationship and provide them with greater economic security. While FTOs enjoyed a period of growth into the 1980s among committed consumers, by the end of the decade the charity-oriented rather than commercially oriented operations common among FTOs began to struggle in the face of growing competition (Littrell & Dickson, 1999; Low & Davenport, 2005, p. 146; Nicholls & Opal, 2005). As Renard (2003, pp. 89–90) notes, although the FTO model "questioned the mechanisms of the dominant market system and proposed a fairer relationship between producers and consumers, it was far from resolving the problems of selling third world products." According to Renard (2003, p. 90), the inconvenience of getting to "alternative" stores and the unattractiveness for the broader population of the political message associated with alternative trade were major impediments to selling more.

In this context a new model of Fair Trade was created to continue to mitigate producers' market risk while at the same time help them to access larger "mainstream" markets. A producer organization in Mexico and Netherlands-based Nongovernment Organization (NGO) Solidaridad developed a product certification and labelling system designed to communicate to mainstream consumers that a product, affixed with the Fairtrade label, had been made and traded under Fairtrade conditions. Using the label as a communicative device would, it was thought, help move Fair Trade products beyond the FTO store. This model was developed and promoted initially by national LIs and then later with the centralized support of the umbrella organization the FLO. FLO instituted a new governance structure in which LI voices were dominant and producer voices marginal and today, FLO is the worldwide standard-setting and certification organization for labelled Fairtrade products with three main responsibilities: setting the international Fairtrade standards, product certification and trade auditing, and producer support services.

Since its inception the Fairtrade certification system has been led by distinct actors who are eager to engage and work with mainstream traders. FLO's mission is to "connect consumers and producers via a label which promotes fairer trading conditions, through which producers who are disadvantaged by conventional trade can combat poverty, strengthen their position and take more control over their lives … ." To achieve its mission FLO's national LIs promote the Fairtrade label in their respective markets, particularly among mainstream distributors, to realize Fairtrade market growth. A practitioner from FLO's national LI in the United States reflected this market-oriented view:

> … our attempt is not to overthrow global capitalism, but to work within the mechanisms of global capitalism, to shift its *benefits* to people in the countries where many of the products we consume originate. We're not anti-WTO protestors, we're not throwing rocks at Starbucks or other companies … we're very much working *with* these companies and see them as actual or potential allies and friends to work with us to develop the growth of Fair Trade and simply to shift more of the benefits back to poor farmers … we're very business-oriented and free-market oriented, and we believe strongly that for Fair Trade to work in the United States, we have to understand the market and we have to embrace it and we have to work within the free market … (fieldwork notes)

It has also evolved into a qualitatively different regulatory model for regulating market risk from the FTO system. Rather than a system of trust and informal and subjective monitoring, the FLO system, though initially based on a strong producer-focus (Audebrand & Pauchant, 2009), has become more market-driven and beholden to market demands and requirements involves specific standards and external, third-party auditing of both traders and producers (Doppler & González Cabañas, 2006; Lockie, 2008; Nicholls & Opal, 2005; Renard & Perez-Grovas, 2007).

According to activists and researchers, this model has stripped the more expansive model of Fair Trade promoted by FTOs of its more radical elements as it does not aim to change the rules and practices of "business as usual" and world trade. Rather it promotes Fairtrade as "a simple extension of conventional trade" with the inclusion of "additional rules and standards" (Bezençon & Blili, forthcoming). As Raynolds (2008, p. 3) puts it, the FLO system "refashion[s] Fair Trade's alternative principles, based on fairness and trust, into a management system, based on formal standards and bureaucratic oversight."

For economically vulnerable producers, the Fairtrade system has become increasingly difficult to understand with reporting requirements and certification criteria becoming more complex and onerous for producer organizations to manage (Doppler & González Cabañas, 2006; Jaffee, Kloppenburg, & Monroy, 2004). Studies also indicate the lack of understanding among producers within the Fairtrade system about what Fairtrade is (Shreck, 2005). In fact, since FLO created an independent auditing arm, FLO-CERT, in 2002 which charged producers costly certification fees for registration, producers have become more akin to anonymous clients rather than genuine beneficiaries of the system. While entry fees give producers access to Fairtrade markets, they do not guarantee business for the producer. This is the producer's responsibility. As FLO-CERT's (2009) website cautions:

> … you [the producer] should find out if there are any buyers who want to buy your products under Fairtrade terms in the countries you want to sell to. Being certified does not guarantee that you will sell your product to the Fairtrade market on Fairtrade terms … [your organisation will also] have to pay for the annual audits and the actual costs … You should decide whether you think the costs are going to be worth the expected benefits.

While traders have a register of producers to buy from, producers remain largely at the whims of buyers, a feature of the Fairtrade system which does little to alleviate producers' lack of information about the market (Doppler & González Cabañas, 2006). This lack of information about or support to navigate the end market heightens the risk of investing in Fairtrade registration.

Through FLO's relatively opaque governance structure small-scale producers have also had little influence over controversial policies that challenge their interests, including a policy to certify plantation farms as Fairtrade and to allow disreputable large-scale traders into the Fairtrade system (Renard & Perez-Grovas, 2007, p. 150).[9] The policy to certify plantations potentially displaces the principle of (and adherents to) cooperative or collective organization for improved information and knowledge sharing in that large-scale traders can work with large-scale farming operations instead of working with small-scale producer groups in need of support.

Other principles affecting producers' access to information, such as direct, transparent, and long-term relations and capacity building, also appear to be rare practices among conventional traders in the FLO system (Bezençon & Blili, 2006; Raynolds, 2008; Renard & Pérez-Grovas, 2007). For instance FLO does not define "long term" in the contractual relations between traders and producers beyond the signing of contracts (Nicholls & Opal, 2005) and as more actors have come into the system and repopulated the Fairtrade supply chain, producers often do not know the end buyer of their crop when they sell to conventional (as opposed to Fair Trade) traders in FLO's system (see, e.g., Raynolds, 2008). Moreover while the Fairtrade system remunerates producers for raw commodity production and provides a social premium for development projects, it does not increase their share of more value-added activities such as branding/retailing (Hutchens, forthcoming); in fact producers have little knowledge of the significant gap between their returns and the end retail price of Fairtrade goods even in the presence of Fairtrade minimum prices and premiums (see Moberg, 2005, p. 10). The absence of these principles for trading relations perpetuates producers' risk burden in the sense that information asymmetries between themselves and traders remain largely untouched.

Moreover, the Fairtrade principles or requirements are also only applicable to those companies that put the Fairtrade label on the product. Retailers, who represent an increasing number of buyers in the system and the majority of sales of Fairtrade stock, are exempt in this case as they tend to *outsource* packing and labelling to other companies. Recent research suggests that retailers have abused this loophole in the system and continued to pursue a largely commercial agenda in Fairtrade production networks. This has resulted in retailers dishonouring or reneging on contracts with producer groups – including switching to other producers, cancelling/reducing orders after shipment, charging "fines" for poor quality after refusing to collect orders on time, and purchasing from the cheapest Fairtrade suppliers available (Barrientos & Smith, 2007, pp. 114–115). These commercial or competitive dynamics common to conventional markets but at a real cost to producers effectively makes the Fairtrade market a new site of risk for producers (in addition to conventional markets) given not only the system's lack of systematic redress of producers' information asymmetry with traders but also the lack of information producers have within and about this system. As Eastern Caribbean banana producers in Moberg's (2005, p. 13) study commented:

> … many of us wonder whether this [Fairtrade] will last. A lot of farmers now know that [Fairtrade] doesn't give him any more control over what he produces, how he produces it, or how he packages it. It's a new kind of dependence.

FLO's approach to institutionalizing the Fairtrade product certification and labelling system reflects the posture of "resistance." As explained earlier, in the process of change the role of resisters is to engage institutional actors in institutionalizing game players' innovative models but as a result of which engagement "resisters often lose the argument and succumb to become a compliant citizen of the regulatory order over time" (Braithwaite et al., 2007, p. 292) and thus vulnerable to institutional "capture" (Ayres & Braithwaite, 1992). While the Fair Trade pioneers in the Netherlands and Mexico held more radical expectations of this model of risk-sharing (Roozen & Vanderhoff, 2002) which sought to *redistribute risk more evenly* among all supply chain actors and *reduce risk asymmetries* suffered by producers, the resisters – FLO/the LIs – have modified and reduced this model to its essential elements to help institutionalize a more market-friendly model of Fairtrade that dominant retailers and manufacturers will support. Though the system is increasingly compatible with mainstream market requirements and other quality assurance schemes (Lockie, 2008), the initial model of risk-regulation promoted in producers' favour has changed to one in which producers bear, once again, a disproportionate share of risk and face new risks (information asymmetries).

While the relatively benign model of risk regulation institutionalized by FLO suggests that the Fair Trade movement has "succumbed" to corporate institutional influence and market demands, several pioneers within the movement – who initially conceived and set up the certification and labelling system – have responded by launching new and more radical models of Fair Trade. These models were designed to recapture and elevate the competitive challenge for conventional traders that have demonstrated minimal commitment to principles of Fair Trade, such as capacity building, that reduce producers' level of risk/vulnerability:

> … [the brands] were designed to achieve a few things. One was – when we started [the brand] Cafédirect, it was designed to give small-scale producers who had really worked *hard* to learn how to access the market, somebody to sell to, someone to call their own … Because you know that old adage "you can lead a horse to water but you can't make it drink?" The thing about Transfair and the [Fair]trade-marking models – … [is that] the [Fairtrade] label made it possible for conventional companies to buy directly from small

> farmers and get some kind of reward for that … but it didn't make [conventional companies] *do* [Fair Trade] with many small-farmer organizations, especially the weaker ones with which they just didn't want to get involved. They tended to pick the ones that were more capable, more able. And that's not very developmental … (fieldwork notes)

This observation highlights pioneers' dissatisfaction with the effect of the Fairtrade system in terms of promoting information and knowledge sharing (such as through capacity building) between traders and producers and the creative nature of their response. Rather than accept the fate of, or be constrained by, the institutional capture of the FLO model, the pioneers in the market opted to re-challenge conventional traders, in effect play competitive games with them, by ratcheting up and shifting the terms of competition. As one pioneer described:

> I always see it as a kind of challenge model, you have to challenge in order to get [others to change] … but if you want to challenge, you have to be able to move up [to the next stage of the "game"] yourself … your influence will diminish when the others are responding … from the moment you stop innovating you're already losing. … if [FLO] don't become the innovators again – if they don't become the standard-setting initiative – they'll be forgotten and others will take their place … [FLO] is just one of the stakeholders [now], not the big guys setting the standards … (fieldwork notes)

In this context, several pioneers in the Fair Trade market began to develop for-profit Fair Trade brands positioned in the mainstream market – ostensibly brand companies that exploited commercial and legal tools of marketing and branding in which the producers were co-owners, board of directors, and shareholders of the trading company. The aim of this model was to enhance producers' control over information and knowledge in the trading relationship in ways not included in the FLO model, such as in the governance of the trading organization and the ownership of intellectual property (the trademark) and economic benefits (brand equity) that flow from it. It was also designed to reduce producers' risk more significantly and with greater certainty than the FLO model in that principles of direct, transparent, and long-term partnerships were given new meaning by creating trading companies jointly owned and controlled by producer organization(s) supplying the brand company (rather than an independent trading firm that purchase from suppliers anywhere in the world). This feature of the organizational structure and governance aimed to increase producers' knowledge and certainty over their trading partner and the prices, premiums *and dividends* they receive, or as the respondent above expressed it "to give small-scale producers somebody to sell to, someone to call their own." In fact, a particularly unorthodox feature of the FTO brand company is producer co-ownership over lucrative informational or "intangible" assets, namely the brand (see Hutchens, 2009). The level of information-sharing in this model, especially capacity building, is enhanced by virtue of the dependence of the success of the brand/product on producers' expertise and capacity.

An example is AgroFair, a farmer-owned banana and fresh fruits company. Spread across Ghana, Ecuador, and Costa Rica, AgroFair fruit farmers and cooperatives own 50 percent of AgroFair's shares and profits (AgroFair, 2006a, 2006b)[10] and new growers are offered company shares after a period of 12 months of trading with AgroFair. AgroFair producers gain direct experience and skills in value-added activities such as sales and marketing (rather than low-value activities such as raw commodity production as per FLO's model).[11] This novel enterprise has had much success in the banana sector in particular (its first product) with the Swiss retailer, *Coop*, which sells 100 percent of its bananas as Fairtrade (AgroFair, 2004, pp. 4, 24). In 2004, AgroFair's turnover increased by 47 percent to €37.6 million and a further 40 percent in 2006, with a turnover of €62 million plus a share dividend of €236,000 (half of which has gone to producers).

Another example is Divine Chocolate Ltd., set up in 1997 primarily between Twin Trading and the Ghanaian cocoa cooperative, Kuapa Kokoo.[12] Kuapa Kokoo producers have Board representation and co-own the brand: 33 percent since 1997 and 45 percent since 2006.[13] Divine's mission is multiform: to "take a quality affordable range of Fair Trade chocolate bars into the mainstream chocolate market," and to "pay a Fair Trade price for all the cocoa used in the products." Positioned consciously among other normal "mainstream" chocolate bars in terms of price, quality and availability, Divine aims to "raise awareness of Fair Trade issues among UK retailers and consumers of all ages" and "be highly visible and vocal in the chocolate industry and thereby act as a catalyst for change." Competing directly with major firms in the UK chocolate industry such as Cadbury and M&M/Mars, Divine Chocolate is available in 5,000 stores in the United Kingdom, including Sainsbury's, the Co-op, and Tesco supermarkets. It has also experimented with private own-label ventures with the UK's Co-op (for its entire own-brand chocolate) as well as Starbucks for all its own-brand chocolate. In 2003, the company reached profitability, and has continued to do so year on year. In 2006, with 18 percent growth, the company received a posttax profit of over £450,000, and after 10 years of business, in 2007 the company made its first dividend of £500/share (Martyn, 2007).

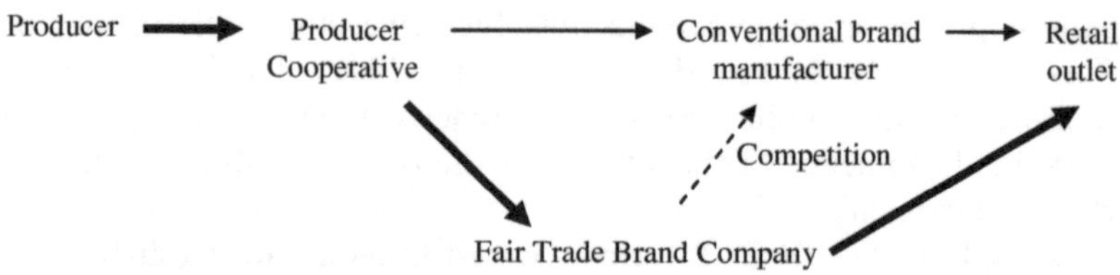

Fig. 1. Pioneers' Strategic Response to Conventional Brands in the Fairtrade System: Fair Trade Brands (adapted from Hutchens, 2009).

The strategic or "game" thinking behind farmer co-owned Fair Trade brands such as AgroFair and Divine was to bypass dominant traders in the Fairtrade market that take a minimalist approach to mitigating producers' market risk (see Fig. 1). Moving around these actors enables producers to gain direct access to mainstream retailers – via a benevolent rather than exploitative intermediary – while also giving them more control over that intermediary organization. The Fair Trade brand model further sought to stimulate competition between themselves and conventional corporate brands on the basis of performance/commitment to Fair Trade principles. They have done so by communicating (or marketing) to consumers their unique and radical features (such as producer co-ownership) as a source of competitive advantage (Doherty & Tranchell, 2007) and, on the basis of their success in doing so, to force conventional brands to respond to the demand generated for Fair Trade brand companies. This amplification of the market challenge is necessary to prevent the movement's regulatory mechanisms from the fate of locking producers into new systems and sites of risk.

The pioneers of the Fair Trade brand companies can be seen as the market's game players. By contrast with resisters, the movement's game players have re-innovated with more radical models of information and knowledge sharing (i.e., FTO brand companies) that aim to advance or ratchet up producers' control over information and knowledge in the trading relationship. This model is premised on principles of direct, transparent, and long-term relations between producer and trader in which producers have greater control over the trading company to which they sell their stock and co-ownership of its informational assets (the trademark). Producer knowledge and capacities are also prioritized as a matter of long-term business sustainability. This model of risk regulation has proved more challenging for institutional actors to coopt (Hutchens, 2009), as Braithwaite highlights, gaming elicits a distinct institutional response from institutional actors compared with resistance – game players keep their opponents "on their toes" and unable to turn their backs on the dynamic competitive tactics of the game player (Braithwaite, 2009, p. 96). The ongoing innovation-response of gaming is critical in the context of resisters' cooption and dilution of models of risk-regulation.

CONCLUSION

An analysis of the Fair Trade movement's experience in regulating risk through the lens of defiance captures the complexity of regulatory actors, motivational postures, and institutional effects that exist within the social sphere. The elaborated framework of defiance outlined in this article offers a psychosocial lens to the study of risk regulation and conceptually frames this space as diverse in agents, models, and institutions of risk regulation that are dynamic and iterative in their interaction but more importantly, explains how this diversity poses challenges for regulating, and threats to the goal of mitigating, market risks faced by weaker market actors in the global market. Understanding the significance of the social sphere in risk regulation pivots on understanding the triggers or switches of creativity and change that the defiance lens brings to the analytical foreground. In particular, the motivational posture of game playing is replete with potential to mitigate the risks generated by economic activity through its continued experimentation and entrepreneurship in transnational risk regulation.

NOTES

1. To clarify industry terminology, "Fair Trade" (written as two words) refers to the movement and the philosophy whereas "Fairtrade" (written as one word) refers specifically to the product certification and labeling system governed by FLO. Finally, unless otherwise indicated, respondent comments are kept anonymous and cited as fieldwork notes, in accordance with respondents' wishes.

2. The study of risk is broad, with little accepted definition or approach to its study across the disciplines (Zinn, 2009). Beck's (1992) definition of risk is used here as a classic which is typically credited with pioneering the study of risk regulation.

3. This article does not address the question of the extent to which those actors in more powerful positions in the global market produce and reproduce the power differential between themselves and less powerful actors. In transnational market structures this is a complex question which relates to individual and collective responsibility which is explored elsewhere (see, e.g., Young, 2004).

4. This idea fits well with Giddens' (1999, pp. 3–4) idea that risk does not only refer to a hazard or danger but also to control or lack thereof.

5. Lack of information is not the only type or source of risk that affects producers living in poverty, or the only one the movement has tackled, but will form the focal point in this article.

6. In the interests of space restrictions this article does not address how or to what extent these principles are achieved in practice.

7. It is outside the scope of this article to address or compare the two types of "authority" in the application of Braithwaite's schema, namely the Australian Taxation Office (a state regulatory authority) and the networked, "private" actors embodied in the Fair Trade accreditation bodies. In this article "authority" is conceived in its broadest sense to accommodate such differences, for instance an agency/organization and a social institution (such as the market) that regulates and constrains behavior with established rules and norms. In the case of Fair Trade, both resisters and game players are responding to the latter type of authority, namely the authority of global neoliberalism.

8. In this context poorer (mostly post-colonial) nations along with international institutions such as the UN Centre for Trade and Development (UNCTAD) were concerned with securing more equal terms of trade between the South and richer nations in the North (Fridell, 2004).

9. While FLO agreed to limit certification of plantations to plantation-only commodities (such as tea) and not in commodity sectors where small-scale production still exists, FLO has begun to certify plantations alongside small-scale producers in the banana and tropical fruit markets (Renard & Pérez-Grovas, 2007; Wilkinson & Mascarenhas, 2007).

10. AgroFair's NGO and ethical investor partners include TWIN, CTM Altromercato, Solidaridad, VIVA Trust, and Triodos Innovation Fund (AgroFair, 2006a).

11. AgroFair's FTO partners take responsibility for the day-to-day operation of sales and marketing in European, United Kingdom/Ireland, and Italian markets. In 2006, AgroFair's Oké-labelled bananas gained market access in the United States through a new Fair trade company, Oké USA. Oké USA is owned by AgroFair, Equal Exchange (US pioneer in Fair Trade coffee), and Red Tomato (Boston-based NGO that helps family farmers in New England to access markets, founded by cofounder of Equal Exchange). AgroFair farmers share ownership of the company's equity in addition receiving Fair Trade minimum prices and premiums.

12. Other investors and/or partners included The Body Shop, SNV, Comic Relief, DFID, the International Cocoa Organization, and Christian Aid (Tiffen, MacDonald, Mazmah & Osei-Opare, 2004, p. 24). Until July 2006, The Body Shop held ownership of 14 percent of shares, and Kuapa Kokoo 33 percent. The Body Shop donated its shares to Kuapa Kokoo which now owns 47 percent of the company.

13. In 2006 The Body Shop, a founding partner and shareholder in Divine, decided to donate its shares to Kaupa Kokoo.

ACKNOWLEDGMENTS

The author would like to gratefully acknowledge Professors Peter Drahos, Valerie Braithwaite, Fiona Haines, and Dr. Bettina Lange for their comments on, and keen engagement with, earlier drafts of this article. The author also wishes to thank Drs. Petrina Schiavi and Bina D'Costa for their encouragement and support during the writing of this article.

REFERENCES

AgroFair. (2004). *The Oke impact: 2004 annual report*. Retrieved from http://www.agrofair.nl/pages/view.php?page_id=318. Accessed on June 12, 2009.

AgroFair. (2006a). *About AgroFair – Profile and structure*. Retrieved from http://www.agrofair.nl/pages/view.php?page_id=320. Accessed on June 13, 2009.

AgroFair. (2006b). *The Oke impact: 2006 annual report*. Retrieved from http://www.agrofair.nl/upload/File/AgroFair_Annual_Report_2006_secure_ENG.pdf. Accessed on June 12, 2009.

Audebrand, L., & Pauchant, T. (2009). Can the fair trade movement enrich traditional business ethics? An historical study of its founders in Mexico. *Journal of Business Ethics*, *87*, 343–353.

Ayres, I., & Braithwaite, J. (1992). *Responsive regulation: Transcending the deregulation debate*. New York, NY: Oxford University Press.

Barratt-Brown, M. (1993). *Fair trade: Reform and realities in the international trading system*. London: Zed Books.

Barrientos, S., & Smith, S. (2007). Mainstreaming fair trade in global production networks fair trade. In L. Raynolds, D. Murray & J. Wilkinson (Eds.), *Fair trade: The challenges of transforming globalization*. New York, NY: Routledge.

Beck, U. (1992). *Risk society: Towards a new modernity*. London: Sage.

Bezençon, V., & Blili, S. (forthcoming). Fair trade managerial practices: Strategy, organisation and engagement. *Journal of Business Ethics*. Retrieved from http://www.springerlink.com/content/g078j6747156h717/?p=78f8b2254ac24653a251b2ff5da84474&pi=2. Accessed on October 24, 2009.

Bezençon, V., & Blili, S. (2006). Fair trade channels: Are we killing the romantics? *International Journal of Environmental, Cultural, Economic and Social Sustainability*, *2*(1), 187–196.

Braithwaite, V. (1998). Designing the process of workplace change through the affirmative action act. In M. Gatens & A. Mackinnon (Eds.), *Gender and institutions. Welfare, work and citizenship* (Chapter 7). Cambridge: Cambridge University Press.

Braithwaite, V. (2009). *Defiance in taxation and governance: Resisting and dismissing authority in a democracy*. Cheltenham, UK: Edward Elgar Publishers.

Braithwaite, J., & Drahos, P. (2000). *Global business regulation*. Cambridge: Cambridge University Press.

Braithwaite, J., Makkai, T., & Braithwaite, V. (2007). *Regulating aged care. Ritualism and the new pyramid*. Cheltenham, UK: Edward Elgar Publishers.

Doherty, B., & Tranchell, S. (2007). "Radical mainstreaming" of fairtrade: The case of the day chocolate company. *International Journal in Culture and Diversity in Marketing*, *26*(7), 315–327.

Doppler, F., & González Cabañas, A. A. (2006). Fair trade: Benefits and drawbacks for producers. *Puente @ Europa*, *4*(2), 53–56.

Fairtrade Labelling Organizations International (FLO-CERT). (2009). *Becoming a Fairtrade producer*. Retrieved from http://www.fairtrade.net/becoming_a_fairtrade_producer.html?&L=1s. Accessed on November 23, 2009.

Fridell, G. (2004). The fair trade network in historical perspective. *Canadian Journal of Development Studies, XXV*(3), 411–428.

Giddens, A. (1999). Risk and responsibility. *Modern Law Review, 62*(1), 1–10.

Hutchens, A. (2007, May 31). *Entrepreneurship, power and defiance: The globalisation of the Fair Trade movement.* Unpublished dissertation. The Regulatory Institutions Network (RegNet), The Australian National University (ANU), Canberra ACT Australia.

Hutchens, A. (2009). *Changing big business: The globalisation of the Fair Trade movement.* Cheltenham, UK: Edward Elgar Publishers.

Jaffee, D., Kloppenburg, J., & Monroy, M. (2004). Bringing the 'moral charge' home: Fair trade within the north and within the south. *Rural Sociology, 69*(2), 169–196.

Littrell, A., & Dickson, M. (1999). *Social responsibility in the global market: Fair Trade of cultural products.* Thousand Oaks, CA: Sage.

Lockie, S. (2008). Conversion or co-option? The implications of 'mainstreaming' for producer and consumer agency within Fair Trade networks. In C. Farnworth, J. Jiggins, & E. Thomas (Eds.), *Creating food futures: Trade, ethics and the environment.* Aldershot, UK: Gower. (Chapter 17.)

Low, W., & Davenport, E. (2005). Postcards from the edge: Maintaining the 'alternative' character of Fair Trade. *Sustainable Development, 13*, 143–153.

Martyn, T. (2007). *Capturing the intangible: Accessing marketing rents through farmer own-brands.* Masters dissertation. Faculty of Economics (Development Studies), London School of Economics (LSE), London.

Moberg, M. (2005). Fair Trade and eastern Caribbean banana farmers: Rhetoric and reality in the anti-globalization movement. *Human Organization, 64*(1), 4–15.

Nicholls, A., & Opal, C. (2005). *Fair Trade. Market driven ethical consumption.* London: Sage.

O'Malley, P., Rose, N., & Valverde, M. (2006). Governmentality. *Annual Review of Law and Social Science, 2*, 83–104.

Pavlich, G., & Wickham, G. (Eds) (2000). *Rethinking law, society and governance: Foucault's bequest.* Oxford: Hart Publishing.

Raynolds, L. (2008). Mainstreaming Fair Trade coffee: From partnership to traceability. *World Development, 37*(6), 1083–1093.

Renard, M.-C. (2003). Fair Trade quality, market and conventions. *Journal of Rural Studies, 19*, 87–96.

Renard, M.-C., & Pérez-Grovas, V. (2007). Fair Trade coffee in Mexico. At the center of the debates. In L. Raynolds, D. Murray & J. Wilkinson (Eds.), *Fair Trade. The challenges of transforming globalization.* New York, NY: Routledge.

Roozen, N., & Vanderhoff, F. (2002). *L'aventure du commerce équitable.* Paris: J.C. Lattès.

Shreck, A. (2005). Resistance, redistribution and power in the Fair Trade banana initiative. *Agriculture and Human Values, 22*, 17–29.

Tallontire, A. (2000). Partnerships in Fair Trade: Reflections from a case study of Cafédirect. *Development in Practice, 10*(2), 166–177.

Tallontire, A. (2002). Challenges facing fair trade: Which way now? *Small Enterprise Development, 13*(3), 12–24.

Tiffen, P., MacDonald, J., Mazmah, H., & Osei-Opare, F. (2004). From tree-minders to global players: Cocoa farmers in Ghana. In M. Carr (Ed.), *Chains of fortune: Linking women producers and workers with global markets.* London: Commonwealth Secretariat.

Wilkinson, J., & Mascarenhas, G. (2007). Southern social movements and Fair Trade. In L. Raynolds, D. Murray & J. Wilkinson (Eds.), *Fair Trade. The challenges of transforming globalisation*. New York, NY: Routledge.
World Fair Trade Organization (WFTO). (2009a). *What is fair trade?* Retrieved from http://www.wfto.com/index.php?option=com_content&task=view&id=1&Itemid=11. Accessed on November 21, 2009.
World Fair Trade Organization (WFTO). (2009b). *A charter of Fair Trade principles*. Retrieved from http://www.wfto.com/index.php?option=com_content&task=view&id=1082&Itemid=11. Accessed on November 29, 2009.
World Fair Trade Organization (WFTO). (2009c). *10 Standards of Fair Trade Organizations (FTOs)*. Retrieved from http://www.wfto.com/index.php?option=com_content&task=view&id=2&Itemid=14. Accessed on November 29, 2009.
Young, I. M. (2004). Responsibility and global justice: A social connections model. Paper presented at 'Global Justice' Conference, October 21–23, Bowling Green State University, Bowling Green, OH.
Zinn, J. (2009). The sociology of risk and uncertainty – Current state and perspectives. Paper delivered at the Australian Sociological Association's (TASA) 2009 conference, December 1–4, Australian National University, Australia.

"ETIQUETTE AND MAGIC": BETWEEN EMBEDDING AND EMBEDDED CORPORATE SOCIAL RESPONSIBILITY

Aurora Voiculescu

ABSTRACT

This article looks at corporate social responsibility (CSR) as a discursive social practice that attempts to interrogate the global market economy and its neoliberal underpinnings and that reflects as well as frames and shapes domestic and global politics and institutions. Drawing upon Karl Polanyi's notions of reciprocity and redistribution while also emphasizing the normative content of the concept, the article inquires into the position that the CSR discourse occupies in addressing the corporate transnational risks derived from social tensions and conflicts and more generally, in answering social expectations for justice. The Polanyian perspective highlights the CSR discursive quest for a missing conceptual consistency and implicitly, for a constructive "critical" core. From this perspective, the article shows CSR to reside within controversial conceptual boundaries; a discursive social practice that engages with the social aspiration of embedding market economy in society while it is

From Economy to Society? Perspectives on Transnational Risk Regulation
Studies in Law, Politics, and Society, Volume 62, 189–216

ISSN: 1059-4337/doi:10.1108/S1059-4337(2013)0000062008

also in need of reclaiming its critical core and its potential for social change.

Keywords: Corporate social responsibility; Polanyi; neoliberalism; social embeddedness; reciprocity and redistribution; civil economy

Writing on the cunning of imperialist reason, Bourdieu and Wacquant noted that the power to universalise particularisms that is linked to a singular historical tradition manifests itself by causing those particularisms to be "misrecognized" as universal (Bourdieu & Wacquant, 1999, p. 41). It is precisely with this kind of misrecognition that one is faced when pausing to reflect on the evolution of the concept of corporate social responsibility (CSR) and of the CSR discourse as a whole in the context of the contemporary (global) market economy paradigm. As a specific discursive practice that purports to bring ethics to business practices and to infuse market economy with social values, CSR attempts to interrogate the central tenets of the economic formula that it addresses. From this point of view, the CSR discourse has been strewn with diversions (Banerjee, 2008), taboos (Kallio, 2007), and with discursive strategies that allow the misrecognition of the market economy paradigm as universal to take place, limitting the actual critique of this paradigm while "[setting] the terms of such critique that they do permit" (Foster, 2009, p. 97).[1]

In a context in which the present global market economy paradigm appears to be characterized by complex social conflicts and tensions (Hutter, 2006, p. 217; Zinn & Taylor-Gooby, 2006, p. 69), is CSR emerging as a consistent concept that addresses the transnational risks associated with these conflicts? From Berlin'88 and Seattle'99 to the "Occupy the City" movement, the signals related to the social expectations for business responsibility and to the complex risks incurred by the present way of doing business are not lacking. CSR can be seen as a discursive practice that addresses various (transnational) risks associated with the global market economy. These risks appear two-faceted. On the one hand, with the sovereign nation state going through profound transformations of its functions and powers of "providing and protecting," there are increased risks for the environment, labor standards, human rights, the rule of law even, as reflections of various both acute and chronic social conflicts. On the other hand, the globalized market economy also creates operational risks for the business organizations themselves (Hutter & Power, 2005; Power, 2005). The risk of far-reaching consumer or other stakeholder actions; the risk of emerging undesirable regulatory instruments at domestic, regional and international level; the reputational risk related to business strategies that might be out of pace with various (global and local) social values, are only some of the most common risks associated with the new social responsibility environment. The two types of risk are often the two sides of the same coin: transnational risks stemming from social conflicts carry as a certain operational risks for the business organizations. In this context, CSR is put forward as "strategic intelligence" (Kytle & Ruggie, 2005) and first of defence against both types of risk (Louche, Idowu, & Filho, 2010).[2] At the same time, at a deeper conceptual level, CSR can also be seen as an interrogating tool that addresses the global market economy system and its neoliberal underpinnings as a risk-generating paradigm (Broomhill, 2007, p. 7; T. Carroll, 2012).

Following Karl Polanyi's critical contribution to the conceptualization of market economy, the article advances the idea that, through the interrogations addressed to it in the CSR discourse, the paradigm of a self-regulating market economy can be understood as a universalized particularism in the sense defined by Bourdieu and Wacquant above. Highlighting labor standards, human rights and environmental issues as being, on the one hand, at the heart of social conflicts and tensions that are increasingly brought about by the processes of global market economy, and on the other hand, at the heart of transnational risks with which business organizations need increasingly to grapple, the article inquires into the position that the CSR discourse occupies in the evolution – if not resolution – of social tensions and conflicts, as well as in offering credible tools for addressing corporate transnational risks. In particular, the article inquires into whether – in the context of global market processes – CSR is *the answer* to conflicts and tensions, or whether CSR is *merely* the question: a normative as well as an increasingly regulatory way of interrogating ideologies. In this sense, the concept of embeddedness as well as the principles of reciprocity and redistribution, such as they were developed by Polanyi,[3] inform the inquiry into the position of the CSR discourse within a rapidly changing – risk-generating and risk-managing – market economy. In particular, the principles of reciprocity and redistribution can be seen to structure the CSR discourse, particularly with respect to the emphasis on the "superabundant noneconomic motivation (Polanyi, 2002, p. 50)" that CSR might propose. Working with an intricate reciprocity map and engaging in complex structured redistribution is proposed from a Polanyian perspective on

CSR as a constructive way of valorizing the relationship with all stakeholders when engaging in economic activities and as a way for CSR to gain theoretical and empirical strength, as well as normative and regulatory consistency.

Drawing on his experience in social anthropology, Karl Polanyi advanced the idea that a laissez-faire economy based on the self-regulating market is a utopia and, as a social project, it proves too deficient to work. In his book *The Great Transformation* (Polanyi, 2002), Polanyi argued that the deficiencies of the liberal design of the market economy – based on minimal intervention and thus on self-referentiality[4] and self-regulation – could neither sustain the market processes nor meet community aspirations without government intervention. He argued that a (self-regulated) market economy could only exist in a "market society" and this, in turn, implied that the two spheres – market and society – were separated from each other. According to Polanyi, this paradigm constitutes a singular departure from previous ways of construing society and economy as interrelated within a web of "etiquette and magic" (Polanyi, 2002, p. 52). The "disembedded" nature of the market economy from its social environment would constitute, in Polanyi's view, the source of the critical failures of the market economy:

> … [The] control of the economic system by the market is of overwhelming consequence to the whole organization of society: it means no less than the running of society as an adjunct to the market. *Instead of economy being embedded in social relations, social relations are embedded in the economic system* […] For once the economic system is organized in separate institutions, based on specific motives and conferring a special status, society must be shaped in such a manner as to allow that system to function according to [*that system's*] own laws. This is the meaning of the familiar assertion that a market economy can function only in a market society. (Polanyi, 2002, p. 60, emphasis added)

This notion of a market that is disembedded from society is potentially relevant in deciphering some of the points of tension from which the CSR discourse has grown. A Polanyi-inspired perspective may help us elucidate CSR's role in linking social normative perspectives to contemporary market processes and to their institutional reflection, as well as understand the perspective from which this linkage is sought and the claims raised by the CSR discourse when interrogating the existing market paradigm. To begin addressing these issues, this article will first look into the way in which the definition and conceptual framework of the CSR discourse attempt to narrow the gap between the normative parameters of the neoliberal market economy and the social expectations related to the market that are characteristic at a given time. It will then look at some of the key perspectives on the morality of the market and of the link between market and morality, building on the neoliberal perspective and some of its critiques. The remaining part will address the way the concept of "embeddedness" and the related principles of reciprocity and redistribution can help with understanding, shaping, and eventually promoting the CSR discourse and the normative/regulatory dimensions that may be attached to it. Finally, the article looks at the place that the concept of CSR holds within a wider array of social practices and at whether such a concept can be seen as part of an "embedding mechanism" that employs both a normative and a regulatory path.

THE UNFINISHED BUSINESS OF THE CSR CONCEPTUAL FRAMEWORK

CSR is one of those concepts characterized by a hard core of ideas, which are present in a multitude of attempts at an institutional definition, and of a set of variable elements that might be part of some definitions but not of others (Corkin, 2008; Dahlsrud, 2006). Writing already three decades ago, Zenisek, for instance, spoke of CSR as meaning "something" but not always the same "something" to everyone (1979). As expected, when definitions are not settled, identifying the "aims and expectations" of a concept also becomes difficult (Boeger, Murray, & Villiers, 2008, p. 2). In principle, however, most definitions – though not all – present CSR as a business way of engaging with its own social environment by taking into consideration elements other than those strictly related to its profit-making functions. The main dimensions included under the umbrella of social responsibility – rather than strictly "corporate responsibility" – are the ones related to labor standards, human rights and environmental protection. Other issues, however, are often included here, either as additional dimensions – such as corporate philanthropy, corporate responsible investment – or as issues that cut across various CSR dimensions or even replace this concept altogether with "alternative thematic frameworks" (A. B. Carroll, 1999), such as social entrepreneurship, corporate ethics, corporate sustainability (van Marrewijk, 2003). Other terms come to add color and symbolism, advancing terms such as "corporate citizenship" (Corkin, 2008) or suggesting the development of a "corporate consciousness" (Selznick, 2002, p. 97).

As a normative approach, the concept of CSR is equally complex. While most of the definitions acknowledge the roots of the concept within voluntary actions, many also acknowledge, in theory and practice, a regulatory – domestic, transnational, international – dimension of CSR as a social phenomenon. This two-pronged approach brought about a complex normative spectrum that spans from voluntary corporate codes of conduct (with or without inbuilt implementation and control mechanisms) and ethical investment schemes, to direct regulatory intervention, passing through a multitude of "interactive," "semi," and "meta" regulatory mechanisms (Zumbansen, 2011).

While three decades ago the normative regulatory spectrum of CSR was much less developed, Carroll's definition of CSR remains to a great extent useful in classifying the various dimensions of the CSR (A. B. Carroll, 1979). Carroll's definition of CSR uses the social expectations placed on business organizations as a structuring concept that encompasses ethical and philanthropic as well as economic and legal responsibilities. The economic responsibility of business organizations corresponds to the business's self-perception of its scope and role in society. It covers what is seen as the business's primary responsibility of producing goods and services in a way that is profitable for its owners. A second dimension of business responsibility refers to the compliance to the rules and regulations that reflect society's values at a certain moment in time and that offer a regulatory framework for the profit-making activities that businesses pursue. This legal dimension of responsibility creates a bridge between the economic role fulfilled for the immediate interest of the business' owners and the social expectations reflected in an unwritten social contract. However, not all dimensions of this social contract are captured in law. This would be both impossible and undesirable. Business organizations, therefore, are also expected to abide by a series of ethical norms that further add to the normative-regulatory spectrum of the social environment within which business organizations operate. Carroll argues that, because these norms are not written down, they are more ambiguous than the requirements captured in the legal norms and, therefore, are more difficult for business organizations to anticipate and follow (A. B. Carroll, 1979, p. 498). Pushing the spectrum of responsibility beyond the social expectations, Carroll defines philanthropy as the fourth dimension of the business organizations' responsibilities. This "discretionary" dimension consists in engaging in activities that go beyond the expectations of society (such as donations to public and nonprofit organizations, sponsorship of philanthropic projects, volunteer work).

As most of the definitions reveal, the concept of CSR is a multifaceted one. It is also a concept that remains attached to an unfinished and still controversial rationale. It takes into account a large normative and regulatory spectrum, from philanthropy to correct book-keeping, from voluntary triple bottom line to legal compliance, environment, human rights, labor rights, poverty, development, security, governance and global governance, as well as many others (Dahlsrud, 2006). All these play a part in defining the concept of CSR and in giving it substance, proposing it as a set of tools capable of handling at least some of the emerging transnational risks that characterize the global market economy.

Illustrating the role that the firm maintains in the contemporary market economy as an economic institution, the discourse of CSR has lately been described as a "discourse of the firm," through which the firm manages its various operational risks derived from potential conflicts between social expectations and values on the one hand and corporate self-interest on the other (Ocler, 2009).[5] From this perspective, the discourse would focus in particular on how firms build and develop the corporate practice in relation to social responsibility and on the way in which this discourse is used to construct and refine a corporate social strategy (Ocler, 2006, 2009; O'Neill, 2002). While acknowledging the potential benefit of a focus on the firm,[6] this article addresses the CSR discourse from a wider perspective, which incorporates the former but is not reduced to it.[7] This perspective looks at specific ideas, concepts, and categorizations that "are produced, reproduced and transformed in a particular set of practices and through which meaning is given to social and physical realities" (Hajer, 1995, p. 44). Starting from this perspective, this article inquires into CSR as a social discursive practice that reflects as well as "frames and shapes" (Healy, 2005, p. 252) domestic and global politics and institutions.[8] The perspective focuses on the process of the conceptualization of CSR such as it is reflected through the processes of analytical distillation and filtering of the various ideas and concepts that underscore CSR. The article, therefore, proceeds to a recontextualization of the CSR discourse as a social practice (Wodak & Meyer, 2009), deconstructing those conceptual underpinnings to which a multitude of CSR perspectives relate. It is within this wider conceptual perspective that a Polanyian contribution can be envisaged as part of a critique of CSR as an institutionalized discourse (Archel, Husillos, & Spence, 2011; Bartlett, Tywoniak, & Hatcher, 2007; Moon, 2004, p. 21).[9]

In this context, it is acknowledged that the CSR phenomenon is made up of a multitude of discursive practices and statements originating in various social spheres (Boeger et al., 2008). Social movements, such as the 1999 Seattle anti-globalization demonstrations and the "Occupy the City" movement, corporate or industry-wide voluntary initiatives toward codes of conduct or other voluntary instruments, the UN, OECD, ILO and other international initiatives, the domestic courts interventions (or even the lack of their intervention) on issues that may enlarge the regulatory sphere of corporate social responsibilities, all these contribute to the bigger discursive picture of CSR.

Fed through various social channels – political, business, civil society, legal – the CSR discourse has one point of consensus going for it: any acceptable definition of CSR foregrounds the aspect of the voluntary undertaking of social responsibilities that go beyond the legal responsibilities of the economic actors. Any other point of consensus would be much more difficult to find. The CSR discourse has sufficient contradiction built into it to be promoting disagreement even about whether it is controversial or not.[10] The contestation of a basic consensus about CSR often relates to the precise meaning of the concept. While the tenets of self-regulation and voluntariness are, to some extent, dominating the spectrum of CSR definitions (Dahlsrud, 2006), even those tenets have been challenged by certain scholars in order to render apparent a rather different normative and regulatory spectrum encountered in the real (regulatory) world (McBarnet, Voiculescu, & Campbell, 2007). As we will see later, CSR comprises several controversial elements: whether the main conceptual source of CSR should be normative or economic; whether the mechanisms through which CSR is to be internalized should be voluntary or regulatory; whether CSR implies a political/ideological dimension; and ultimately, whether there is such a thing as CSR.

Of course, all these controversial dimensions complicate any attempt at analysis. In spite of this, there is a certain agreement that, regardless of those parts that potentially overlap with the regulatory domain, CSR will require economic agents to strive normatively beyond existing regulatory frameworks. The CSR discourse, therefore, proposes and promotes a reconciliation of ethics and business in a bottom-up movement that feeds upon a certain ethos of the business actors. It also proposes a diffusion, if not institutionalization, of socially mindful behavior throughout the capillarity of the global market economy structures.

The amorality of the firm and, more widely, of the market, promoted actively among business actors, complicates the CSR agenda and riddles it with contradictions. The amorality of the market and of its economic agents, it is said, should never be confused with "immorality." The amoral dimension of the market has been derived from Adam Smith' argument in *The Wealth of Nations* (1776), according to which, in the long run, everybody – individuals and society – benefits from everyone pursuing freely their economic interest, with market mechanisms as the only regulator (Smith, 2008). Economic agents are not "fitted" with a "morality barometer," as this would have been both ontologically impossible[11] and superfluous from a utility point of view. Individual economic actors pursuing freely and selfishly their interests is all that is required for the market economy – and thus for individuals and society – to thrive.

Starting from this premise, for example, Friedman took a stance against CSR's contamination of the neoliberal economic model. The title of his 1970 article in *The New York Times Magazine* sums up the gist of his intervention: "The Social Responsibility of Business Is to Increase Its Profit" (Friedman, 1970). By making profit, Friedman and supporters mean, of course, making profit legally, according to the rules and regulations of the country. Despite this, however, making profit *legally* in the corporate context is often a complex issue in itself (McBarnet, 2003).

Along the lines of the self-regulation of market mechanisms, one can conceive of a "subjectively anarchic, objectively harmonious" market (Habermas, 1991, p. 86), a market that organizes itself, generating its own mechanisms of correction: supply and demand become naturally tuned, unbridled creativity and competition stimulate a steady increase in the quality of products and services and, medium to long term, the distribution of overall benefits becomes fair. However, these are not exactly the parameters that describe the global market economy, nor indeed the domestic one. The global economic context is very complex and it remains a challenge to demonstrate that laissez-faire and self-regulation precepts are spontaneously compatible with a thriving social economy. Indeed, Smith himself cautioned against – in the words of John Gray – the "morally corrosive effects" of market institutions and market life (John Templeton Foundation, 2008) and pointed out the government role in preventing malignant greed that would translate into unhealthy pursuit of profit, through dishonesty and fraud (Smith, 1759).[12] Of course, one can see this position as arguing for a benevolent yet rather distant regulator, capable of ensuring the minimum amount of regulation in order to keep the most dangerous inclinations in check (Vico, 1984 [1744]) while not impeding business creativity and the healthy pursuit of profit. The question, of course, remains as to what would be the level of minimum regulatory intervention that can strike the right balance between the healthy and the unhealthy business practices in pursuit of profit.

The CSR discourse appears thus to address at least two dimensions of market behavior, albeit not always simultaneously or consistently. On the one hand, the CSR discourse suggests a need for a revisiting of the legal environment within which domestic and global markets develop, in order to narrow down those gaps that reveal sources of social conflict and market system vulnerabilities. This implies addressing corporate activities that can give occasion to illegal corporate behavior either in *hard* domestic systems or according to international standards that are sometimes of *softer* regulatory implementation, though not necessarily deprived of normative effectiveness. On the other hand, as a potentially complementing dimension that is, nevertheless, not always clearly acknowledged – the CSR discourse promotes a move toward an infusion of morality into market mechanisms, or even into the economic system as a whole.

Chronologically, it would be difficult to separate the two approaches, although conceptually – as we shall see later – they are rather different and can lead to very different (regulatory) strategies. In principle, however, there is a two-and-fro between the two perspectives, with their respective deployment being influenced by specific discursive practices that thus give meaning to social realities. Both dimensions have been met with strong reactions and anxiety not only from the neoliberal market lobbies, but also from a legal regulatory perspective that is supposed to find innovative – that is radical yet plausible – regulatory answers. Both normative and regulatory approaches depend, however, on the perspective one adopts in relation to the nexus between markets and social moral values (Bruni & Zamagni, 2007).

THE MARKET AND THE NORMATIVE AND REGULATORY DIMENSIONS OF CSR

The ethical dimension of the market was an object of inquiry well before the relatively young CSR discourse. Scholars have developed competing normative constructs and techniques that can now be instrumental in analyzing the position and potential of the CSR discourse within the normative and regulatory spectrum.[13]

As ironic as this might seem at the time of writing this article, with a deep economic crisis clearly here to stay some time, at least among the developed countries, the contemporary institutionalized perspective on the social role of the market is derived from Montesquieu's notion of *doux-commerce*/gentle commerce (de Montesquieu, 1751, bk. XX). This concept is centered on the idea that commerce is one of the central civilizing activities that societies can entertain. Competing markets are seen as the best means not only to fulfill the individual pursuit of satisfaction and happiness, but also as the best means to accomplish the efficient distribution of resources. Selfishness, as a basic human inclination, is raised at the rank of supreme mechanism that caters not only for individual but also for social and communitarian aspirations. This happens through a process of selection and deselection of individual choices in the marketplace, with aggregating individual choices constituted in market and social trends.

Some of the classic formulations of the *doux-commerce* thesis are telling. Montesquieu, for instance, dedicated an important part of his masterpiece, *The Spirit of the Laws* (1748), to commerce as the cure to the most destructive prejudices:

> ... It is almost a general rule that wherever manners are gentle there is commerce; and wherever there is commerce, manners are gentle.
>
> [...] "... Commerce ... polishes and softens barbaric ways as we can see every day." (de Montesquieu, 1751, *The Spirit of the Laws*, Bk. 2, pp. 1, 2)

Similarly, Thomas Paine, in *The Rights of Man* (1792), picked up the same idea:

> ... [Commerce] is a pacific system, operating to cordialise mankind, by rendering Nations, as well as individuals, useful to each other ... The invention of commerce [...] is the greatest approach towards universal civilization that has yet been made by any means not immediately flowing from moral principles. (Paine, 2000, p. 215)

According to Montesquieu, still, countries that do commerce rarely fight, a position echoed later by the forefathers of the European Union. However, Montesquieu also recognized that while this effect was obvious in the case of countries, it was less obvious in the case of individuals. On the contrary, he recognized that commerce can bring out the worst in human relationships:

> ... if the spirit of commerce unites nations, it does not in the same manner unite individuals ... in countries where the people are actuated only by the spirit of commerce, they make a traffic of all the humane, all the moral virtues; the most trifling things, those which humanity would demand, are there done, or there given, only for money. (de Montesquieu, 1751, Vols. 2, p. 8)

Adam Smith, however, brought even individual selfishness into the civilizing paradigm, casting it, in effect, as the engine of the civilizing force of commerce.

> It is not from the benevolence of the butcher, the brewer, or the baker, that we expect our dinner, but from their regard to their own self-interest. We address ourselves, not to their humanity but to their self-love ... (Smith, 2008, p. 15)

Smith thus contends here that our interest and the community interest will be best served by the selfish pursuit of profit by the butcher and the baker. It is their self-interest that will drive them – in most situations – to be honest and civil and to cooperate where appropriate and needed. Some would go even further and set commerce as a precondition to human progress and as an important component to political freedom (Friedman, 2002). Moreover, one of the strongest tenets of this perspective refers to the creativity and innovation that the market can unleash if allowed the greatest possible freedom to self-organize and self-regulate. The market system would be an amoral but virtuous system that secures progress precisely because of the selfishness of its individual actors. The quest for profit of each individual actor is kept in check by other similar pursuits. This is done via the communicative of commerce (McCloskey, 2007) or via a utilitarian perspective that prompts economic actors to cultivate religiously their credibility and reputation (Fourcade & Healy, 2007, p. 288).

The role of law and regulation, from this perspective, is minimal. The state remains the invisible hand that intervenes only when absolutely necessary in order to adjust occasional and, we might add, non-systemic market imperfections. Inevitably, this perspective altered fundamentally the equilibrium between authority and market, transforming radically the relationship between state and society. This redefined the purposes and the extent to which government could legitimately intervene and regulate domestic economy. As Ruggie put it, "[t]he role of the state became to institute and safeguard the self-regulatory market ..." (1982, p. 386).

The legislator's job would, therefore, be restricted to the most basic of legal frameworks for economic activity and the government's regulatory powers could not be used according to its whims. Instead, it is for the market to produce – directly and indirectly – social harmony as well as goods and services that we may need or desire.

The social responsibility discourse finds it difficult to accommodate such a perspective without questioning its consistency and without challenging its tenets. However, the CSR discourse does feel the pressure of the universalized neoliberal particularism, and this is reflected in its inconsistencies. Branded as a "fundamentally subversive doctrine" (Friedman, 2002, p. 135), the CSR discourse does its best to prove the contrary. Faced with the dominant doctrine, the discourse falls into self-censorship, with all the inherent inconsistencies and loss of substance that may derive from this.

Noninstitutional Approaches to Market and Morality

The neoliberal perspective on markets and morality is not the only way of looking at the role of markets in society and at the ethical dimension that this may or may not entail. It is, however, the main institutionalized economic discourse that the CSR discourse (as well as the legal discourse) needs to contend with.

The critics of the liberal market economy system have promoted a rather different perspective on the self-regulating market and its effects on society. While, in theory, the commerce may be *doux*, gentle and civilizing, with very little apparent need for regulatory intervention, the reality, it is argued, is often harsher, with not much being left of the civilizing functions that the theory assumes. Virtue would be replaced by greed or envy, cooperation by wasteful competition and rivalry, free trade and commerce by coercion, monopoly, and exploitation. The confusion of democratic freedom with market populism is also exposed,[14] as is the dramatic expansion of copyright laws, that stifle rather than stimulate creativity and the emergence of new cultural forms (Fourcade & Healy, 2007, p. 292ff).

This view is often backed by hard sociological and statistical data that at least support, if not also prove the point (Dale, 2010). Some authors have dwelt particularly upon the issue of the morality of the market, offering a rather novel perspective on this. In his book *The Social Limits to Growth*, Fred Hirsch, for instance, presented the idea of a market economy system that does have a capacity for growth, but not an inherent one (1976). According to Hirsch, this capacity is checked by social limits. These limits are in fact inbuilt into the market mechanisms, pertaining to its very ontology. He acknowledges the system's capacity for material productivity, but also its generating of social demand that cannot be satisfied any longer. In this context, "one man's gain is often another's loss; and both may lose from the struggle" (Hirsch, 1976, p. 118).[15] Hirsch questions in this way the beneficial influence of the individualistic orientation of the market economy, which allegedly keeps the system functioning with very little regulatory intervention and with even less need for individual morality on the part of the economic actors.

As mentioned above, the selfishness of the individual actors was being acclaimed as the guarantor of the system's value ethics that makes the butcher and the baker give us the best possible service. Hirsch, however, reassembles the evidence related to the market economy value ethics. His main argument is based upon the idea that the hard individualism of market economy can only function when contained by a strict social morality. Hirsch suggests that such a strong social morality is not inherent to or generated by market economy, but is in fact a social inheritance from the (precapitalist and preindustrial) past. This deep rooting of the liberal market system into the traditional values of the past is exemplified with respect to the British system:

> The resulting deficiencies in this individualistic approach were obscured for a long time by *the special, and largely unconscious, influences of the English tradition of enlightened paternalism* ... Keynes's interpretation of managed capitalism retains a vital importance precisely because of its *unquestioning reliance on obligations and instincts deriving from an earlier preindustrial culture*. (Hirsch, 1976, p. 123, emphasis added)

Later on, John Ruggie echoed the same idea by noting that:

> ... nowhere did [the role of state as mere guardian of the self-regulatory market] take hold so deeply and for so long a period as in Great Britain. Great Britain's supremacy in the world economy had much to do with the global expansion of this new economic order, *and even more with its stability and longevity*. (Ruggie, 1982, p. 386, emphasis added)

According to Hirsch, rather than strengthening the much needed social morality that would bound the market actors,[16] the individualism that constitutes the basis of the market has actually been corroding it. In other words, market economy has developed based on borrowed social moral capital that now appears as spent:

> ... This legacy has diminished with time and with the corrosive contact of the active capitalist values – and more generally with the greater anonymity and greater mobility of industrial society. (Hirsch, 1976, p. 118ff)

Hirsch seems to open a new perspective not only upon the evolution of the morality of the markets – past and present – but also upon social morality as a contributing factor to the calls for government intervention and CSR discourse institutionalization and regulation. As individual market behavior is feeding upon a depleted social morality deposit (Rodrigues & Carvalho, 2005, p. 10ff), "habits and instincts based on communal attitudes and objectives have lost out" (Hirsch, 1976, p. 118). One might speculate, therefore, that had the market economy mechanisms – with their strong individualism as a guiding star – added to, rather than unsustainably fed upon, the past social moral capital, social values proposed through the CSR discourse would have potentially been organically enmeshed in the corporate ethos.

THE CSR DISCOURSE AND ITS CONTACT POINTS WITH EMBEDDEDNESS

Hirsch's emphasis on the economic system's need for feeding upon a stratum of socially constructed values that would accompany its reproduction brings to light the potential of Polanyi's concept of embeddedness. In his use of the embedded/disembedded concept of economy, Polanyi emphasized the unusual nature of the liberal market economy paradigm as opposed to other economic and social paradigms of the past.[17] Drawing upon a wealth of anthropological data that lends a credible alternative logic to that of the self-regulating market (Munck, 2003, p. 2), Polanyi identified reciprocity and redistribution as the main principles characterizing a social economy that remains in contact with the social values that constitute its source, thus ensuring that the market economy system remains embedded in society. As we shall see next, these principles are identified as being at the root of the CSR discourse, as well as of those other social discourses that attempt to challenge the imperialist reasoning of the neoliberal paradigm. Indeed, Polanyi himself noted that these principles are not primarily associated with economics, but are rooted much deeper in non-economically oriented social practices (2002, p. 262).

The Reciprocity Dimension of the CSR Discourse

Emphasizing the social role of economic activities – as opposed to just the economic – and the equal status of the social actors – beyond the hierarchy that is usually established through law, the CSR discourse appears centered largely upon the principle of reciprocity. The complex parameters of reciprocity, according to Polanyi, rest on a "superabundant noneconomic motivation for every act performed in the frame of the social system as a whole" (Polanyi, 2002, p. 50). In the contemporary CSR debate, reciprocity of this caliber – going beyond the offering of a "fair price" – is revealed as one of the points of tension at the interface between traditional societies and the corporate world. As an example, one could only look at the challenges of stakeholder consultations, when stakeholders are indigenous populations (Harris & Wasilewski, 2004; Welker, 2009), or indeed, when stakeholders' "stake" is not easily quantifiable. In this sense, a number of claims and movements that develop synergies with the CSR discourse appear to suggest a similar "embedding" dimension, based on the principle of reciprocity. This is the case of some anti-globalization movements (Christakis, 2004, p. 479; Munck, 2003; Starr, 2005) or of those movements aiming to establish reciprocity channels as a way of reclaiming social space from the dominant market discourse, that is, the market discourse that uses money as its only exchange mechanism.

Identifying CSR as one of the social discourses that reflect a call for reciprocity, Bruni proposes a complex "reciprocity map," largely involving three dimensions (2008). First, CSR is undertaken as part of the "cost" the economic agents have to pay for the privilege of operating in society. In this case, CSR reciprocity is endorsed under civil or political pressure or as part of the calculation of direct or indirect economic profits. This dimension of reciprocity may well appear of a less generous nature. According to Bruni though, this is a necessary dimension, which comes to complement the others. However, it is not from the actors that endorse solely this type of reciprocity that one can expect the emergence of a new corporate culture such as the one centered on social responsibility.

The CSR discourse entails two additional dimensions of reciprocity that are more conducive to innovation and to the regeneration of the "civil quality of economic development" (Bruni, 2008, p. 91). The first of these two reciprocity dimensions is expressed by those agents that embrace certain values and answer social expectations based on instinct, market analysis, or strongly influenced by ethical or environmental concerns. In this case, economic agents, while not inspired by intrinsic – purely altruistic – motivations, are however capable of internalizing new social values predominantly as part of what is called "the business case" for CSR (Carroll & Shabana, 2010; Unerman & O'Dwyer, 2007; Vogel, 2005). Third, there is the "gratuitous reciprocity" characterized by unconditionality. In the case of "gratuitous reciprocity," the economic actor's commitment to certain civil values of the economic life ensures that those values are pursued regardless of the cost. Bruni argues that a combination of the various dimensions of reciprocity is probably the best way to reinforce the channels of communication between society and economy as well as social value creation (Bruni, 2008, p. 94). In Polanyi's definition of the reciprocity principle and in the anthropological examples he used in order to back his analysis of the principle, one can identify a similarly complex reciprocity mosaic.[18]

The Redistributive Dimension of the CSR Discourse

Polanyi argued persuasively for redistribution as an essential embedding dimension of a socially healthy economic life.[19] The process of redistribution takes place through a central institutional setup, with an intercommunity symmetry dimension that secures a benign level of personalization in the process of reciprocity and with a centricity dimension that secures both the economic and the social coming together of the community.[20] Polanyi's harmonious *mandala* of socially centered economic relationships is contrasted by some authors to "the anarchy of exchange as this is mediated through price-making markets in a disembedded and potentially self-regulating economy" (Jessop, 2003, p. 2).

In Polanyi's account, redistribution takes the economic interactions of society at a higher societal level, moving beyond the "sharing" instituted through complex systems of reciprocity – "today's giving will be recompensed by tomorrow's taking" (Polanyi, 2002, p. 52) – to a "redistribution proper" performed, through an "intermediary" that holds a special central place in the political set up of the community (Polanyi, 2002, p. 53). These redistribution mechanisms tend, according to Polanyi, to enmesh the economic system proper in social relationships (Polanyi, 2002, p. 55).

In the CSR discourse itself, the principle of redistribution plays an important role in defining the concept's normative parameters (Baron, 2001, p. 7; A. B. Carroll, 1979; Freeman, 2010; Preston & Post, 1975; Wood, 1991). In this sense, economic actors are expected to actively engage in structured redistribution practices that valorize relationships with all stakeholders. Of course, this engagement can have several sources (Baron, 2001). It can be based on the desire to avoid government regulatory intervention or it can be the result of marketing calculations that sum up to a convincing business case for CSR.[21] At the same time, the CSR discourse promotes the principle of redistribution based on normative grounds (such as, for instance, the ones derived from the human rights discourse) that can guide the fine-tuning between the economic actors' financial and social performance (Baron, 2001; Gray, Kouhy, & Lavers, 1995; Kolk, 2005).[22]

CSR – PERSPECTIVES FOR A THEORY OF SOCIAL CHANGE

The CSR discourse appears thus to host within its controversial boundaries the principles of reciprocity and redistribution that are also key tools of the Polanyian double movement of embedding/disembedding market economy and society. Reciprocity and redistribution complement each other in building and securing social ties through the development of "civil economy" and, ultimately, of the foundation of *pubblica felicita*, or "civil happiness" (Bruni, 2004; Grab, 1986; Vico, 1984).[23] While promoting the same principles does not necessarily secure social change, a refined CSR concept can gain theoretical and empirical strength by being linked to Polanyian thinking. The theoretical gain refers to the fact that CSR – at least at its "subversive" beginnings[24] – challenged to a great extent the same neoliberal utopia that Polanyi addresses comprehensively in his book. The empirical reinforcement comes from Polanyi's proposed principles (Munck, 2003) as principles of general application that are not limited to a particular type of society, such as small communities or indigenous populations. On the contrary, supporting his arguments with historical examples and empirical anthropological data (Dale, 2010), Polanyi argues that the principles of reciprocity and redistribution have functioned and can function in big and complex societies as well. Accordingly, an embedded economic life can be conceived regardless of the size of the community and of the complexity of its economic activities (Harris & Wasilewski, 2004; Jessop, 2003; Polanyi, 2002, p. 258).

Building on Hirsch's image of the individualist, neoliberal market behavior that feeds upon an eroding social morality deposit, CSR can be understood as a discourse that aims to revive habits and instincts – such as the ones reflected in reciprocity and redistribution – based on communal attitudes and objectives (Hirsch, 1976, p. 118). The *closing* of the embedding circle achieved by Polanyi with his perspective on economy and society – a *closing* that takes Hirsch to a higher level – was summarized by Glasman. Glasman identifies in Polanyi not only a sharp critique of the idea of a self-regulating economy – grounded in individualism and feeding upon more generous moral values inherited from the past – but also a critique of the idea of a self-regulating system that is based "on an impoverished conception of the *importance of the economy and its institutions in the reproduction of ethics and society*" (Glasman, 1996, p. 7, emphasis added). Through this lens, the CSR discourse becomes part of a new call for embeddedness not only because economic life is deemed to reflect social values, but also because economic processes, structures and even their underlying ideology are essential for the reproduction of ethics and society. If the former are somewhat deficient or affected by a certain "pathology" (Driver, 2006), the processes of the reproduction of ethics and society can only become themselves deficient or pathological.

However, one can argue that Polanyi's vision supports the sublimation of the CSR discourse in a more fundamental way as well, shedding a new light upon some of CSR's key points of contention, and in particular upon the economic/normative choice of foundations for CSR and upon the voluntary/regulatory dilemma that haunts the CSR discourse. Through a process of soft institutionalization (Kallio, 2007), the CSR discourse builds largely on an economic foundation (Unerman & O'Dwyer, 2007), in other words, on the business case for CSR.[25] Apart from the inherent conceptual inconsistencies of this approach that refer to the attempt to build "business *ethics*" on a "*business* case" – that is on a profit-focused case for CSR (A. B. Carroll & Shabana, 2010) – this type of unilateral tuning of the social and political agenda under the pressure of the neoliberal market imperatives can also be shown to be ineffective according to the Polanyian model. Allowing for the market to impose its values would deepen rather than alleviate the disembedding spiral and the erosion of social values that the CSR is aspiring to mend (Unerman & O'Dwyer, 2007).

On the other hand, the normative rationale put forward – often more timidly – in the CSR discourse can now be seen in a new light, as part of the distillation of social values that can contribute to the embeddedness of market economy into society. A genuine embedding could only take place through a normative path, distilled from the complexity of social life and reflected in the political and legislative/regulatory dimensions of that life.

Looking at the CSR discourse from this perspective, the proposed set of concepts and practices, if inconsistent, may still be seen as a ("timidly radical") way of interrogating the prevailing, dominant ideology that universalizes the particularism of the neoliberal market system. This view on CSR could be consistent with Hoff and Stiglitz' perspective regarding the role of ideas in economic change. Following their model for social change (Hoff & Stiglitz, 2010, p. 13), one can see CSR as a "higher-order-belief" that may propose an intrinsic value, a "überideology" that incrementally gnaws away at the dominant paradigm. It is precisely this potential that is to a certain extent obscured by higher order taboos related to CSR, the taboo of the political dimension of CSR being an example in point (Kallio, 2007). The Polanyian concept of embeddedness, with its principles of reciprocity, redistribution and normativity rooted outside pure economic values, appears to support that dimension of CSR that can render it into part of an emerging "überideology."

CSR between Normativity, Regulation and Freedom in a Complex Society

Assuming a normative dimension implies facing one of the main contested areas of CSR, namely what some have called the taboo of the political dimension of CSR (Kallio, 2007, p. 170). This political dimension refers to the need to incorporate into CSR a dimension of social legitimacy of the business practices that would justify the promotion of business actors' and other stakeholders' own interests (Kallio, 2007, p. 170). It also refers to the incorporation into CSR of a potential for the promotion of common social interests through government intervention (Bruni, 2004; Grab, 1986; Hamilton, 2004; Polanyi, 2002, p. 48).

Assuming a normative dimension is part of the mechanisms of selection of social values, including the ones selected through legislative and regulatory processes, values that are meant to condition and embed economic activities in the complex social set-up. Following Polanyi (2002, p. 146f), these mechanisms can be politically structured and backed by legislative and regulatory tools, but can also be spontaneous, reflecting civil society signals that have not been institutionalized, yet can contribute to the discourse aimed at embedding economy in society. Though not institutionalized, there is increasing evidence that these signals often inform and feed legislative imagination and regulatory initiative (McBarnet et al., 2007). An acknowledgment of the normative dimension of CSR does not necessarily imply a complete obliteration of all aspects of the economic arguments that are usually seen to stem from a "business case." The ethical values of economic inspiration become just some of the values competing for normative and regulatory endorsement in the social arena, rather than being the dominant ones.[26]

With reciprocity and redistribution at the basis of a normative perspective on CSR as an embedding tool, one is not heading for an unconditional subsuming of market and political institutions to social communitarian values. On the contrary, from the Polanyian perspective, the individual freedom(s) remain of paramount importance. Institutions, argues Polanyi, "are embodiments of human meaning and purpose. We cannot achieve the freedom we seek, unless we comprehend the true significance of freedom in a complex society" (Polanyi, 2002, p. 262).

The question is, of course, where can one go from here? Can the CSR discourse contribute in any way to addressing the multilevel crisis within society and within itself? Schwaninger, for instance, proposes the cybernetics model for addressing crises as "crises of regulation" (2004, p. 515f) which would probably make CSR and other normative systems appropriate crisis tools. However, is CSR itself part of a deeper conceptual regulatory crisis? The challenge of dealing with the contemporary crises of the neoliberal market economy model as crises of regulation also echoes Gianbatista Vico's statement about the social engineering – if not civilizing – nature of law. Incidentally, Vico himself highlights "avarice" or the individual pursuit of selfish goals, which is also the cornerstone of the neoliberal ideology, but emphasizes its destructive force in society in the absence of guiding laws (1984, p. 62). Legislation, argues Vico, considers humans in their most basic and negative features and sublimates those features, converting them for the benefit of the society:

> Out of ferocity, avarice, and ambition, the three vices which run throughout the human race, [legislation] creates the military, merchant, and governing classes, and thus the strength, riches, and wisdom of commonwealths. Out of the three great vices, which could certainly destroy all mankind on the face of the earth, [legislation] makes civil happiness. (Vico, 1984, p. 62 [1744])

In this perspective, the CSR discourse, as embedding discourse, might well become a mosaic of both ethical normative elements that contribute to an embedded economy and of regulatory normative elements that structure and channel the complex embedding processes. This mosaic includes a set of global regulatory structures that can place limits on the disembedding pull of market forces (Block, 2003).[27] Polanyi acknowledges that embedding regulation restricts freedom but it also extends it. In his opinion though, "only the balance of the freedoms lost and won is significant" (Polanyi, 2002, p. 262f). In this sense, the CSR discourse, both in its voluntary and regulatory dimensions, is potentially a negotiating terrain where individual freedom – as paramount value – can be continuously shaped and enlarged without the crushing dominance of the self-regulating market that can take away freedom from individuals and governments alike.[28]

CONCLUSION

Straddling across a vast normative area, between voluntariness and regulation, the CSR discourse appears as a complex set of ideas aimed both at answering changing social expectations and at managing the risk associated with these changes and with the global market economy processes. From this perspective, CSR can be seen as interrogating and challenging the dominant market economy paradigm. Both interrogation and challenge, it has been suggested earlier, are supported conceptually by elements related to the Polanyian concept of embeddedness, in particular by the principles of reciprocity and redistribution and by the role assigned to the regulatory functions of the government in the process of embedding economy in society. As such, CSR may be becoming part of those social choices that "get aggregated into a new social construct" and ultimately into a "überi-deology" that will be pervasively influencing economic change until there is a sudden qualitative transformation, "a tilting of the social perception" (Hoff & Stiglitz, 2010) of the dominant ideology.

While there is sufficient evidence indicating that CSR may be part of such a model of social change, there are also indications – supported empirically as well as highlighted by the normative inconsistencies of the CSR concept – that CSR is being absorbed within the dominant market paradigm. As a social discourse, therefore, CSR oscillates between the status of *embedding* "higher-order-beliefs" – that is, a complex set of ideas and practices that contribute to the process of embedding economy into society, and the status of *embedded* (in the neoliberal paradigm) concept that got absorbed through the "cunning imperialist reason" of the dominant (neoliberal) ideology before it had the time to ripen and become positively subversive, an integral part of the embedding "etiquette and magic" that would strive toward a global "civil economy."

NOTES

1. See also Fourcade and Healy (2007) on "prevailing classifications"; Perry-Kessaris (2011) on "economics imperialism"; Boje, Luhman, and Baack (1999) on the "hegemonic stories"; O'Neill's (2002) account of the "story telling" in organizations; and Lary May on "pseudo-unities" proposed as facts.
2. In relation to making CSR systemic, see Altschuller and Smith (2011).
3. For how the concept has been taken forward by Granovetter, see Gareth (Dale, 2010).
4. See Bob Jassop's analysis for the specific link between the market economy perspective proposed by Polanyi and an autopoietic perspective (Jessop, 2003).
5. For a systematic account of the use of CSR as a risk management set of tools, see Zumbansen (2011) on private regulation and transnational law and Parker (2007) on meta-regulation.
6. According to Van Marrewijk, a successful CSR strategy "has to be context specific for each individual business" and further knowledge of how CSR is socially constructed in a specific context must be obtained "by other means than through a definition of CSR" (2003).
7. For a conceptual framework for identifying stakeholders see Mitchell, Agle, and Wood (1997).
8. Regarding the benefits of such discursive inquiry, see Schwaninger's analysis of the contribution of cybernetics to the conscious evolution of organizations and society (2004, p. 528ff).
9. Quoting Link, van Leeuwen speaks for instance about "institutionalized way of talking that regulates and reinforces action and thereby exerts power" (2009).

10. For more details, see Knippenberg and Jong (2010, p. 17ff) and also Blowfield (2005, p. 175ff) and Moon (2004).

11. See for instance the debate on corporate personality and corporate responsibility in the literature on corporate criminal responsibility.

12. John Gray, for instance, emphasizes that "... Smith is as important as a critic of the market as a defender of the market." See John Gray in one of his interventions at the London Round Table on "Does the Free Market Corrode Moral Character?" (John Templeton Foundation, 2008, p. 20).

13. See the three ideologies of individualism identified by Greene (2008).

14. "The road to the free market was opened and kept open by an enormous increase in continuous, centrally organized and controlled interventionism. *To make Adam Smith's 'simple and natural liberty' compatible with the needs of a human society was a most complicated affair.* Witness the complexity of the provisions in the innumerable enclosure laws; the amount of bureaucratic control involved in the administration of the New Poor Laws ... ." (Polanyi, 2002, p. 146f, emphasis added)

15. See also Kallio's article in relation to CSR and the issues of "continuous growth" (2007).

16. See for instance, how Hirsch describes the loss of the support related to religion: "Truth, trust, acceptance, restraint, obligation – these are among the social virtues grounded in religious belief which are also now seen to play a central role in the functioning of an individualistic, contractual economy." [...] "... The market system was, at bottom, more dependent on religious binding than the feudal system, having abandoned direct social ties maintained by the obligations of custom and status. Yet, the individualistic, rationalistic base of the market undermined the unseen religious support." (Hirsch, 1976, pp. 143, 145)

17. See Bruni and Zamagni (2007) for an explanation as to why the civil approach to economics disappeared from the public arena, cultural debates and scientific enquiries at the end of the 18th century, only to surface again in more recent times.

18. For an overview of the various dimensions of reciprocity, see Bruni (2008, Appendix 1).

19. See Bruni (2004) and also Grab (1986) on the concept of "civil economy."

20. Polanyi also highlighted the role of "householding" as a key element that is geared toward the production that satisfies the needs of largely self-sufficient units (family, settlement, manor, etc.).
In short, the capitalist market economy is only one form of organizing economic activity and should not be used as a transhistorical model for interpreting other economies (Jessop, 2003, p. 2).

21. For an analysis of the business case for regulation of CSR see Unerman and O'Dwyer (2007).

22. Barron, for instance, equates corporate social performance with redistribution (2001, p. 15).

23. Writing about Antonio Genovesi's initial coining of the concept, Grab writes that "civil economy" combines ethical dimensions including justice, government duties to the people and its relationship with the people, as well as "human needs and motivations."

24. For a critique of CSR as "establishment," as part of the neoliberal hijacking of the discourse of justice in the market place, see Bobby Banerjee (2008).

25. "The domain of corporate social responsibility cannot be assessed by primarily economic criteria and neither can an environmental ethic be developed through an 'ethically pragmatic managerial' morality that primarily serves organizational interests." (Banerjee, 2008, p. 73)

26. "CSR research then focuses not on which behaviors are normatively better, which is likely to mire it in just the kind of stalemate we have found in the literature. Instead it can focus on the extent to which behaviors reflect multiple voices and complex dialog and investigations of responsibility that do not have to determine which behaviors are more right but which behaviors reflect a more multidimensional dialog. In a sense, replacing debates over what is right and wrong in practice with investigations into how a more decentered organizational self-narrative encompasses a more systemic approach to responsibility in practice simply because it includes more voices, more dialog and more complex reasoning." (Driver, 2006, p. 352)

27. "Polanyi's vision depends on expanding the role of government both domestically and internationally. He challenges the now fashionable view that more government will inevitably lead to both bad economic results and excessive state control of social life." (Block, 2003)

28. The recent EU crisis with Greece at its heart is a very good illustration of the way in which governments' decision power and democratic processes are vastly curtailed by the blind (global) market forces. See *The Economist*, the "Charlemagne" section in particular, across 2011–2012 (available at http://www.economist.com).

ACKNOWLEDGEMENTS

The author would like to thank the participants to the workshop "Socializing Economic Relationships: New Perspectives and Methods for Analysing Transnational Risk Regulation" at the Centre for Socio-Legal Studies, Oxford, where an initial draft of this article was presented. The author is also indebted to the two anonymous reviewers from *Studies in Law, Politics and Society* as well as to Grazia Necsutu and Bettina Lange. Any errors and inconsistencies remain the author's.

REFERENCES

Altschuller, S. A., & Smith, G. A. (2011). Making corporate social responsibility systemic. *Executive Council*, February/March 2011. Available at www.executivecounsel.info. Accessed 8 April 2012.

Archel, P., Husillos, J., & Spence, C. (2011). The institutionalisation of unaccountability: Loading the dice of corporate social responsibility discourse. *Accounting, Organizations and Society*, *36*(66), 327–343.

Banerjee, S. B. (2008). Corporate social responsibility: The good, the bad and the ugly. *Critical Sociology*, *34*(1), 51–79.

Baron, D. P. (2001). Private politics, corporate social responsibility, and integrated strategy. *Journal of Economics & Management Strategy*, *10*(1), 7–45.

Bartlett, J. L., Tywoniak, S., & Hatcher, C. (2007). Public relations professional practice and the institutionalisation of CSR. *Journal of Communication Management*, *11*(4), 281–299.

Block, F. (2003). Karl Polanyi and the writing of "The great transformation." *Theory and Society*, *32*(3), 275–306.

Blowfield, M. (2005). Corporate social responsibility – The failing discipline and why it matters for international relations. *International Relations*, *19*(2), 173–191.

Boeger, N., Murray, R., & Villiers, C. (Eds.) (2008). *Perspectives on corporate social responsibility: Corporations, globalisation and the law*. Cheltenham, UK: Edward Elgar Publishing.

Boje, D. M., Luhman, J. T., & Baack, D. E. (1999). Hegemonic stories and encounters between storytelling organizations. *Journal of Management Inquiry*, *8*(4), 340–360.

Bourdieu, P., & Wacquant, L. (1999). On the cunning of imperialist reason. *Theory, Culture & Society*, *16*(1), 41–58.

Broomhill, R. (2007). *Corporate social responsibility: Key issues and debates*. Dunstan Papers Series No. 1. Don Dunstan Foundation, Adelaide, Australia.

Bruni, L. (2004). The "technology of happiness" and the tradition of economic science. *Journal of the History of Economic Thought*, *26*(01), 19–44.

Bruni, L. (2008). *Reciprocity, altruism and the civil society: In praise of heterogeneity*. Abingdon, Oxon, UK: Routledge.

Bruni, L., & Zamagni, S. (2007). *Civil economy: Efficiency, equity, public happiness*. Bern, Swizerland: Peter Lang.

Carroll, A. B. (1979). A three-dimensional conceptual model of corporate social performance. *Academy of Management Review*, *4*, 497–505.

Carroll, A. B. (1999). Corporate social responsibility: Evolution of a definitional construct. *Business and Society*, *38*(3), 268–295.

Carroll, A. B., & Shabana, K. M. (2010). The business case for corporate social responsibility: A review of concepts, research and practice. *International Journal of Management Reviews*, *12*(1), 85–105.

Carroll, T. (2012). The cutting edge of accumulation: Neoliberal risk mitigation, the Baku-Tbilisi-Ceyhan pipeline and its impact. *Antipode*, *44*(2), 281–302.

Christakis, A. N. (2004). Wisdom of the people. *Systems Research and Behavioral Science*, *21*, 479–488.

Corkin, J. (2008). Misappropriating citizenship: The limits of corporate social responsibility. In N. Boeger, R. Murray, & C. Villiers (Eds.), *Perspectives on corporate social responsibility: Corporations, globalisation and the law* (pp. 39–63). Cheltenham, UK: Edward Elgar Publishing.

Dahlsrud, A. (2006). How corporate social responsibility is defined: An analysis of 37 definitions. *Corporate Social Responsibility and Environmental Management*. Published online in Wiley InterScience. doi:10.1002/csr.132. Accessed on 8 April 2006.

Dale, G. (2010). Polanyian meditations on economy and society: A review of "market society: The great transformation today." *Dialectical Anthropology*, *34*(1), 29–41.

Driver, M. (2006). Beyond the stalemate of economics versus ethics: Corporate social responsibility and the discourse of the organizational self. *Journal of Business Ethics*, *66*, 337–356.

Foster, R. J. (2009). Corporate oxymorons and the anthropology of corporations. *Dialectical Anthropology*, *34*(1), 95–102.

Fourcade, M., & Healy, K. (2007). Moral views of market society. *Annual Review of Sociology*, *33*, 285–311.

Freeman, R. E. (2010). *Strategic management: A stakeholder approach.* Cambridge, UK: Cambridge University Press.

Friedman, M. (1970). The social responsibility of business is to increase its profits. *New York Times Magazine*, September 13, p. SM17.

Friedman, M. (2002). *Capitalism and freedom* (40th anniversary ed.). Chicago and London: University of Chicago Press.

Glasman, M. (1996). *Unnecessary suffering: Managing market Utopia.* London and New York: Verso.

Grab, A. (1986). Book review: Antonio Genovesi dalla politica economica alla "political civile" by Eluggero Pii. *The Journal of Modern History*, *58*(4), 963–965.

Gray, R., Kouhy, R., & Lavers, S. (1995). Corporate social and environmental reporting: A review of the literature and a longitudinal study of UK disclosure. *Accounting, Auditing & Accountability Journal*, *8*(2), 47–77.

Greene, T. W. (2008). Three ideologies of individualism: Toward assimilating a theory of individualisms and their consequences. *Critical Sociology*, *34*(1), 117–137.

Habermas, J. (1992). *The structural transformation of the public sphere: An inquiry into a category of bourgeois society*. Cambridge, UK: Polity Press.

Hajer, M. (1995). *The politics of environmental discourse: Ecological modernization and the policy process*. Oxford: Clarendon Press.

Hamilton, C. (2004). *Growth fetish*. London/Sterling, Virginia: Pluto Press.

Harris, L. D., & Wasilewski, J. (2004). Indigeneity, an alternative worldview: Four R's (relationship, responsibility, reciprocity, redistribution) vs. two P's (power and profit). Sharing the journey towards conscious evolution. *Systems Research and Behavioral Science*, *21*(5), 489–503.

Healy, S. (2005). Toward a vocabulary for speaking of the engagement of things into discourse. *Journal of Environmental Policy & Planning*, *7*, 239–256.

Hirsch, F. (1977). *Social limits to growth*. London: Routledge and Kegan Paul Ltd.

Hoff, K., & Stiglitz, J. E. (2010). *Equilibrium fictions: A cognitive approach to societal rigidity*. World Bank Policy Research Working Paper No. 5219. The World Bank, Washington, DC.

Hutter, B. (2006). Risk, regulation and management. In P. Taylor-Gooby & J. O. Zinn (Eds.), *Risk in social science* (pp. 202–227). Oxford, UK: Oxford University Press.

Hutter, B., & Power, M. (Eds.) (2005). *Organizational encounters with risk*. Cambridge, UK: Cambridge University Press.

Jessop, B. (2003, December). *Regulationist and autopoieticist reflections on Polanyi's account of market economies and the market society*. Department of Sociology, Lancaster University. Retrieved from http://www.comp.lancs.ac.uk/sociology/papers/Jessop-Regulationist-and-Autopoieticist-Reflections.pdf

John Templeton Foundation. (2008, December). *London Round Table on "Does the Free Market Corrode Moral Character?"*. Retrieved from http://www.templeton.org/market/PDF/templeton-london-event.pdf

Kallio, T. J. (2007). Taboos in corporate social responsibility discourse. *Journal of Business Ethics*, *74*(2), 165–175.

Knippenberg, L., & Jong, E. B. P. (2010). Moralising the market by moralising the firm. *Journal of Business Ethics*, *96*(1), 17–31.

Kolk, A. (2005). Corporate social responsibility in the coffee sector: The dynamics of MNC responses and code development. *European Management Journal*, *23*(2), 228–236.

Kytle, B., & Ruggie, J. G. (2005). *Corporate social responsibility as risk management: A model for multinationals*. Corporate Social Responsibility Initiative Working Paper No. 10. John F. Kennedy School of Government, Harvard University, Cambridge, MA.

Louche, C., Idowu, S. O., & Filho, W. L. (Eds.) (2010). *Innovative CSR: From risk management to value creation*. Sheffield, UK: Greenleaf Publishing.

McBarnet, D. J. (2003). When compliance is not the solution but the problem: From changes in law to changes in attitude. In V. Braithwaite (Ed.), *Taxing democracy: Understanding tax avoidance and evasion* (illustrated ed., pp. 229–244). Aldershot, UK: Ashgate Publishing Limited.

McBarnet, D. J., Voiculescu, A., & Campbell, T. (Eds.) (2007). *The new corporate accountability: Corporate social responsibility and the law*. Cambridge: Cambridge University Press.

McCloskey, D. N. (2007). *The bourgeois virtues: Ethics for an age of commerce* (1st ed.). Chicago and London: University of Chicago Press.

Mitchell, R. K., Agle, B. R., & Wood, D. J. (1997). Toward a theory of stakeholder identification and salience: Defining the principle of who and what really counts. *The Academy of Management Review*, *22*(4), 853–886.

Montesquieu, C. de S. (1751). *The spirit of laws*. Printed for G. and A. Ewing and G. Faulkner.

Moon, J. (2004). *Government as a driver of corporate social responsibility*. Research Paper Series. International Centre for Corporate Social Responsibility. Nottingham University, UK.

Munck, R. (2003). *Globalisation, labour and the Polanyi problem or, the issue of counter hegemony*. Retrieved from http://www.theglobalsite.ac.uk/press/402munck.htm. Accessed on July 3, 2011.

Ocler, R. (2006). From what we say to what we tell: The rhetoric of social responsibility in France. *Social Responsibility Journal*, *2*(3/4), 300–307.

Ocler, R. (2009). Discourse analysis and corporate social responsibility: A qualitative approach. *Society and Business Review*, *4*(3), 175–186.

O'Neill, J. W. (2002). The role of storytelling in affecting organizational reality in the strategic management process. *The Journal of Behavioral and Applied Management*, *4*(1), 3.

Paine, T. (2000). *The rights of man*. Mineaola, NY: Dover Publications Inc. Original work published 1791/1792.

Parker, C. (2007). Meta-regulation: Legal accountability for corporate social responsibility. In D. J. McBarnet, A. Voiculescu, & T. Campbell (Eds.), *The new corporate accountability: Corporate social responsibility and the law*. Cambridge: Cambridge University Press.

Perry-Kessaris, A. (2011). Prepare your indicators: Economics imperialism on the shores of law and development. *International Journal of Law in Context*, *7*(4), 401–421.

Polanyi, K. (2002). *The great transformation: The political and economic origins of our time* (2nd ed.). Boston, Massachusetts: Beacon Press. Original work published 1944.

Power, M. (2005). Organizational responses to risk: The rise of the chief officer. In B. Hutter & M. Power (Eds.), *Organizational encounters with risk* (pp. 132–148). Cambridge, UK: Cambridge University Press.

Preston, L. E., & Post, J. E. (1975). *Private management and public policy: Principle of public responsibility*. Englewood Cliffs, NJ: Prentice Hall.

Rodrigues, J., & Carvalho, L. F. (2005, June). *The continuing relevance of Fred Hirsch's insights on markets and morality*. WP No. 2005/43, ISCTE – Instituto Superior de Ciencias do Trabalho e da Empresa.

Ruggie, J. G. (1982). International regimes, transactions, and change: Embedded liberalism in the postwar economic order. *International Organization*, *36*(2), 379–415.

Schwaninger, M. (2004). What can cybernetics contribute to the conscious evolution of organizations and society? *Systems Research and Behavioral Science*, *21*, 515–527.

Selznick, P. (2002). *The communitarian persuasion*. Washington, DC: Woodrow Wilson Center Press.

Smith, A. (2002). *The theory of moral sentiments*. Gloucestershire, UK: Clarendon Press Original work published 1759.

Smith, A. (2008). *An inquiry into the nature and causes of the wealth of nations* (1st ed., *Vol. I*, p. 1776). Charleston, South Carolina: BiblioBazaar.

Starr, A. (2005). *Global revolt: A guide to the movements against globalization*. London and New York: Zed Books.

Unerman, J., & O'Dwyer, B. (2007). The business case for regulation of corporate social responsibility and accountability. *Accounting Forum*, *31*(4), 332–353.

van Leeuwen, T. (2009). Discourse as the recontextualization of social practice: A guide. In R. Wodak & M. Meyer (Eds.), *Methods of critical discourse analysis* (pp. 144–161). London; New Delhi; Singapore: Sage.

van Marrewijk, M. (2003). Concepts and definitions of CSR and corporate sustainability: Between agency and communion. *Journal of Business Ethics*, *44*(2), 95–105.

Vico, G. (1984). *The new science of Giambattista Vico*. New York: Cornell University Press. Original work published 1744.

Vogel, D. J. (2005). Is there a market for virtue? The business case for corporate social responsibility. *California Management Review*, *47*(4), 19–45.

Welker, M. A. (2009). "Corporate security begins in the community": Mining, the corporate social responsibility industry, and environmental advocacy in Indonesia. *Cultural Anthropology 24*(1), 142–179.

Wodak, R., & Meyer, M. (Eds.). (2009). *Methods of critical discourse analysis*. London; New Delhi; Singapore: Sage.

Wood, D. J. (1991). Corporate social performance revisited. *Academy of Management Review*, *18*, 691–718.

Zenisek, T. J. (1979). Corporate social responsibility: A conceptualisa- tion based on organisational literature. *Academy of Management Review*, *4*(3), 359–368.

Zinn, J. O., & Taylor-Gooby, P. (2006). The challenge of (managing) new risks. In P. Taylor-Gooby & J. O. Zinn (Eds.), *Risk in social science* (pp. 54–75). Oxford: Oxford University Press.

Zumbansen, P. (2011). Neither "public" nor "private", "national" nor "international": Transnational corporate governance from a legal pluralist perspective. *Journal of Law and Society*, *38*(1), 50–75.

THEME 3
EMBEDDING ECONOMIC ACTIVITY THROUGH EMOTIONS?

EMOTIONS AND RISK REGULATION

Susan A. Bandes

ABSTRACT

The concept of risk is often approached as if it is self-defining. Yet placing an event or activity in the category of "risk" is a categorization with consequences. Framing normatively complex problems like immigration, terrorism, or monetary crisis as risks that require regulating suggests that certain cognitive tools are best suited for analyzing them. It suggests that the problems are measurable or quantifiable, that they lend themselves to utilitarian calculus, and that they have ascertainably correct solutions that require no value judgments. This article employs emotion theory to illustrate the difficulties with approaching normatively complex areas of governmental policy through the framework of risk regulation. It argues that interdisciplinary inquiry into the role of emotion in human behavior sheds light on how risks are assessed, prioritized, and ameliorated, on how the category of risk is constructed, and on how that categorization affects the cognitive tools and approaches we bring to normatively complex problems. The article begins with a brief discussion of behavioral law and economics, which styles itself a corrective to law and economics, but which replicates its fatal flaw: its unrealistic view of human behavior. Next it turns to two more specific problems with the

From Economy to Society? Perspectives on Transnational Risk Regulation
Studies in Law, Politics, and Society, Volume 62, 219–237

ISSN: 1059-4337/doi:10.1108/S1059-4337(2013)0000062009

standard notion of risk formulation. First, the standard notion reads out the essential role of emotion in deliberation about risk regulation and overvalues top-down expert knowledge. Second, it reads out the heuristics that erase patterns and maintain the status quo. Finally, the article will focus on two illustrative case studies, the Chicago heat wave of 1995, and Hurricane Katrina.

Keywords: Behavioral law and economics; emotion theory; risk regulation; bounded rationality; heuristics and bias; cognitive bias

Risk regulation is a rapidly growing area of inquiry: an effort to systemize principles for identifying, prioritizing, and ameliorating risk in a variety of contexts. Placing an event or activity in the category of "risk," or the assessment of an event or activity in the category of "risk regulation" or "risk management," is a categorization with consequences. Yet the concept of risk is often approached as if it is self-defining.

Framing an inquiry in terms of risk assessment or risk management may seem unproblematic when the question appears quantifiable: for example, whether a speed limit of 60 miles per hour saves more lives than a speed limit of 50 miles per hour. Even when data appears quantifiable, issues of interpretation and evaluation are unavoidable. But the less salient and therefore more pernicious problem is that the very use of risk analysis implies a certain way of framing and approaching a problem. Framing normatively complex problems like immigration, terrorism, or monetary crisis as risks that require regulating suggests that certain cognitive tools are best suited for analyzing them. It suggests that the problems are measurable or quantifiable, that they lend themselves to utilitarian calculus, and that they have ascertainably correct solutions that require no value judgments. The notion of ascertainably correct solutions, moreover, implies that risk regulation is best left to the experts – those with education and access to information that will enable them to reach those right answers unimpeded by emotion and other hurdles to rational measurement. This view is dangerous both because it elides the initial choices implicit in defining social, political, and economic problems – and even natural disasters – as regulable risks, and because it denies, and therefore insulates from scrutiny, the emotional and moral assumptions that influence our approach to those problems.

This article will employ emotion theory to illustrate the difficulties with approaching normatively complex areas of governmental policy through the framework of risk regulation. Emotion theory is an emerging interdisciplinary field that explores the role of emotion in human behavior in general and in the dynamics of decision making in particular, drawing on a range of fields that includes psychology, cognitive neuroscience, sociology, anthropology, philosophy, and literary studies.[1] Even in fields like psychology that take the human psyche as their central subject, the study of emotion has not always been embraced. But in fields that style themselves as scientific or autonomous, as trafficking in the measurable rather than the subjective, the study of emotion is a particularly hard sell. This resistance is problematic when it leads to conclusions drawn and policies adopted based on assumptions about emotion – assumptions that go unexamined.

The study of the perception and assessment of risk is rife with issues about how people make decisions in conditions of uncertainty, and about how to assess, predict, and influence human behavior. It is rife with issues about the role of fear, hope, denial, and other emotions that influence planning and avoidance. Yet risk analysis too rarely makes use of the rapidly growing knowledge in the fields of psychology and cognitive neuroscience about how decisions are made, or in the field of sociology about how group and institutional structure influence decision making. This article argues that interdisciplinary inquiry into the role of emotion in human behavior sheds important light on how risks are assessed, prioritized, and ameliorated, on how the category of "risk" is constructed, and on how that categorization affects the cognitive tools and approaches we bring to normatively complex problems.

First, the choice of category is influenced by assumptions about human behavior: what motivations are inferred, what causal links are drawn, what behaviors are viewed as isolated and atomistic, what is regarded as "natural" or unavoidable, and how responsibility and blame are allocated. Emotion theory helps reveal and evaluate these hidden assumptions.

Second, and particularly germane to the topic of governmental and global risk regulation, institutions are designed and maintained based on assumptions not just about individual actors, but about how group dynamics transform emotion. Emotion theory is increasingly focusing on how these rules of behavior operate in varying institutional contexts. In addition, institutional structure influences attitudes and motivations, both through top-down regulation and modeling of behavior, and through the interpretive and enforcement actions of institutional agents (see generally Bandes, 2009a).

Third, social norms and attitudes about crime, immigration, foreign aid, and even the role of governmental and intergovernmental institutions in regulating financial behavior and addressing financial crisis are animated by emotionally laden views about how the world ought to work. These assumptions and values arise and evolve through social exchange and deliberation.

Finally, emotion theory sheds light on the tenacity with which we defend our assumptions and categories, even as they lose their coherence or prove unworkable. Bettina Lange insightfully describes the "negative emotion associated with revealing the emotional aspects of decision making" (2002). There is a distinct but overlapping phenomenon at work as well: negative emotion associated with threats to the foundations of one's discipline. As mentioned above, these negative emotional reactions have been in evidence in fields like economics and law that view themselves as autonomous, scientific disciplines that can operate without reference to unruly human nature (for discussion of these reactions, see Abrams & Keren, 2010; Bandes, 2009b).

This article will seek to illustrate some of the traps and perils of the risk framework, particularly when normatively complex issues are at stake. It will begin with a brief discussion of behavioral law and economics, which styles itself a corrective to law and economics, but which replicates its fatal flaw: its unrealistic view of human behavior. Next it will turn to two more specific problems with the standard notion of risk formulation. First, it reads out the essential role of emotion in deliberation about risk regulation and overvalues top-down expert knowledge. Second, it reads out the heuristics that erase patterns and maintain the status quo. Finally, the article will focus on two case studies, the Chicago heat wave of 1995, and the multifaceted disaster known as Hurricane Katrina. These case studies are offered to illustrate the extent to which assumptions and value judgments about human emotion and human behavior pervade policymaking about risk assessment and avoidance, and the perils of leaving such evaluations to the experts.

THE INTERTWINED NATURE OF THE ECONOMIC AND SOCIAL SPHERES

Although emotion theory is a wide ranging and contentious field, scholars across the range of disciplines that study cognitive processes are in substantial agreement on one central point: that emotion is a fundamental aspect of cognition rather than a force that operates in necessary opposition to rational thought (Bandes, 2000, 2009a). In this central regard, emotion theory is at odds with not only law and economics, but behavioral law and economics. Behavioral law and economics has styled itself as a corrective to classical economic theories; one that takes the vagaries of human behavior into account (Sunstein, 2000). It acknowledges that human beings do not always behave as rational actors; that they often act under conditions of bounded rationality, circumscribed by lack of time, lack of information, and other conditions that interfere with rational decision making. In short, like classical law and economics, behavioral law and economics assumes that emotions, heuristics, and other deviations from the rational actor model are interferences with an ideal. It assumes that the rational economic actor is not only an attainable but a worthy model for behavior. Although it acknowledges the influence of emotion, it treats emotion as an unfortunate and ultimately eradicable interference with rational thought and action. This central assumption underlying both the rational actor model and behavioral law and economics is flawed as both a descriptive matter and a normative one.

One of Karl Polanyi's enduring insights is that the economic sphere cannot be understood without reference to knowledge about human behavior and social norms. What Polanyi wrote in the 1940s is unsettlingly germane today: an essential reminder that the market economy is an artifact, a political and social construct, rather than the natural and inevitable state of affairs it is often assumed to be. Adam Smith's notion of the invisible hand has proved astoundingly resilient (1902).[2] It rests on assumptions about human behavior as profit-maximizing, about markets as self-regulating, and about the public interest as self-interest in its aggregate form, that "go without saying" and that thus escape scrutiny (see, e.g., Polanyi, 1944).[3] As the economic sociologist Fred Block observed about the enduring relevance of Polanyi's work: "History … has shown us again and again that market-based societies only work because markets are embedded within legal and political rules that prevent opportunistic and predatory behaviors" (2008).

The lesson bears repeating yet again. Those who approach economics or other disciplines as autonomous, as somehow exempt from the usual rules and vagaries of human behavior, do so at their peril – and ours. As has been widely reported, former U.S. Federal Reserve Chairman Alan Greenspan recently acknowledged that there was a flaw in his model of financial risk management. The flaw had to do with a misapprehension about human nature – as became evident, unregulated self-interest did not necessarily lead to shareholder well-being or a self-regulating market. Greenspan had failed to properly account for human greed, self-dealing, and self-deception. Greenspan's acknowledgment that the reigning economic paradigm was flawed was accompanied by an acknowledgment (perhaps even more significant) *that it was in fact a model* – a conceptual framework, not a self-contained and accurate representation of the economic landscape. And as Polanyi's work emphasizes, no matter how internally consistent a model is, it is a dangerous thing in the world of actual policymaking if it is premised on inaccurate assumptions. It is a dangerous thing if it is perceived, not as a model with uses and limitations, but as an accurate description of the natural world, useful for all purposes and without limitation. Here is the germane portion of Greenspan's testimony:

> Representative Henry Waxman: Do you feel that your ideology pushed you to make decisions that you wished you had not made?
>
> Greenspan: Well, remember what an ideology is: it is a conceptual framework about the way people deal with reality; everyone has one; you have to; to exist you need an ideology. The question is, whether it is accurate or not. What I'm saying to you is, yes, I found a flaw. I don't know how significant or permanent it is. But I have been very distressed by that fact. (European Institute, 2009)

Greenspan acknowledges that everyone has a conceptual framework about the way the world works – some more accurate than others. This acknowledgment strikes at the heart of the reigning economic paradigm. Because economists must begin with a conceptual framework about how human beings behave both individually and collectively, economics cannot be a self-contained field. It must inevitably rest on assumptions about the social sphere. As David Brooks recently argued in *The New York Times*, the economists gained coherence for their model by "amputating most of human nature." He predicted that economists, now that they have acknowledged the relevance of human nature, will soon find that "the moral and social yearnings of fully realized human beings are not reducible to universal laws and cannot be studied like physics." He quoted Keynes' observation that "Economics is a moral science. It deals with motives, expectations, psychological uncertainties" (Brooks, 2010). But this moral science is not economics as currently constituted, and it is increasingly hard to deny the obvious lesson that those trained as economists are not therefore adept at the study of motives, expectations, and moral quandaries. Indeed the evidence to the contrary seems to mount daily (see, e.g., Morgenson & Rosner, 2011; and Morgenson & Story, 2011).[4]

This observation leads to another key point, one particularly relevant to the literature on decision making about risk. Experts are as liable as laypeople to make cognitive errors about human behavior. They may in fact be more likely to make certain cognitive errors. Studies show that experts often possess overconfidence in their own judgments (Dana, 2003; Tesser & Leone, 1977). In addition, there are strong incentives for experts to remain loyal to the organizing principles of their fields of expertise (Cassidy, 2010: conversations with many of the key economists of the Chicago School about how they now view their theories). And there is a related problem. Risks that do not conform to recognized areas of expertise might remain unrecognized or miscategorized.

Greenspan's model assumed away the complexity of human nature. The flaw is not only that it assumed individuals who act in a way that no individual actually acts – that it assumed away denial, greed, conflicts of interest, and overoptimism. The flaw is also that the model's unit of analysis is the individual (Ahdeih, 2009). It assumes away not only individual human nature but also social dynamics. Because it assumes that group behavior is simply the aggregate of individual preferences, it fails to focus on how individuals make decisions about collective or institutional goals. For the same reason, it fails to focus on how group dynamics and institutionalized incentives and disincentives affect decision making.

As it happens, this second flaw in Greenspan's model is one that until recently beset the study of emotion in a number of disciplines as well. The individual was the unit of analysis. Motivation, moral development, and norm-creation were assumed to be private, individual, and internally driven. But more recently psychology, sociology, anthropology, political science, risk management, and other disciplines have recognized the importance of studying emotion not as a private, internal, individual phenomenon, but as a dynamic social process (Bandes, 2009a, 2011). For those who study law, economics, and other fields that focus on governmental systems and other institutional dynamics, this was a crucial step. It is the crucial next step for behavioral law and economics if it is to investigate the institutional role in regulating self-dealing, self-deception, groupthink, and other predictable human behaviors and behavioral dynamics (see e.g. Bazerman & Gino, 2012).

It would be an overstatement to say that either economic discourse or the discourse of risk regulation has ignored emotion. Yet the role emotion has played in these fora has been revealing. The rational actor paradigm has somewhat grudgingly incorporated the bounded rationality critique of Herbert Simon (1957) and others, which argues that economic actors are prone to certain recurring cognitive errors. But this notion of bounded rationality, which has given rise to the subdisciplines of behavioral economics and behavioral law and economics, should not be regarded as a challenge to the core belief in the rational actor. Behavioral economics, while acknowledging that people often deviate from the rational actor ideal, for the most part shares the assumption that pure rationality, untouched by affect, is desirable and, in some utopian sense, possible, if only one could address the systematic deviations, biases, and mental shortcuts that cloud judgment. It has not grappled with, much less embraced, the current view of cognition and emotion as inextricably intertwined, and of heuristics as a pervasive part of reasoning (Bandes, 2008).

More specifically, the bounded rationality literature acknowledges the operation of certain heuristics; generally those that it regards as imperfect shortcuts to accurate calculation of measurable risks (e.g., anchoring bias, the endowment effect, the representativeness heuristic). Yet heuristics are far more pervasive than this account suggests, and indeed the use of heuristics is essential to human functioning. Without the ability to screen, organize, and prioritize incoming stimuli and data, we would be unable to function. The question is not whether to employ heuristics; it is which heuristics are best suited to the cognitive tasks at hand.

The connection between heuristics and emotions is woefully underexplored. But as I will discuss shortly, emotion plays an unavoidable and in some respects essential role in the everyday screening, organizing, and prioritizing of stimuli that enable us to function. It assists in identifying who to fear or to trust, what to care about, when to act. Emotion does not always lead to optimal decisions, of course, but people without access to their emotions, or to the ability to make quick, instinctual judgments, tend to make very bad decisions indeed, if they can bring themselves to make a decision at all (Damasio, 1994).[5] Current cognitive theorists describe two interwoven systems, which together allow for both quick, instinctual "gut" reactions and slower, more conscious deliberation. Both are essential to good decision making, and contrary to much of the conventional wisdom, both utilize emotion – for better or for worse (Bandes, 2008, p. 429). The behavioral economists, as I will discuss shortly, remain loyal to the outmoded view that emotion is, for the most part, an impediment.

LAY EMOTION AND EXPERT RATIONALITY

Emotion – the emotion of fear at least – receives some acknowledgment in the risk regulation literature. Nevertheless, the role it plays is telling. In the behavioral economics lexicon, emotion, or affect, is a heuristic. Heuristics are shortcuts. They are the province of laypeople. Laypeople are portrayed as having fears and other strong emotions toward risk that are often unjustified by the empirical evidence. Emotion and other heuristics are considered proper subjects of study, albeit grudgingly, because it is important to understand lay perceptions. Lay perceptions need to be studied so they can be addressed and, more often than not, corrected. In this account laypeople's perceptions of risk are affected by emotion and cognitive bias because laypeople, unlike experts or governmental officials, do not have access to the best science or to all the facts about the scope of the problem at hand. This is a deeply flawed account of decision making; one that misperceives the role of both emotion and heuristics, and that overstates the boundary between assessment of fact and perception of value.

Current emotion research views emotion as shaping perceptions of fact as well as perceptions of value, and as influencing deliberative as well as intuitive reasoning. The initial factual assumptions underlying intuitive processing continue to exert a strong influence on the more deliberative processing that follows. For example, the debate in the United States about the causes of and solutions to the recent housing crisis is raged not merely on the level of values but on the level of fact. Proponents and opponents have different assumptions about human behavior, and these tend to be tightly intertwined with their assumptions about the role of government. They differ, for example, on the role of naïve or greedy first time buyers in precipitating the crisis, on the importance of home ownership as a core American value, on the role of self-dealing and greed among private institutional players and therefore the need for government oversight of those players, and on whether governmental agencies were too intrusive or asleep at the wheel.[6]

These are initial intuitions and perspectives about crisis that combine constructions of fact with constructions of value. Unless those who hold these views come to question their initial assumptions – something people rarely do of their own accord – the deliberation that follows will simply build upon and reinforce those initial assumptions. This dynamic has implications for the question of experts. If the intuitive process leads to errors and distortions, deliberation will not correct these unless they are brought into consciousness – and this is true for experts as well as laypeople (Bandes, 2008).

Early work on risk perception, like the work of Peter Sandman, found that feelings of dread were a major determinant of public perception and acceptance of risk (1989, cited in Slovic, 2004). Paul Slovic in his work on the affect heuristic has focused on fear, dread, outrage, and other emotions that drive individual perceptions about risk. Slovic is engaged in sophisticated and important work on the role of emotion, instinct, and morality in judgments about global policy. In an early work, he and his coauthors coined the term "affect heuristic" to describe the role of emotion in risk assessment. The term is misleading and in need of revision, and has been relied on to unfortunate effect. Here is Slovic's description of the affect heuristic:

> Using an overall, readily available affective impression can be easier and more efficient than weighing the pros and cons of various reasons or retrieving relevant examples from memory, especially when the required judgment or decision is complex or mental resources are limited. This characterization of a mental short-cut has led to labeling the use of affect a "heuristic." (Slovic, 2004, p. 976)

In this account, affect (emotion) is portrayed as a heuristic, a shortcut, rather than a component of the reasoning process. The "judgment under uncertainty"[7] literature that undergirds behavioral economics defines a heuristic as "a mental shortcut for a more careful evaluation" (Sunstein, 2002). It does not accept that emotion adds any value to the inquiry – it is a second best shortcut when there is insufficient time for careful deliberation.

Slovic observes that different types of decision making require different cognitive tools: a crucial observation. But this is where the construction of the category of risk becomes essential. The scholars who study judgment under uncertainty, and the heuristics and biases it employs, generally approach risk assessment as an essentially computational task – a task of finding the most accurate way to determine and measure quantifiable threats. Their works are filled with studies about probability estimates in situations with a mathematically correct answer (see Slovic, 2004, pp. 980–982; and sources cited in Bandes, 2008, p. 247, n. 28). They rely on computational games – visual games estimating numbers of jelly beans, numerical brain twisters. The sorts of risks they discuss involve probability and relative frequency – perception versus reality of the frequency of shark attacks, of air crash deaths versus highway deaths, of deaths caused by radiation versus exposure to the sun, of lives saved by lowering the speed limit. In these examples, people use shortcuts and get things wrong – they reach demonstrably inaccurate results because they rely on intuition rather than a slower, more deliberative process. If risks are readily identifiable and quantifiable, all that remains is to bring to bear the best methods for measuring the risks and then to determine the appropriate calculus for weighing them.

The problem is that the field has moved beyond the study of computational processes to address questions about governmental and global policy that are both empirically and normatively complex and that have no definitive, value-neutral answers. Distinguishing helpful heuristics from unhelpful biases requires examining particular emotional influences on particular judgmental tasks and making a normative decision about whether they advance or distort judgment. These evaluations may differ depending on whether the reasoning is purely computational or involves more complex normative social judgments.

If affect were a heuristic mainly employed by the uninformed or those pressed for time, it would make sense to be very cautious about according normative weight to beliefs that are the product of – or are unduly influenced by – these substitute processes and to prefer the conclusions reached by those with more time and better information. Thus Cass Sunstein and others writing in this field, including Slovic himself, assume that experts will have a more accurate view of the prevalence and seriousness of risks.[8] As I mentioned above, this assumption is problematic on two counts: first, it treats experts as immune from normal cognitive processes and outside the flow of general social norms, and second, it reads out the essential role of emotion in cognition for both experts and laypeople.

Identifying risk requires crafting a coherent narrative of a problem amenable to policy recommendations. The task implicates a cognitive process that is both normative and affect-laden. Causation is never solely a factual calculation – it always requires a standard of proof, a decision about the relevance of motive, fault, or blameworthiness, and a way of comparing contributory factors. Any discussion of solutions will be influenced, in part, by evaluative assumptions and biases about who is deserving of aid, what is fixable and what is inevitable, which factors are most relevant, and who is within our circle of empathy and compassion.

Sunstein and others assume that when risks are debated by non-experts, that debate will exacerbate misconceptions. Sunstein, for example, talks of availability cascades, availability errors, probability neglect, and other distortions that make certain measurable risks seem more salient than they actually are. He argues that "senseless policies result from social influences, through which some risks come to seem serious and other trivial, only because of what other people seem to think" (Sunstein, 2002).[9] He is willing to acknowledge the importance of taking lay perceptions of risk into account on occasion, but only because he views it as important to acquiesce, at times, to irrational but deeply held fears. This is very different from acknowledging that as to certain categories of regulation, emotion is an inescapable and sometimes essential aspect of the deliberative process rather than a hindrance to it.

RISK: AGGREGATED OR ATOMIZED?

The cognitive errors on which the behavioral economists tend to focus are those that identify patterns that don't exist or that overestimate measurable risks. One obvious limitation to this approach, as I discussed, is that many risks are not quantifiable – risks to civil liberties for example. But in addition there are heuristics, frames, and biases that erase or minimize certain risk patterns, and these are not discussed in the behavioral economic literature. It is painful and destabilizing to acknowledge and address deeply rooted systemic inequalities and structural deficits, and various mechanisms exist that help us shield ourselves from this discomfort (Bandes, 1999, pp. 1320–1322). For instance "just world thinking" describes the deeply rooted need to believe the world is a just place (Lerner & Miller, 1978). When inequities present themselves, there is a strong impulse to explain them away or assume they are deserved (Bandes, 1999; see also Blasi & Jost, 2006). Persistent economic inequities may be recast as social problems, and moreover, as attributable to individual character. One common way to avoid cognitive dissonance is through the fundamental attribution error, which leads us to perceive our own bad fortune as situational, whereas others' bad fortune is due, not to systemic problems, but to their bad character (Ross, 1977). Bad fortune may also be attributed to nature, evolution, biology, god's will, or the aforementioned invisible hand of the market (Hanson & Hanson, 2006, p. 427). The upshot is that government is off the hook, and cognitive dissonance is ameliorated.

TWO ILLUSTRATIONS: THE CHICAGO HEATWAVE AND HURRICANE KATRINA

I will briefly discuss two disasters that illustrate the perils of cordoning off the inquiry into emotion and human behavior from the process of identifying, addressing, and preventing risk. These case studies illustrate the elasticity of the concept of a disaster, and the importance of the choice of frame and cognitive tools, for defining the nature and causes of a disaster and the sorts of expertise required to address it.[10]

In 1995, Chicago had a record breaking heat wave that led to 739 deaths in a six-day period. At the time and long thereafter the deaths were viewed not as a unified event, but rather as a string of individual tragedies. The deaths were portrayed as natural and unavoidable, or at times, as the fault of the victims' families or even the victims themselves. Sociologist Eric Klinenberg analyzed the factors that made it so difficult for this tragedy to be seen, first, as a unified phenomenon at all, and second, as anything other than a natural and inevitable disaster. He concluded that the deaths were the result of a complex combination of factors, most of which were man-made and therefore susceptible to correction. The most compelling message of the book is that many of the factors that caused and defined this disaster did not fall into familiar categories of risk or catastrophe and thus failed to register with experts or opinion makers. In part, this was an issue of salience, or availability – heat waves simply don't generate the tangible physical damage (or the spectacular, camera-ready images) that floods, fires, and hurricanes do. But in addition, the social factors that contributed to the mortality rate also contributed to the masking of the scope and nature of the disaster. The vast majority of the victims were poor, isolated, and "invisible" – that is, off the radar of the general populace and the "social scientific experts on disasters" (Bandes, 2008). Klinenberg noted that the methods and theories used in conventional health and climate studies deprive scientists of the instruments they need to conduct a thorough investigation. There is little in their professional tool kit to help explain the social sources of the disaster. Although every major study and report found that medical and meteorological approaches are inadequate to explain why so many Chicago residents died, no one analyzed how the city's social environment contributed to the devastation. As Klinenberg argues, before an unexpected situation can be perceived as a disaster or a risk, it needs to fit certain frames that prompt certain types of experts to ask – or to be asked – the questions they are used to addressing. In this case, "political officials, journalists, and research scientists established the dominant analyses of the heat wave as well as the basic categories that organized public discourse about the trauma" (Bandes, 2008). Because the disaster was viewed as a naturally occurring phenomenon, for years afterward experts and government officials saw no need to determine how to prevent such a disaster from happening again.

Even as to more easily recognizable disasters and tragedies, affect-laden assumptions about human behavior and causality affect risk assessment. Consider, for example, the response to the multifaceted tragedy known as Hurricane Katrina. What lessons about risk regulation can be learned from the facts of the disaster? The questions of causation and remedy require complex judgments of fact and value, and are rife with assumptions about human behavior.

To some, Katrina was a natural disaster, or at least a natural disaster in a place that is below sea level and therefore never should have been settled. To others, governmental acts and omissions, such as the failure to maintain an adequate seawall, were to blame. To many, Katrina reflected a failure of empathy – a searing indictment of a city that seemed to abandon its poor, minority citizens. Yet as legal scholars John Hanson and Kathleen Hanson have argued, inequality of the sort Katrina laid bare is hard to acknowledge, and there are ways of screening out such information. A common theme was that if the disaster fell most heavily on poor, minority residents, it was due to their own, individual poor choices – such as building shoddy homes on low ground or failing to implement an exit plan. This view overlooked systemic economic barriers that left large portions of the population without viable means to flee New Orleans or arrange alternative housing, and in many cases, without adequate warning of the evacuation (Hanson & Hanson, 2006, pp. 452–454). This "blame the individual victims" frame was buttressed by a portrayal of New Orleans in the immediate aftermath of Katrina as:

> a place where social norms had disintegrated and dangerous, uncontrolled lawlessness prevailed. The anarchy narrative was not limited to media stories based on unconfirmed sources, but was employed and perpetuated by New Orleans' highest public officials, including its chief of police and mayor, whose reports of terrible atrocities proved exaggerated at best. (Sun, 2011)

This myth proved mightily resistant to correction, though it was demonstrably incorrect. One heuristic at work here is implicit racial bias, a "linkage of blackness, badness, violence, and criminality" (Hanson & Hanson, 2006, p. 480). Such portrayals have consequences. As one scholar points out in reference to the response to Katrina:

> [this portrayal] may make it more likely that the president will deploy federal troops in a law enforcement capacity … and … less likely that the president will be willing to commit federal troops to humanitarian missions. Second, belief in exaggerated reports of looting and violence distorts implementation of response priorities outlined in disaster plans. Third, exaggerated fears of looting and violence lead public officials to implement restrictions on freedom and freedom of movement, many of which are authorized in state disaster laws, that may be counterproductive to relief efforts, including delaying return of evacuees to their homes. (Sun, 2011, pp. 13–14)

New Orleans stands to lose as much as 80% of its pre-Katrina minority population.

This diaspora is often portrayed as the inevitable result of a natural disaster. Representative Richard Baker, Republican Congressman from Baton Rouge, made this all too representative comment: "We finally cleaned up public housing in New Orleans. We couldn't do it. But God did" (Saulny, 2006, A14). The aftermath of the disaster was portrayed as the result of forces beyond the control of government: whether nature, or God, or the market. In part this reflects an omission bias – a reluctance to impute blame for failures to act (see Bandes, 1990; Hanson & Hanson, 2006). Yet governmental aid that was heavily skewed toward homeowners rather than renters, government decisions to demolish or fail to rebuild certain low-income housing projects and to offer no alternative housing, combined with a dearth of legal aid for those struggling with recalcitrant insurance companies and a lack of public pressure or oversight of patterns of insurance claim denials or price gouging by private renters, are just some of the factors that have helped produced a recovery that is shockingly skewed toward the non-minority and affluent areas and citizens (Inniss, 2007).

CONCLUSION

As Klinenberg's study, the Katrina tragedy, and for that matter Alan Greenspan's testimony, well illustrate, experts as well as laypeople will gather and evaluate data in light of implicit assumptions about how the world works – or ought to work. For experts to add value to the equation, they need more than just additional data. They need a means of identifying their own background assumptions and recognizing the emotional influences that animate them, as well as a means of splitting off pernicious biases and other influences that interfere with sound judgment. Current research suggests that people are not very good at identifying their own fallibilities. Indeed, left to their own devices, people screen out dissonant information, block out sources that don't validate their assumptions, and in short, become increasingly sure of their own convictions (Kunda, 1990). Correction is more likely to come from debate with others and exposure to differing viewpoints than from continued private deliberation.

Slovic, in his discussion of the importance of communication in the crafting of anti-terrorism policies, emphasizes the importance of top-down actions emanating from the government: actions taken to gain the public's trust and to address its fears and vulnerabilities (2004, pp. 988–999). Yet we should also focus on the public's own role in national and international conversations on issues like the appropriate balance of safety and security, or the acceptability of torture, or the balance between executive power and transparency, or more broadly, whether a polity should be defined by its fears or its hopes. Norms and values arise as part of – and are tested through – the social process of deliberation (Bandes, 2008; see also Moran, 2002).[11] Ideally, policy-making is an ongoing dialogue.

Emotion plays an essential role in that process. Slovic calls emotion a visceral factor, and generally regards it as a factor that misleads us. It can mislead us, but it is also crucial to the cognitive process, particularly once we move beyond number problems and word games to difficult policy issues requiring normative judgment. Empathy, for example, is an essential capacity for social beings, and an essential part of effective moral judgment – the kind that leads us to be concerned not only about our immediate neighbors, but also about the loss of life or hunger or human rights violations in countries far away. By itself, empathy provides no metric for making difficult allocational decisions – and it may pull us in directions that do not reflect our best collective judgment. It may lead us to misallocate to the attractive or the immediate, and to overlook genocide because it is far away or because it is easier to care about one person than thousands (Slovic, 2004, p. 983). Thus it is certainly right that government should not simply reflect individual fears and empathies; that it needs expert advice; that its role is to take a broader view of the common welfare; and that sometimes it needs to model and encourage values, not merely reflect them. Nevertheless, although empathy cannot provide a metric, it is one of a range of emotions and emotional capacities that are always part of the calculus. There is no "correct" metric for governmental obligation, and there exists no rational calculus uninfluenced by loyalty, compassion, and affect-based judgments of need and desert. There are no experts with the "view from nowhere" (Nagel, 1989). Government policy should not simply reflect emotion, but emotion per se is not the problem. The challenge is to encourage the helpful emotions, and discourage, educate, or cabin the unhelpful ones (Bandes, 2008, pp. 426–427). That is an ongoing conversation. Just as that conversation has a moral component; it has an emotional one – which we ignore at our peril.

NOTES

1. For introductions to the emerging field of law and emotion, see Bandes (2000) and Maroney (2006). For an introduction to emotion theory, see generally the *Emotion Review*, a publication of the International Society for Research on Emotion.

2. The individual, intending "only his own gain" is "led by an invisible hand to promote an end which was no part of his intention" and "by pursuing his own interest he frequently promotes that of society more effectually than when he really intends to promote it" (pp. 160–161).

3. "The transformation [from an agricultural to an industrial society] implied a change in the motive of action on the part of the members of society: for the motive of subsistence that of gain must be substituted. All transactions are turned into money transactions ... But the most startling peculiarity of the [market] system lies in the fact that once it is established, it must be allowed to function without outside interference." (p. 41)

4. Reporting on the report of Senator Levin's Permanent Subcommittee on Investigations' report entitled "Wall Street and the Financial Crisis: Anatomy of a Financial Collapse," finding rampant self-dealing, predatory behavior, and conflict of interest in the financial and regulatory communities.

5. For example, Damasio discusses his patient Elliot, who has lost access to his emotions, suggesting that "the cold-bloodedness of Elliot's reasoning prevented him from assigning different values to different options, and made his decision-making landscape hopelessly flat (p. 51)."

6. The report of the Financial Crisis Inquiry Commission (2011) on the causes of the current financial crisis splits along party lines in its assumptions about what aspects of human behavior caused the crisis – the greed and naivety of individual first time and unschooled investors or the greed, self-dealing, and conflicts of interest that beset financial industries and regulatory agencies.

7. The literature focuses on estimation and assessment of the likelihood of uncertain events occurring. The classic collection of essays on the topic is Kahneman, Slovic, and Tyersky (1982).

8. However, Slovic's discussion at least implicitly recognized that experts are subject to the same cognitive biases. See, for example, his studies of experienced forensic psychologists and psychiatrists assessing the likelihood that a mental patient would commit an act of violence soon after discharge (2004, pp. 980–981).

9. Sunstein does acknowledge and discuss the claim that laypeople have a "richer rationality" in that they focus on values other than a pure cost benefit analysis. However, he is generally skeptical of these claims (2002, pp. 58–61).

10. The following discussion of the Chicago Heat Wave and of Hurricane Katrina appeared, in somewhat different form, in Bandes (2008).

11. "Emotional sensations like fear result from socialization that links physiological responses to acceptable cognitive understandings and courses of action. Through this process, emotions become not simply individual conditions but products of collective normative judgments."

ACKNOWLEDGMENT

The author wishes to thank Bettina Lange for the invitation to participate in this written symposium and the conference on which the articles are based. She also wishes to thank the two anonymous reviewers for very helpful comments.

REFERENCES

Abrams, K., & Keren, H. (2010). Who's afraid of law and emotion. *Michigan Law Review, 94*, 1997–1074.

Ahdeih, R. (2011). *Beyond individualism in law and economics. Boston Univ. Law Review, 91*, 43–85.

Bandes, S. A. (1990). The negative constitution: A critique. *Michigan Law Review, 88*, 2271–2347.

Bandes, S. A. (1999). Patterns of injustice: Police brutality in the courts. *Buffalo Law Review, 47*, 1275–1341.

Bandes, S. A. (Ed.). (2000). *The passions of law*. New York, NY: NYU Press.

Bandes, S. A. (2008). Emotions, values, and the construction of risk. *University of Pennsylvania Law Review – PENNumbra, 156*, 421–434. Retrieved from http://www.pennumbra.com/responses/response.php?rid = 39

Bandes, S. A. (2009a). Foreword: Exploring the interaction between emotions and legal institutions. *Vermont Law Review, 33*, 387–394.

Bandes, S. A. (2009b). Repellent crimes and rational deliberation: Emotion and the death penalty. *Vermont Law Review, 33*, 489, 491–495.

Bandes, S. A. (2013). Emotion and deliberation: The autonomous citizen in the social world. In Fleming (Ed.), NOMOS LIII: Passions and Emotions. New York: NYU Press.

Bazerman, M. H., & Gino, F. (2012). Behavioral ethics: Toward a deeper understanding of moral judgment and dishonesty. *Annual Review of Law and Social Science, 8*, 85–104.

Blasi, G., & Jost, J. T. (2006). System justification theory and research: Implications for law, legal advocacy, and social justice. *California Law Review, 94*, 1119–1168.

Block, F. (2008). *No such thing as a free market*. Retrieved from http://www.longviewinstitute.org/nosuchthing

Brooks, D. (2010). The return of history. *The New York Times*, March 26. Retrieved from http://www.nytimes.com/2010/03/26/opinion/26brooks.html

Cassidy, J. (2010). After the blowup. *The New Yorker*, January 11. Retrieved from http://www.newyorker.com/reporting/2010/01/11/100111fa_fact_cassidy

Damasio, A. R. (1994). *Descartes' error: Emotion, reason, and the human brain*. New York, NY: HarperCollins Publishers.

Dana, D. A. (2003). A behavioral economic defense of the precautionary principle. *Northwestern University Law Review, 97*, 1315–1345.

European Institute. (2009). Alan Greenspan explains mistake behind global meltdown. Retrieved from http://www.europeaninstitute.org/2008120224/Winter/Spring-2009/alan-greenspan-explains-mistake-behind-global-meltdown.html

Financial Crisis Inquiry Commission. (2011). *The financial crisis inquiry report*. Retrieved from http://cybercemetery.unt.edu/archive/fcic/20110310173538/http://www.fcic.gov/report

Hanson, J. D., & Hanson, K. (2006). The blame frame: Justifying (racial) injustice in America. *Harvard Civil Rights-Civil Liberties Law Review, 41*, 413–480.

Inniss, L. B. (2007). A domestic right of return? Race, rights, and residency in New Orleans in the aftermath of Hurricane Katrina. *Boston College Third World Law Journal, 27*, 325–373.

International Society for Research on Emotion. *Emotion review*. Retrieved from http://emr.sagepub.com/

Kahneman, D., Slovic, P., & Tyersky, A. (Eds.). (1982). *Judgment under uncertainty: Heuristics and biases*. Cambridge, UK: Cambridge University Press.

Kunda, Z. (1990). The case for motivated reasoning. *Psychological Bulletin, 108*(3), 480–498.

Lange, B. (2002). The emotional dimension in legal regulation. *Journal of Law and Society, 29*(1), 197–225.

Lerner, M. J., & Miller, D. T. (1978). Just world research and the attribution process: Looking back and ahead. *Psychological Bulletin, 85*(5), 1030–1051.

Maroney, T. A. (2006). Law and emotion: A proposed taxonomy of an emerging field. *Law and Human Behavior, 30*(2), 119–142.

Moran, R. F. (2002). Fear unbound: A reply to Professor Sunstein. *Washburn Law Journal, 42*, 1–30.

Morgenson, G., & Rosner, J. (2011). *Reckless endangerment: How outsized ambition, greed, and corruption led to economic Armageddon.* New York, NY: Times Books.

Morgenson, G. & Story, L. (2011). Naming culprits in the financial crisis. *The New York Times.* Retrieved from http://www.nytimes.com/2011/04/14/business/14crisis.html

Nagel, T. (1989). *The view from nowhere.* Oxford, UK: Oxford University Press.

Polanyi, K. (1944). *The great transformation: The political and economic origins of our time.* Boston, MA: Beacon Press.

Ross, L. (1977). The intuitive psychologist and his shortcomings: Distortions in the attribution process. In L. Berkowitz (Ed.), *Advances in Experimental Social Psychology, 10*, 173. New York, NY: Academic Press.

Sandman, P. (1989). Hazard versus outrage in the public perception of risk. In V. T. Covello, D. B. McCallum, & M. T. Pavlova (Eds.), *Effective risk communication: The role and responsibility of government and nongovernment organizations.* New York, NY: Plenum Press.

Saulny, S. (2006). Residents clamoring to come home to New Orleans projects. *The New York Times*, June 6. Retrieved from http://www.nytimes.com/2006/06/06/us/nationalspecial/06housing.html

Simon, H. A. (1957). *Models of man: Social and rational.* New York, NY: Wiley.

Slovic, P. (2004). What's fear got to do with it? It's affect we need to worry about. *Missouri Law Review, 69*, 971–990.

Smith, A. (1902). The wealth of nations. New York: P.F. Collier & Son.

Sun, L. G. (2011). *Disaster mythology and the law.* Cornell L. Rev. 1131–1208.

Sunstein, C. R. (Ed.). (2000). *Behavioral law and economics.* Cambridge, UK: Cambridge University Press.

Sunstein, C. R. (2002). *Risk and reason: Safety, law, and the environment.* Cambridge, UK: Cambridge University Press.

Tesser, A., & Leone, C. (1977). Cognitive schemas and thought as determinants of attitude change. *Journal of Experimental Social Psychology, 13*, 340–356.

TRUST AND REGULATION: INSIGHTS FROM THE MINING INDUSTRY

Petrina Schiavi

ABSTRACT

This article develops Polanyi's (2001) theme of harnessing the regulatory capacity of a social sphere by focusing on trust as an emotion for framing risk regulatory regimes. Using the global mining sector as its focus, it explores the role of trust in the regulation and corporate management of social and environmental risk.

Sociological perspectives on trust are employed to identify and analyze dynamics of trust in the mining industry. The article draws on data collected between 2004 and 2008 by way of participant observation, document analysis, and in-depth qualitative interviews with around 40 representatives of the mining industry, NGOs, and regulators. Trust-relationships are an example of harnessing the regulatory capacity of a social sphere, but they can also undermine regulatory effort where trust is abused. The effectiveness of trust-based regulation would be enhanced by sanctions for nonperformance that target corporate motivations and financial performance. This research focused on a selection of large, multinational mining corporations with a presence in Australia.

From Economy to Society? Perspectives on Transnational Risk Regulation
Studies in Law, Politics, and Society, Volume 62, 239–261

ISSN: 1059-4337/doi:10.1108/S1059-4337(2013)0000062010

Generalizations could not be made from this research about smaller mining entities or single-country or state-owned corporations.

A better understanding of corporate trust-building behaviors and motivations can help inform more effective regulatory strategy for improving corporate, social, and environmental impacts. This article contributes to the body of knowledge about the regulation of the social and environmental performance of the mining industry. This is important as many of the remaining accessible mineral deposits across the globe are in areas of environmental and social significance.

Keywords: Regulation; mining industry; trust; risk; corporate responsibility

INTRODUCTION

Global mining corporations are large and powerful entities which are in the business of converting natural resources into material wealth. Host countries can benefit significantly from mining development through royalties, taxes, rents, and local employment, but the potential for environmental- and social-risk is high. Economic development through large-scale mining rarely comes without environmental and social costs. For this reason, the mining sector is a useful site for exploring the dynamics of the market economy in a practical setting.

In his thesis, Polanyi (2001) observes that the market economy reduces land to property, and people to workers for the purpose of making money. Left unchecked by government regulation, he warns that a self-adjusting market "annihilat(es) the human and natural substance of society … destroy(ing) man and transform(ing) his (sic) surroundings into a wilderness" (Polanyi, 2001, p. 13). This was indeed the case in the first half of the 20th century, when mining development was left mostly unchecked and unregulated by government intervention to the detriment of environmental and social health. In the 1960s and 1970s, public uprising against corporate environmental damage led to the development of environmental law in various jurisdictions across the world. Since the late 1990s, many governments have enacted legislation that requires mining corporations to address the social impacts of their activities in addition to their environmental impacts.

As Polanyi (2001) observes, government curtailment of a self-regulated market economy rarely comes without a cost to material welfare. It follows that business entities such as corporations would prefer to regulate themselves than to have regulation thrust upon them. Indeed, since the beginning of the 21st century, there has been a marked increase in corporate voluntary initiatives in the mining sector, with many of the world's largest mining corporations keen to demonstrate their commitment to the self-regulation of their social and environmental impacts as part of their broader management of transnational risk by signing up to voluntary codes of conduct. In doing so, these corporations are seeking to demonstrate that they can be trusted to regulate themselves.

Regulation is about "steering the flow of events and behavior" (Braithwaite, Coglianese, & Levi-Faur, 2007, p. 3). Formal regulatory instruments such as laws and voluntary initiatives may set standards for performance and sanctions for noncompliance, but the existence of such mechanisms alone does not provide the full picture of regulation. Regulation is also a "social activity that includes persuasion, influence, voluntary compliance, and self-regulation" (Braithwaite, 2006, p. 1–2). This article develops Polanyi's (2001) theme of harnessing the regulatory capacity of a social sphere by focusing on trust as an emotion for framing risk-regulatory regimes.

Large-scale mining developments have significant environmental, social, and economic impacts, both positive and negative. In order to obtain approval for mining development (or the expansion of existing developments), mining corporations must negotiate with those who are affected by and have legal interest in the land under which the mineral deposit lies. It is in this context that the social and environmental risks of mining become subject to scrutiny and vulnerable to regulation. It is also in this context that trust plays a central role.

The social and environmental transnational risks that are being considered to be addressed here through regulatory regimes, including regulatory regimes mobilizing trust, can be broadly understood as all of the negative impacts of mining developments on the environment and people. While the actual risks of mining activities will be specific to the characteristics of the surrounding landscape and population (e.g., the risks involved in the expansion of an existing mine site near a traditional mining township in Australia will be different from a proposed mine site near an environmentally sensitive area in a developing country), some of the generalized environmental and social risks of mining include: land clearing and its impact on biodiversity and local populations; waste rock disposal; water usage; pollution of air, water, and land; the relocation of local communities; the health and safety of mine site workers; the use of chemicals such as cyanide; and the transportation of minerals. Large, multinational mining corporations recognize that the way in which they address site-specific risks has an impact on their global reputation. This is especially the case following high-profile disasters such as chemical spills or mine site accidents that harm or kill workers. For this reason, site-specific environmental and social risks are considered to be transnational risks by multinational mining corporations, predominantly because of their potential impact on their global reputation.

This article is comprised of four main parts. The first part reviews relevant literature, commencing with regulatory theory that demonstrates the link between high trust/low regulation and low trust/high regulation. It commences with a review of relevant literature on trust-based regulation and then goes on to review the regulatory and sociological literature on trust-based regulation. It explores trust-based regulation in the mining industry from a sociological perspective. The second part of the article describes the broad characteristics of the global mining industry, and explains why the activities of large mining corporations offer a useful case study for exploring the dynamics of trust-based regulation in the market economy. This section also includes a discussion of methodology. The findings that emerged from the research around trust-based regulation are then presented, ranging from the reflections of government regulators on trust-based regulation, to insights from mining executives on corporate motivations for trust-building. The article concludes by considering the limitations of trust-based regulation for the market economy and other forms of regulating it, including the Polanyian approach of "harnessing the regulatory capacity of a social sphere."

TRUST AND LEGAL REGULATION

Trust is significant to the form that regulation takes and also in the way in which regulatory mechanisms are applied and enforced. For example, it has been noted that high levels of public trust in a corporation or a business sector can help to facilitate self-regulation (Eden, 1994). Indeed, it has been suggested that it can be politically costly for governments to attempt to regulate parties that are imbued with higher levels of public trust than the government itself (e.g., Braithwaite, Makkai, & Braithwaite, 2007).

In contrast, low levels of trust in certain industry sectors or professional groups can result in more demands for corporate accountability (Swift, 2001, p. 21) and greater public pressure for increased government regulation and control (Edelman, 2009, p. 15; Eden, 1994). An example of this can be seen in the dramatic loss of public trust in the accountancy profession following the Enron collapse (see Walker, 2005). The strong public demands for greater accountability following the Enron collapse and other corporate scandals resulted in the US government implementing the Sarbanes Oxley Act 2002 in an effort to regulate the accountability profession. Where there is a lack of trust in corporations, there will also be a greater demand for transparency in the form of assurance mechanisms (Wade, 2005, p. 188).

Relationships based on trust between the government regulator and the regulated party are central to the way in which legal regulation plays out. It has been suggested that high levels of trust between the government and the party being regulated encourages greater compliance with the law (Murphy, 2004). Others have demonstrated that government regulators who trust the party being regulated are more likely to employ a strategy of negotiated compliance-seeking than use punitive strategies for enforcement (Hawkins, 1984, 2002). As Hawkins (2002, p. 47) explains,

> Compliance strategy is regularly found, therefore, when a continuing or personal relationship exists between inspector and employer because it is based on and creates the conditions for the growth of trust. Trust is central to the viability of informal law enforcement.

In contrast, mistrust in the regulated party is more likely to foster a ritualistic approach to regulation (Braithwaite, 1993), and it is also more likely to result in prosecution rather than negotiated compliance-seeking. For example:

> Prosecution is more likely to be used (by regulatory agencies) where trust has broken down, or where an act or even is so serious that trust is trumped by other demands to act to which the regulatory agency feels vulnerable. (Hawkins, 2002, p. 421)

The dynamic of trust in regulation can be understood in the context of a "regulatory pyramid" (Ayres & Braithwaite, 1992), or a "pyramid of enforcement" (Fisse & Braithwaite, 1993), whereby strategies such as negotiated compliance-seeking sit at its base, and prosecution at its tip. If levels of trust between the regulator and the regulated party decrease, regulators move up the pyramid to employ more punitive and prescriptive regulatory strategies. For example, Fisse and Braithwaite (1993, p. 152) talk about their Accountability Model for dealing with corporate offenders in the following terms:

> The strategy of the Accountability Model is to appeal in the first instance to the responsibility of a wrongdoer to voluntarily put things right, and to back up that appeal by

> providing an array of sanctions that can be escalated in the event of non-compliance (the pyramid of enforcement). The tectonic plates of trust and rational self-interest may buckle, however, and where this happens, or is likely to happen, provision needs to be made for more intrusive methods of controlling corporate behaviour. The dynamisms of the Accountability Model is to shift our assumptions about corporate offenders from an assumption of trustworthiness, to an assumption of the corporation as a rational cheat which must be deterred, to an assumption that the corporation is an untrustworthy irrational resister to the law which must be incapacitated from further offending.

The escalation strategy of Fisse's and Braithwaite's Accountability Model can be seen in terms of a pyramid of enforcement. The base of the pyramid is the area where there is an assumption of trustworthiness of the intentions of the corporation to "put things right," where the tip of the pyramid is the point at which the corporation is seen as an "untrustworthy irrational resister to the law":

Fisse and Braithwaite (1993, p. 197) warn that laws that treat corporations as unworthy of trust to be good corporate citizens will find their assumptions to be a self-fulfilling prophecy. They go on to say that:

> Courts which operate from starting assumptions that corporations have good faith to right the wrongs of the past will mostly have that trust rewarded. Moreover, in the case where the axe of sanctions for non-compliance is poised over the corporation, the detection of abused trust can be readily remedied by allowing the forces of gravity to operate on the axe ... The community has little to lose from trust in the shadow of the axe, and a lot to gain. (Fisse & Braithwaite, 1993, p. 197)

TRUST AND REGULATORY STRATEGY

Of interest to this article is how trust might be leveraged or used strategically in regulatory contexts to achieve certain purposes. From a corporate perspective, the purposeful building of trust with key stakeholders such as communities and NGOs may reduce the need for true accountability (see Swift, 2001, p. 23). High levels of trust in corporations can help facilitate self-regulation as well as reduce demands for the government regulation of corporate behavior, while relationships based on trust between corporations and regulators can reduce the risk of prosecution by supporting negotiated compliance-seeking (Hawkins, 1984, 2002).

From the perspective of government regulators, trust may be used strategically to achieve regulatory outcomes through the threat of damage to corporate trustworthiness and reputation. For example, Hawkins (1984, p. 190) found that the public stigma and reputational damage that flows from an association with the machinery of the legal process and appearance in court can even have more impact on corporations that value their trustworthiness than the punishment meted out. Trust can strategically be used to encourage compliance with regulation. Regulatory strategies that use "naming and shaming" similarly work by affecting the trustworthiness of the "named and shamed" party. Further, if high levels of trust between government and the regulated party results in greater compliance with the law (Murphy, 2004), regulators who work on building trust with corporations may be able to improve levels of corporate compliance with the law.

WHAT IS TRUST?

Trust is a dynamic that is particularly important in the context of behavior that is going to happen in the future, or that is otherwise unobservable (Dasgupta, 1998, p.53). As Misztal (1996, p. 9) explains, "To trust is to believe that results of somebody's intended action will be appropriate from our point of view." Alternatively, when an organization has lost public trust, it means "many members of the public and stakeholder groups believe that the organization (and its contractors) neither intends to take their interests into account nor would it have the competence/capability to act effectively even if it tried to do so" (La Porte & Metlay, 1996, p. 342).

Trust has been identified as being hard to construct and easy to destroy (Dasgupta, 1988, p. 50). Because it is so easy to destroy, trust has been described as a "fragile commodity" (Levi, 1998, p. 81) that must be negotiated and bargained for (Giddens, 1994). It has been suggested that every action of an institution has an impact on an organization's trustworthiness (La Porte & Metlay, 1996, p. 345). Some of the main actions that have been identified as contributing to the building of trust include: transparency (Giddens, 1994; Misztal, 1996), integrity, and making credible commitments (Bennis, 1989; La Porte & Metlay, 1996; Whetten & Mackey, 2002); consistency in leadership (La Porte & Metlay, 1996, p. 345); sincerity and participation (Levi, 1988; Rothstein, 2005); having a good reputation (Dasgupta, 1988; Good, 1988; Granovetter, 1985); and being embedded in a trustworthy institution (or, "guardians of trust") (Hardin, 2002; Shapiro, 1987).

THE MINING INDUSTRY AS A SITE FOR EXPLORING TRUST

There are around 30–40 large, multinational mining corporations in the global mining industry (IIED & WBCSD, 2002). These corporations dominate the global mining scene, representing over 80% of the industry in terms of market capitalization (PWC, 2007). The remaining 20% of the mining industry in terms of market capitalization comprises of "intermediates" or middle-sized corporations that are engaged mainly in production and acquisition and which are often the subject of mergers and takeovers, as well as "junior" mining firms that concentrate on exploration and the sale of ore bodies to larger companies (IIED & WBCSD, 2002, p. 60–61).

The focus of this research is on the large global mining corporations that dominate the industry. In addition to the construction and operation of large-scale mine sites and related infrastructure necessary for the extraction and transportation of minerals, these corporations are engaged in exploration, refining, smelting, and the sale of metals, and concentrates on world markets (IIED & WBCSD, 2002, p. 60–61). They are able to engage in these activities because they have the financial resources to weather the long lead times and high costs involved in bringing a large mining development to fruition (Lenegan, 2006). These global corporations operate across a number of different countries, and are required to negotiate a range of regulatory requirements with regard to their environmental impacts. The environmental impacts of mining activities can be significant, not only at the initial stages of the construction of large-scale mine site operations, but also from the ongoing activities of mineral extraction, transportation, and processing.

The site of mining operations is dictated by the location of the mineral or ore body. This means that mining corporations cannot simply relocate their mining activities to a site where local communities and governments are more amenable to their development proposals. Instead, they have little choice but to engage in relationships with those who are affected by or have an interest in the environmental impacts of a proposed mining development in order to obtain development approval. This means that the ability to build relationships based on trust with key stakeholders is of increasing importance to many of these large mining corporations, especially those in the business of mineral extraction.

Disputes often arise between the mining industry and its stakeholders in relation to the actual and perceived distribution of the social, environmental, and economic burdens and benefits of mining. These conflicts can have a negative impact on mining corporations in terms of delays and work stoppages. Disputes between mining corporations and their key stakeholders can also make it difficult to obtain a legal license to construct a mining development, or to continue with their existing operations. Consequently, there has been a growing recognition within the mining industry that mining corporations need to address the expectations of local communities and other key stakeholders who have concerns over the impacts of mining activities in order to minimize the risk of conflict. This has become known as obtaining a "social license to operate." In the context of the mining industry, the "social license to operate" has been described as an "unwritten social contract" between the mining corporation and its stakeholders (MCA, 2005) that represents support from stakeholders for a mining project over and above meeting any legal requirements (BSR, 2003, p. 4). It is typically seen as complementary to the legal license to operate that is issued by government (MCA, 2004, p. 2). Trust plays a central role in obtaining a "social license to operate."

Mine site operations have a finite life. Once the mineral deposit is depleted, the mine site closes and the mining personnel usually move on to another development. However, the mining industry is running out of safe and easily accessible mining deposits in areas where there are few social and environmental issues to negotiate. Much new mining development is already taking place in or near ecologically fragile regions around the world (Sampat, 2003, p. 115). Large mining developments of the future are more likely to be in areas that have previously been considered marginal (PWC, 2007, p. 6), or "less desirable from a social or environmental perspective" (IIED & WBCSD, 2002, p. 83). Accordingly, there will be an increased pressure on mining corporations to demonstrate that they can address the environmental impacts of their operations in the future if they wish to gain access to new deposits.

METHODOLOGY

This article develops Polanyi's (2001) theme of harnessing the regulatory capacity of a social sphere by focusing on trust as an emotion for framing risk regulatory regimes. Using the global mining sector as its focus, it explores the role of trust in the regulation and corporate management of social and environmental risk. In-depth, semi-structured interviews were used to collect data in this project. This form of interviewing is consistent with a qualitative methodology and involves the use of open-ended questions that interviewees are encouraged to answer freely (Flick, 1998). Interviews were conducted with a cross-section of stakeholders that have an interest in the social and environmental performance of the mining industry. Interview subjects included: national and international NGOs; regulators at state and national levels, site level managers, and corporate executives from global mining corporations; lawyers; and other relevant stakeholders from the broader community of the "triad" of state, industry, and civil society (Ballard & Banks, 2003, p. 289). A total of 39 interviews were conducted between August 2003 and June 2007 in Australia and the United States. The first stage of identifying suitable interview participants involved a desktop review of the structure and composition of the global mining industry, the public and private organizations that helped to regulate the social and environmental performance of the mining industry, and the NGOs and other interest groups that had an active interest in the social and environmental performance of the mining industry. From this research, key personnel – both senior managers and front-line personnel – in the mining industry, regulatory agencies, and NGOs and other interest groups were identified.

Another source of data was the annual social and environmental reports published by large mining corporations. These reports represent the corporation's perspective on how the mining corporation has performed both socially and environmentally over a set period of time. The public discourses contained in these reports are written by corporations with many audiences in mind, including regulators, local communities, NGOs, and employees. The sample of reports selected for analysis is those published in 2006 by the world's largest mining corporations. These reports discuss the social and environmental performance of the mining corporation after 2005. Different mining corporations have different names for these reports, including: "Sustainability Report," "Responsibility Report," and "Report to Society," but the content of these reports is essentially the same. This report is the key publication issued by a mining corporation in which the corporation presents its perspective of its social and environmental performance over a period of one year. Some corporations discuss their performance against a specific set of goals, while others offer a general discussion of the achievements and challenges they have experienced in relation to their social and environmental impacts. Many reports also contain reference to the corporation's performance goals for the future.

FINDINGS

Regulators' Perspectives on Trust-Based Regulation

Regulators who participated in the research identified trust as playing a central role in the way in which they did their job. As can be seen in the following interview extract, one regulator quite specifically noted that the higher the level of trust between the regulator and the corporation, the less control the regulator exercises over them, and vice versa. For example:

> There's the whole issue of the relationship as a regulator of the issue of trust as against control: the higher the trust, the less control you want. The less trust, the higher control. And that tends to have a reflection in the sorts of conditions that you'll actually put on onto a project. (Regulator No. 3)

One of the responsibilities of the regulator in question was the processing of development approvals for mining. The final sentence in the above extract suggests that trust also has an impact on the kinds of conditions the regulator places on the development approval. It could be assumed that higher trust would result in more lenient conditions, and vice versa. This is one example of how relationships based on trust between a mining corporation and government regulator can result in regulatory outcomes that may be of benefit to the corporation.

Other research on corporate environmental regulation has suggested that larger corporations are generally viewed by regulators as being more trustworthy and as having more expertise than smaller corporations (Hawkins, 1984, p. 114). A similar finding emerged from this research data, with some regulators noting the differences between their dealings with large and small mining entities in terms of their trustworthiness. For example:

> Resource projects with mining sector, for example, tend to be pretty straightforward because they've been through the mill, most of the companies, um, know a lot. So if you are dealing with the larger companies, generally we don't have any problems at all. If you are dealing with the small to medium, small enterprises, they see us more of an imposition rather than as part of their core business. And as a result you can end up with, you tend to deal with the laggard end, if you like, and that all becomes about, well, can you trust the information that they give you? Are they taking shortcuts? Are there alternate ways of doing this because they are not thinking broadly? (Regulator No. 3)

Some of the key social and environmental issues affecting the mining industry that were identified by participants in the research included: waste generation and disposal; the pollution of air, land, and water; habitat destruction; the use of cyanide and other chemicals; energy and water usage; the negative impacts of mining activities on local communities; and, the health and safety of mining workers. Government regulators who participated in this study were asked what they believed may be some of the best ways to drive improved social and environmental performance in the mining industry in terms of addressing many of these areas. A number of respondents advocated the use of trust-based regulatory strategies. For example, Regulator No. 4 described how the preferred regulatory approach of their regulatory agency would be to build in rewards for excellence in performance. As the regulator explains below, in the case of large, reputation-sensitive corporations, a suitable reward may be improved reputation and trustworthiness:

> You don't have to be a great psychologist to know that people react to being rewarded, or having an incentive system is a very simple notion and it needn't even be a financial reward, if when you are dealing with large companies, if a large company can perceive some significant benefit to its image or to its public relations, to the perception that the community has of it, they often move very willingly and quite, go a long way. (Regulator No. 4)

The "strategic shaming" of large corporations is a strategy suggested by McMullen (1992, p. 123) as an effective means of regulating corporate behavior, which he suggests "is directed at the reputation of the firm and of corporate executives." This viewpoint was supported by the interview data. For example, one mining executive suggested that the best way to address corporate behavior is to strategically target the reputation or trustworthiness of corporations:

> Being continuously ranked on publicly available rankings on safety performance would be a very strong driver [of improved social and environmental performance], but the enforcement on that is potentially quite expensive. But yeah, if every company was put on a list of how they scored against enforcement or regulatory criteria, it would be a very strong driver for both public and private companies. (Mining Executive No. 3)

Trust is hard to build and easy to lose. Indeed, the legacy of past performance has been identified by the mining industry as one of the key challenges for the industry in the context of building trust (IIED & WBCSD, 2002). What this means for reputation-sensitive mining corporations is that exposure for poor performance can have a potentially devastating impact on the corporation's reputation and trustworthiness. This can then have an impact on their ability to access new resources or expand existing operations, both of which are essential for corporate longevity when in the business of exploiting natural resources.

THE "SOCIAL LICENSE TO OPERATE" AS A DRIVER OF CORPORATE PERFORMANCE

The mining industry has gone through a significant period of change over the past few decades in relation to the way in which it addresses its environmental performance. Participants in this research identified the late 1970s and early 1980s as the period when the mining industry first began to acknowledge that it had certain responsibilities in relation to its environmental impacts. Prior to this time, the industry was characterized as having little concern in relation to environmental issues. During the late-1980s, many mining corporations started to develop and implement environmental management systems. Most mining executives agreed that by the mid-1990s, large mining companies had a strong focus on the technical aspects of environmental management. As one mining executive observed, certain standards of performance in relation to the environmental impacts of mining, such as pollution, that were viewed as secondary issues for mining companies in the 1970s and 1980s, are "now seen as fundamental in terms of licenses and operations get shut down [for noncompliance]" (Mining Executive No. 5).

Four major drivers of change within the mining industry were identified by research participants. These were: government regulation, NGO activism, the global media and internet, and "external expectations." The driver singled out as the most significant in effecting change in the mining industry was "external expectations," or, the expectations from communities and other stakeholders in relation to how the corporation should behave. The source of these expectations was variously described as coming from "local communities," "stakeholders," or "the public" at both local and global levels. A number of mining executives specifically stated that it was a key priority for mining corporations to act in ways that meet community or external expectations in order to obtain their "social license to operate." For example,

> The community [driver] is at the forefront, because I guess it's just so clear that when you are a mine situated in the local community that these are the people who really need to want you to be there and that's definitely the number one side of things. (Mining Executive No. 2)

One mining executive even described the precedence of community expectations over government requirements in terms of a complete turnaround in priority:

> I think in the past a lot of companies hid behind government, and they hid behind legislation and they used their permits as a kind of shield. Basically just turning up in a remote location, waving their permit around and saying, "We don't care what you

> think, we're legally entitled to be here." I think that's moved entirely almost the other way where the priority is given to local communities and you tell government afterwards. It's a tricky thing and you have to balance those things ... (Mining Executive No. 9)

The research found that mining corporations that feel driven by "external expectations" are those who perceived that there would be financial consequences for failure to respond to those expectations. In other words, it is the real or perceived financial impact of external expectations that drives change in the mining industry. External expectations in relation to the social and environmental impacts of mining appeared to be most keenly felt by mining corporations in the context of the longevity and long-term success of the corporation, and were most often mentioned in relation to gaining access to new mineral deposits. For example:

> There are at least 10 projects in the world today, over the last few years, worth about $2–$4 billion that have been stopped because of community concerns. Nothing to do with regulation. Nothing to do with any permitting. (Mining Executive No. 9)

What becomes evident from these interview extracts is how keenly these mining executives are conscious of the impact of regulation through the social sphere on the business of the corporation, even more so than the impact of regulation through law. For example,

> But I think we will never be successful if we don't look at non-state or non-regulatory regulation of industry because it's the social one that's going to pass or fail us, not the regulatory one. The regulatory one is the operating license to stay in business, you know. Our social license... [if] you haven't got that, you going to have to say "Bye." That's the big one, that's the big risk to our business. (Mining Executive No. 4)

In the above responses, mining executives make a distinction between state or government regulation and regulation through the social sphere. State regulation can be understood as legal requirements of government on the activities of the mining corporation, and includes government legislation, conditions on development projects, and other legal contracts, all of which are enforceable by law. "Harnessing the regulatory capacity of a social sphere" is typically used to refer to non-state forms of regulation. In the context of the mining industry, it includes the need to obtain a social license to operate, and involves the negotiation of expectations from external stakeholders (at which point relationships based on trust are important) as well as the management of risk. In practice, however, the distinction is not always clear-cut. The interview data with regulators discussed in the previous section contained evidence that "harnessing the regulatory capacity of a social sphere" can also occur between government regulators and mining corporations. For example, regulators identified how relationships based on trust with mining corporations had an impact on the way in which they enforced government regulation, and trust was also a significant factor in the negotiation of legal contracts between the government and the corporation in terms of the imposition of conditions in development contracts. Similarly, mining corporations consider government regulators to be one of their key stakeholders when they are seeking to obtain a social license to operate.

TRUST AND CORPORATE BEHAVIOR

Corporate documents, such as annual reports, websites, and prospectuses, are a means by which organizations represent themselves to the outside world and create versions of reality (Atkinson & Coffey, 2004). The reports typically represent the corporation's perspective of their social and environmental performance over the period of one year. These reports are intended for a wide audience, from NGOs to shareholders to employees. While the "public relations" function of these reports cannot be denied in terms of the opportunity they provide to tell positive stories about the corporation, the reports also offer a forum for mining corporations to give their perspective on accidents or incidents that have occurred at their mine sites. Such reports also include information about corporate behavior and intentions. As such, the social and environmental reports published by a number of large mining corporations also offered a useful source of data for this research.

Corporate, social, and environmental reports published by the world's largest mining corporations in 2006 – namely, Rio Tinto, BHP Billiton, Anglo American, Newmont, Xstrata and Barrick Gold – were analyzed as part of this research in order to better understand corporate perspectives on trust, and to identify some of the ways in which trust had an impact on corporates' performances. The scope of the analysis was broadened from "trust" to include references to "reputation" which is one of the building blocks of trust. The analysis found that, in their corporate reports, mining corporations talked about their desire to be trusted, they communicated their belief that there was a "business case" for trust, and they talked about their views on how trust might be built and the activities that they were engaging in for the specific purpose of building trust. High-level commitments to trust-building were found in the sections of "Letter from the

CEO," and CEOs talked about building trust with a wide range of stakeholders, such as the "public at large," NGOs, employees, communities, suppliers, and shareholders.

In the body of reports, trust-building was discussed in specific circumstances in the context of the management of corporate behavior and stakeholder engagement. Some examples were also given in relation to specific instances in which the corporation actively sought to build trust with nearby communities and local residents. Corporations emphasized that trust was built through interactions with others, and characteristics that were seen to be necessary for trust-building included: transparency, integrity, delivering on commitments, and being forthright in communications. Internal management systems were also identified by some mining corporations as important in the context of trust-building.

Corporate references to "reputation" in corporate reports were also analyzed, and it was found that, like references to trust, corporations talked about their desire to build corporate reputation, the "business case for corporate reputation," and how they believed reputation could be built. Commitments to reputation-building were also found in "Message from the CEO" sections in reports. In addition, the term "reputational risk" was used by two corporations, Rio Tinto and BHP Billiton. BHP Billiton even had measurement indices for different levels of severity of types of reputational risk. The main tools and strategies that were identified in the context of reputation-building were internal management systems and corporate behavior that met performance objectives.

The large mining corporations studied for this research believed that they could build trust and reputation through certain actions and behaviors. There were some differences between the ways in which corporations believed that trust and reputation could be built. From a corporate perspective, the behaviors that were identified as contributing to the building, enhancement, and protection of corporate reputation related primarily to an aspiration toward high standards of social and environmental performance. Internal management systems that supported the achievement of these high levels of performance were seen to play an integral role in this regard. These included a variety of internal standards, procedures, and systems that were intended to guide and direct the behavior of the employees and agents of the corporation in relation to the social and environmental impacts of corporate activities.

Trust, on the other hand, was viewed by large, reputation-sensitive mining corporations as something that is primarily built through personal interactions with others. The characteristics of the party involved in the interaction – either the corporation as a whole or employees of the corporation – were viewed by mining corporations as a crucial factor in this context. Internal management systems were also seen to play a role in the building of trust, but they were not viewed as being as integral to trust-building as they were seen to be in relation to the building of reputation.

In the reports, corporations mostly talked about their aim of building trust and respect with local communities for the purpose of addressing misconceptions and lack of trust. Trust-building was especially identified as a benefit to corporations in circumstances where distrust threatened the business of the corporation. For example, Newmont stated that they were committed to building trust in order to "reassure communities" about the mine's impact at Cerro Quilish, Peru, where protests had resulted in preventing the planned expansion of Newmont's mining activities. Similarly, BHP Billiton talked about their focus on earning the "trust and respect of the nearby community" in a context where the local community was in fundamental opposition to any kind of corporate development on their land.

The interview data supported the findings from the document analysis. In particular, mining executives emphasized the role of trust in building a "social license to operate" through the building of personal relationships with others. For example:

> Social license to operate is not about doing X, Y, and Z, it's about a culture, it's about building trust, and it's about integrity, and it's about – you know, it's about building relationships with people that creates value for everybody on both sides. (Mining Executive No. 6 (emphasis added))

Some beneficial outcomes were noted by some mining executives as a direct result of their efforts to build relationships based on trust with key stakeholders, such as NGOs that were in opposition to their mining activities. For example:

> Interviewer: What sort of outcomes have you seen in your engagement with [oppositional] NGOs?
>
> Mining Executive No. 9: I think we've had fruitful discussions, perhaps less law suits. We had a shareholder resolution put earlier this year, pushed along by [another NGO]. After we spent a day talking to the people involved they withdrew that resolution on the condition we have continuing dialogue, which we're having.

One of the strategies used by large mining corporations to build trust and reputation is through the development of standardized social and environmental performance indicators across different sites globally, and they appoint personnel at the head office level to oversee international on-site performance. This is typically achieved through the use of performance criteria and indicators, and some mining corporations also engage independent auditors to visit individual mine sites to judge their performance against this standardized criteria. An edited version of the results is usually published as part of the corporation's annual social and environmental reports. One mining executive explained how the corporation's reputation for a commitment to high levels of performance across all of their mine site operations resulted in the corporation in obtaining development approval in one country in record time. As can be seen in the following extract, the mining executive explained this in terms of the corporation's "trusted brand" in terms of their standardized performance across all of their mine site operations:

> [Having the same operating standards to "best practice" level across all sites] is a little bit like brand and brand building. Not that I want to draw a parallel between [our corporation] and McDonalds, but let's talk about sushi restaurants. Basically, if you go into a sushi restaurant anywhere in the world, it's the same. They make it the same, virtually everywhere it's just as fresh, the same sort of menu items, and so on. And people can trust going into a sushi restaurant. I would hope that because of what the [the government of Country C] saw in [Country A] and in [Country B] that they would have been comfortable with [our corporation] coming to [Country C], because it wasn't just all promises, it wasn't just all what we're going to do, it was what we'd already done and we're very comfortable, you know, to do. So it's about knowing that there is one way that this company does things and that it's a positive, favourable one, which then gives you easier access to a new country. It allows you to achieve your investment agreements with governments more easily and you have much more to show communities, even if they're isolated and not familiar with what happens in the rest of the world. ...[As a result, we had] an investment agreement signed off by the whole of Parliament in December; kind of a record agreement. I think a lot of that was just about them feeling comfortable with [our corporation]. It's an advantage, definitely. (Mining Executive No. 9)

These findings link back into the sociological literature on trust that identifies the role of trust in facilitating cooperation between parties with competing interests (Hardin, 2002), and the observation that trust can help people reconcile their interests with others (Misztal, 1996). It also supports the conjecture that people are more likely to enter into economic arrangements with parties that they can trust (Granovetter, 1985).

LIMITATIONS OF TRUST-BASED REGULATION

Parties who are trusted are less likely to be scrutinized, and others take less effort to monitor their behavior, or to find out about their trustworthiness

(Levi, 1998). In the context of trust-based regulation, this highlights the inherent danger that as mining corporations become more trusted, their behavior will be less scrutinized and they will be less pressured to follow through on their promises. Accordingly, there will always be a central role for "distrust" in trust-based regulation by which stakeholders refuse to accept the corporations' version of events or claims about their past, current, or future activities. In the mining industry, this might take the form of informed, engaged, distrustful parties who care about the potential environmental impacts of mining and who can have an impact on the business of the corporation for trust-based regulation. This might include local communities and NGOs, but it is noted that many of these groups have less power and resources than mining corporations, which can reduce their ability to pose a substantial threat to the corporation's business.

Trust-based regulation also relies upon the motivation of the corporation to be trusted. In the context of the mining industry, trust-building was seen as fundamental to obtaining a "social license to operate," a priority that often seemed to eclipse the importance of a legal license to operate. For other industry sectors, the business value of trustworthiness might not be as apparent. Even within the mining sector, there are some corporations for whom trustworthiness is not a priority. For example, state-owned corporations in some countries may not be as reliant on a "social license to operate" as large, western corporations operating in developing countries. In addition, some smaller mining corporations that are created to have a short life span may also not be convinced of the business value of high trustworthiness.

The idea of "trust in the shadow of the axe" (Fisse & Braithwaite, 1993, p. 197) is especially compelling for addressing the limitations of trust-based regulation. As Fisse and Braithwaite (1993, p. 197) so vividly explain, where there are sanctions for noncompliance poised over a corporation, abused trust can be readily addressed by "allowing the forces of gravity to operate on the axe." Without sanctions for abuse of trust, mining corporations have little motivation for building or maintaining trust, and are unlikely candidates for steering through trust-based regulation. Sanctions for abuse of trust need not only take the form of legal sanctions in the form of legal prosecution, fines, and penalties, although these can indeed be successful. Depending on the context, socially based sanctions might also prove effective, such as the withdrawal of the "social license to operate" upon which many mining corporations depend for "smoothing the way," for their continued growth through access to land and mineral resources.

CONCLUSION

Polanyi (2001) argues that we need to prioritize human values above and beyond financial gain, and warns of the dangers of a market economy left unfettered in its pursuit of profit at the expense of our social and environmental health. This signals one of the key dangers of trust-based regulation. Key personnel with responsibilities for the social and environmental impacts of large mining corporations are well aware that if they can successfully build relationships based on trust with key stakeholders, including regulators and interest groups, the corporation is more likely to obtain approvals for mining development, and the corporation's activities are likely to be less scrutinized. Higher levels of trustworthiness can offer corporations greater freedom from outside interference in their pursuit of profit in a market economy.

If we are to be convinced that mining corporations are capable of internalizing human values, and of holding social, environmental, and financial considerations in equal stead, then we might justifiably trust them to self-regulate in a trust-based system. But the primary consideration of corporations in the 21st century is to provide financial return to their shareholders, no matter how earnestly they present their environmental and social performance in glossy annual reports. Corporations were borne of the market economy, created as an instrument for building material worth. Despite the best intentions and sincerity of mining corporations' social and environmental management teams, the long-term financial interests of the corporation are paramount.

This research looked specifically at the regulation of the social and environmental impacts of large mining corporations, and there was evidence in the data that trust does play a crucial role in the environmental regulation of the mining industry. Regulators in this study talked about the relevance of trust relationships with mining corporations in their assessment of development applications, as well as in the context of seeking "negotiated compliance" as distinct from the strict enforcement of the law. These findings support other empirical studies (e.g., Hawkins, 1994, 2002) in demonstrating that a relationship of trust or mistrust between the regulator and the regulated has an impact on the way in which laws are enforced. Of particular note was the comment by one regulator that the higher the trust between the regulator and the mining corporation, the less control that was needed (and vice versa), and this was reflected in the conditions placed onto mining projects.

For trust-based regulation to be effective, both parties involved must be willing to enter into a relationship of trust. In considering how trust might be leveraged within regulation to achieve improved regulatory outcomes, it is therefore critical to understand why corporations are interested in building and maintaining relationships based on trust with others. The research found that mining corporations are motivated to build trust with key stakeholders because this would help them to gain a "social license to operate," an increasingly necessary prerequisite for development approvals for the commencement or expansion of mine site operations. A trusted corporation is also less likely to have conflicts with local communities and other key stakeholders, and this reduces the risk of work stoppages and other business disruptions. Both of these reasons are important for the financial bottom line of the corporation.

Linking to the Polanyian theme of "harnessing the regulatory capacity of a social sphere" raises an interesting paradox in the context of mobilizing trust for risk regulation. On the one hand, trust relationships are an example of harnessing the regulatory capacity of a social sphere, but, on the other hand, they can also undermine regulatory effort where trust is abused. While trust may be successfully leveraged to achieve improved regulatory outcomes in the context of corporate, social, and environmental performance, there is a risk of relying on trust-based regulation without a safety net in the form of sanctions for nonperformance. Strategies that increase reputational risk, such as greater corporate transparency and accountability, are important in this regard, as are legal sanctions for nonperformance that have a financial impact on the corporation.

REFERENCES

Atkinson, P., & Coffey, A. (2004). Analysing documentary realities. In D. Silverman (Ed.), *Qualitative research: Theory, method and practice* (pp. 56–75). New York, NY: Sage.

Ayres, I., & Braithwaite, J. (1992). *Responsive regulation: Transcending the deregulation debate*. Oxford: Oxford University Press.

Ballard, C., & Banks, G. (2003). Resource wars: The anthropology of mining. *Annual Review of Anthropology*, 287–313.

Bennis, W. (1989). *On becoming a leader*. Reading, MA: Addison-Wesley.

Braithwaite, J. (1993). The nursing home industry. In M. Tonry & A. J. Reiss Jr. (Eds.), *Beyond the law: Crime in complex organizations* (pp. 11–54). Chicago, IL: The University of Chicago Press.

Braithwaite, V. (2006). Ten things you need to know about regulation but never wanted to ask. *Australian Law Librarian, 14*, 19–28.

Braithwaite, J., Coglianese, C., & Levi-Faur, D. (2007). Can regulation and governance make a difference? *Regulation & Governance*, *1*, 1–7.

Braithwaite, J., Makkai, T., & Braithwaite, V. (2007). *Regulating aged care: Ritualism and the new pyramid.* Northampton, MA: Edward Elgar.

Business for Social Responsibility (BSR). (2003). *The social license to operate*. San Francisco, CA: Business for Social Responsibility.

Dasgupta, P. (1988). Trust as a commodity. In D. Gambetta (Ed.), *Trust: Making and breaking cooperative relations* (pp. 49–71). Oxford: Blackwell.

Dasgupta, P. (1998). Trust as a commodity. In D. Gambetta (Ed.), *Trust: Making and breaking cooperative relations* (pp. 44–71). Oxford, UK: Blackwell.

Edelman. (2009). *2009 Edelman trust barometer: The tenth global business leaders' survey*. London: Edelman.

Eden, S. (1994). Business, trust and environmental information: Perceptions from consumers and retailers. *Business Strategy and the Environment*, *3*, 1–8.

Fisse, B., & Braithwaite, J. (1993). *Corporations, crime and accountability*. Cambridge: Cambridge University Press.

Flick, U. (1998). *An introduction to sociological research*. New Delhi: Sage Publications.

Giddens, A. (1994). Replies and critiques: Risk, trust, reflexivity. In U. Beck, A. Giddens & S. Lash (Eds.), *Reflexive modernization: Politics, tradition and aesthetics in the modern social order* (pp. 184–197). Cambridge: Polity Press.

Good, D. (1988). Individuals, interpersonal relations and trust. In D. Gambetta (Ed.), *Trust: Making and breaking cooperative relations* (pp. 31–47). Oxford: Blackwell.

Granovetter, M. (1985). Economic action and social structure: The problem of embeddedness. *The American Journal of Sociology*, *91*, 481–510.

Hardin, R. (2002). *Trust and trustworthiness*. New York, NY: Russell Sage Foundation.

Hawkins, K. (1984). *Environment and enforcement: Regulation and the social definition of pollution*. Oxford: Clarendon Press.

Hawkins, K. (2002). *Law as last resort: Prosecution decision-making in a regulatory agency*. Oxford, NY: Oxford University Press.

International Institute for Environmental Development (IIED), & World Business Council for Sustainable Development (WBCSD). (2002). *Breaking new ground: Mining, minerals and sustainable development*. London: Earthscan.

La Porte, T. R., & Metlay, D. S. (1996). Hazards and institutional trustworthiness: Facing a deficit of trust. *Public Administration Review*, *56*, 341–47.

Lenegan, C. (2006). The mining industry, learning from the past, preparing for the future, *American chamber of commerce & SAP Business Briefing*. Sydney, Australia.

Levi, M. (1998). A State of trust. In V. A. Braithwaite & M. Levi (Eds.), *Trust and governance* (pp. 77–101). New York, NY: Russell Sage Foundation.

McMullen, J. L. (1992). *Beyond the limits of the law*. Halifax: Fernwood Publishing.

Minerals Council of Australia (MCA). (2004). *Enduring value: The Australian minerals industry framework for sustainable development. Implementation guidance* (p. 36). Canberra, Australia: Minerals Council of Australia.

Minerals Council of Australia (MCA). (2005). *Enduring value: The Australian minerals industry framework for sustainable development. summary booklet* (p. 24). Canberra: Minerals Council of Australia.

Misztal, B. A. (1996). *Trust in modern societies: The search for the bases of social order*. Cambridge: Polity Press.

Murphy, K. (2004). The role of trust in nurturing compliance: A study of accused tax avoiders. *Law and Human Behavior*, *28*, 187–209.

Polanyi, K. (2001). *The great transformation: The political and economic origins of our time*. Boston, MA: Beacon Press.

PriceWaterhouse Coopers (PWC). (2007). *Mine: Riding the wave*. London: PriceWaterhouse Coopers LLP.

Rothstein, B. (2005). *Social traps and the problem of trust*. Cambridge, UK: Cambridge University Press.

Sampat, P. (2003). *Scrapping mining dependence, State of the World 2003* (pp. 110–137). Washington, DC: The WorldWatch Institute.

Shapiro, S. P. (1987). The social control of interpersonal trust. *American Journal of Sociology*, *93*, 623–658.

Swift, T. (2001). Trust, reputation and corporate accountability to stakeholders. *Business Ethics: A European Review*, *10*, 16–26.

Wade, M. (2005). Good company citizenship: Does governance change the role of companies in society? In U. Petschow, J. Rosenau, & E. U. v. Weizsäcker (Eds.), *Governance and sustainability: New challenges for states, companies and civil society* (pp. 186–199). Sheffield, UK: Greenleaf Publishing.

Walker, D. M. (2005). Restoring trust after recent accountability failures. In J. O'Brien (Ed.), *Governing the corporation: Regulation and corporate governance in an age of scandal and global markets* (pp. 21–46). Chichester, England: Wiley.

Whetten, D. A., & Mackey, A. (2002). A social actor conception of organizational identity and its implications for the study of organizational reputation. *Business & Society*, *41*, 393–414.

DISCUSSION PIECE

SEPARATE SPHERES? THE CULTURAL CONTRADICTIONS OF MARKETS

Mitchel Y. Abolafia

ABSTRACT

This article argues that the economic, political, and cultural spheres of society are not separate but rather mutually embedded in one another. The market is not just an economic phenomenon, but a political and cultural one as well. Markets, in this reframing, include not just the convenient fiction of atomized buyers and sellers but trade and professional associations and a field of public actors including assorted regulators and courts. It is the interaction of these parties that creates a market culture. These cultures exhibit contradictory tendencies that are generated by exchange relations and resolved by power dynamics. The contradictory tendencies reflect the tension between accumulative and regulative norms in market cultures. These include opportunism versus restraint, innovation versus standard practice, and growth versus stability. The resolution of the cultural contradictions of markets is not a natural tendency toward equilibrium, but rather an ideal of public policy to be attained by countervailing power in effective legal and regulatory institutions.

Keywords: Markets; market culture; regulation

From Economy to Society? Perspectives on Transnational Risk Regulation
Studies in Law, Politics, and Society, Volume 62, 265–271

ISSN: 1059-4337/doi:10.1108/S1059-4337(2013)0000062011

The articles in this special issue of Studies in Law, Politics, and Society all argue, in one way or another, that economy, polity, and culture are analytical conveniences fostered by the disciplinary illusion that these are separate spheres. In particular, this illusion is reflected in the belief that there is a separate economic sphere that has a logic and rationality of its own that is sufficient to explain market-based behavior. The articles show that this illusion conflicts with reality and narrows policy debate. The field of economic sociology, much inspired over the last quarter century by the work of Karl Polonyi, has elaborated both evidence and theory to reject this analytic convenience and to argue that the economy is always embedded in politics, culture, and social relations. The articles presented here illustrate how economy is embedded in law, a hybrid product of politics and culture.

Increasingly, the varieties of capitalism in the global economy are not seen as converging on the ideal type reflected in economics, but rather as variations that reflect the social dynamics in different societies. These dynamics reflect real differences in class structure, political structure, and the resulting distributions of power and authority. One may argue that law and the rule of law precede the emergence of modern capitalism or that regulation is created as a "protective countermove" to the free market, but in both cases it seems clear that law and regulation are constituted by the interweaving of the political and cultural systems. The result is that every economic transaction is embedded in its own institutional environment including courts, regulators, a central bank, a patent system, trade associations, and an educational system. The understanding of economic transaction cannot be separated from these institutions and from the history of the social conflicts through which they emerged. Transactions across national boundaries remain embedded in this variety of capitalisms.

THE "ALWAYS EMBEDDED ECONOMY"

With this phrase, sociologist Fred Block characterized the Polanyian idea that market societies must maintain some threshold level of embeddedness to avert social and economic disaster (Block, 2003). As Frerichs shows in her paper, Polanyi believed that the self-regulating market was a 19th-century ideal that never really existed; an ideal that puts society at risk because of the inherent volatility and displacement caused by such arrangements. Bettina Lange goes further, explaining that terms like economy and society are discourses, historically contingent fields of knowledge that regulate what can be imagined, talked, and written. This is a helpful way to think about the interwoven spheres in that it highlights that they are convenient concepts more than representations of reality. They have become tacit proxies for competing interests. An economic discourse favors the concerns of producers and a society discourse favors the concerns of consumers.

Schiavi offers what may be the most fundamental argument against the separation of the spheres, showing how both regulators and regulated believe that a culture of trust allows both parties to manage their relationship. This is an example of the wider argument that says that transactions, whether market or regulatory, are embedded in a social relationship. Firms may try to build trust to reduce direct control by the regulator and to reduce the risk of prosecution. Regulators may use a firms' need for trust to encourage compliance. As such, regulation becomes a social relationship and the management of legitimacy and reputation are critical to successful operation. In fact, trust is at the heart of all transaction. Contracts are inherently incomplete and performance often relies on the norms of trust and reciprocity. Political and economic systems without a culture of trust are inherently fragile and ineffective. The imagery of an atomized, hyper-individualistic society distorts the basis of social relations, even those that seem relatively impersonal.

A second related theme emerging in this special issue is the illusion created by the taken-for-granted imagery of a stand-alone economic sphere. The myths of market fundamentalism literally obscure behaviors that are part of everyday economic relations. Weidemaier and Gulati present a puzzle whose solution is based on this illusion. They find that lawyers who work on contracts in the sovereign debt market claim that such contracts are standardized even as they make innovations in the contracts to adjust them to new contexts. Weidemaier and Gulati's explanation for this modesty on the part of the lawyers is that they need space to do their work. The claim of standardization mollifies the bankers and finance officials who hire them. The belief that the contracts have been commodified enhances the illusion of frictionless exchange on which these markets are built. Going further, the lawyers are using the illusion of the model to reduce their own transactional friction. This is a lovely story of an adaptation in occupational culture in an embedded market setting.

Susan A. Bandes addresses another illusion created by the belief in a disembedded economic sphere. She notes that economists often treat emotions as an unfortunate interference with rational thought. Even "behavioral" economists seem to believe that unfortunate inclinations can be "nudged" aside. But, Bandes argues that human nature is both more complex and more persistent. The over-rationalization of the economic model leads to failed predictions and policy errors. The recent financial crisis is, of course, the most salient example of this. Society is still susceptible to speculative bubbles, manias, and panics. The "animal spirits" that Keynes described are still with us. Any model of economic behavior that excludes these emotions will be wanting. A model that assumes away collective mania and panic, that forgets that economic transaction exists in an emotional climate, is doomed to failed prediction.

THE CULTURAL CONTRADICTIONS OF MARKETS

In the remainder of these comments I will discuss another implication of the social nature of economic relations. This perspective is also derived from the thinking of Karl Polanyi. It refocuses our attention from "the economy" as a stand-alone sphere to markets as their own social systems. In this view, every market becomes a microcosm where economy, politics, and culture interweave. These micro-social systems are shown to exhibit contradictory tendencies generated by exchange relations and resolved through power dynamics among the participants and through institutions that reflect the history of conflict in that market. Each market is its own center of gravity that creates its own culture. The balance of contradictory tendencies in a market is specific to *that* market. This article identifies three pairs of contradictory tendencies that appear across many markets.

The contradictory tendencies reflect the balance or tension between accumulative and regulative norms in market cultures. These include opportunism versus restraint, innovation versus standard practice, and growth versus stability. If markets were people, we might think of these as existential questions, such as "Should I press my advantage with or should I worry about my reputation and self-image?" "Should I try to create a better product or should I mimic the practices of other firms in my market?" "Should I risk my capital by investing in my venture or should I be happy with low-risk and an acceptable level of profit?" But these are meant not to be personal questions. Markets are social phenomena and these contradictory tendencies exist at the level of the market, reflecting the predominance of either accumulative or regulative norms or scripts in that market. Such scripts are guides defining appropriate behavior in the market.

Opportunism refers to the use of guile in transacting with a trading partner. The tendency to opportunism was common in early financial markets and a threat to the traders in these markets, referred to as market makers (Abolafia, 2001). Market makers formed associations or "exchanges" that made rules to keep the trading ongoing. These rules mostly prevented the members from destroying their market by extreme opportunism, such as cornering the market and driving each other out of business. This maintained the going concern. But these rules were not designed to protect participants in the market who were not members of the exchange, that is, outsiders who traded through brokers. There was a strong norm about fouling the nest, not destroying the stream of income, but outsider participants, or the wider public, who were plentiful, were fair game and opportunism was rampant. Market cultures make these distinctions and enforce them.

A second cultural contradiction in markets lies in the tension between innovation and standard practice. Firms don't like rapid changes. If their members have grown accustomed to standards contracts (Weidemaier and Gulati), standard transactional procedures, and a familiar commodity, they are likely to continue with them as long as there is money to be made. But occasionally, a deviant innovator comes along and shakes things up. In financial markets, this innovator usually tells a story about enhanced profits without increased risk. At first, the establishment firms are resistant. They say things like "good firms don't do that." But as the recent financial crisis showed, the profits are too tempting and stockholder expectations too demanding. Even first-tier investment banks engaged in the creation and sale of innovative instruments that they knew were more risky than they revealed to customers. Standard practice was superseded.

A third cultural contradiction lies in the tension between the values of growth versus stability. Markets with low barriers to entry and high profits have a tendency to grow, attracting more sellers and increasing competition. At first, participants put their highest value on growth, as it creates new profit opportunities for them. But, over time, as competition increases, participants create niches they can defend, and look to each other for shared understandings, attempting to restrain trade through cartels, or cartel-like associations, or attempting to capture regulatory relief in search of stability. The market for money and credit is a good example of this. In the United States it was bankers themselves who lobbied most strenuously for a central bank at the end of the 19th century. It became clear that they could no longer tolerate the volatility in the market for money and credit. Panics had become too frequent, resulting in widespread bank closures. The market had become so large that not even J. P. Morgan, the wealthiest banker in the United States, could support the market in a panic. The banking community united and lobbied for a central bank that would manage growth and maintain stability.

From the examples given so far, it should be clear that "markets as cultures" are not like independent, distant villages. They exist in the context of, and rely upon, an institutional environment. Market culture exists in the context of laws, courts, regulators, a banking system, a patent system, trade associations, and an educational system. This institutional environment resolves conflicts over the tendencies identified earlier and lets participants know the normative boundaries accepted in the market. In fact, the differing outcomes to the perennial contradictory tendencies observed in markets are largely explained by the resolution of earlier conflicts that have been sedimented into institutions. The stock exchange, discussed earlier, is itself just such an institution. Its rules and roles were created by traders over the course of 200 years so that they might have more predictable streams of income over the long term. The institution is infused with cultural values.

Economic institutions, whether private or public, are formalized expressions of prior conflicts over the contradictory tendencies in market culture. Institutions reflect earlier resolutions of these conflicts and the winner's determination to make outcomes more predictable and favorable. The recent financial crisis is once again a good example of this. The crisis began with imbalances between opportunism and restraint as well as innovation and standard practice in mortgage backed securities and the derivatives markets. New versions of mortgage-backed securities and insurance on these securities, credit default swaps, that were far riskier than most understood, were created and sold. What permitted these imbalances to occur was an institutional failure. Institutions like the Securities and Exchange Commission and the Federal Reserve reflected the resolution of earlier financial crises and had been given the tools to prevent the extremes of opportunism and deviant innovation that developed. These institutions were themselves undermined. They were undermined by a political process that allowed the lessons of economic history to be replaced by a distorted ideology of deregulation reflecting powerful financial interests.

The contradictory tendencies of market culture are kept in balance by economic institutions that represent diverse stakeholders and are inclusive of their interests. How did institutions like the Securities and Exchange Commission and the Federal Reserve come to forget the lessons of the Great Depression? The answer lies in a political process that delegitimated regulation and elevated market fundamentalism to an organizing principle. The "markets as cultures" perspective suggests that markets are not natural phenomena that normally reach equilibrium, but rather social arrangements prone to conflict and disequlibrium that are supported by moral, political, and economic sanctions. When the political process fails to enforce these sanctions, then cultural contradictions go too far toward either accumulative or regulative norms. Effective political process requires countervailing power.

CONCLUSION

Culture, economy, and polity are not separate spheres. Rather, they interpenetrate and shape each other. Research on economic exchange must start from this premise. Economic development cannot be managed and market failure cannot be prevented without clear recognition that market culture emerges at the transaction level, but that its contradictions are resolved by institutions that are tied to the political process and a fair representation of a cross-section of its interests. This is as true in labor and production markets as it is in the financial markets. It is the responsibility of politicians and administrators to build trust in those institutions, based on equal treatment and access. The resolution of the cultural contradictions of markets is not a natural tendency toward equilibrium, but rather an ideal of pubic policy to be attained by effective institutions.

REFERENCES

Abolafia, M. Y. (2001). *Making markets: Opportunism and restraint on wall street*. Cambridge, MA: Harvard University Press.

Block, F. (2003). Karl polonyi and the writing of the great transformation. *Theory and Society*, *32*, 275–306.

